Advance Praise for
Multiracial Experiences in Higher Education

"This book offers unique and complex explorations of diverse Multiracial experiences in higher education. Unlike many volumes, it highlights the lives of Multiracial faculty, staff, and graduate and undergraduate students who differ across racial backgrounds, racial identities, and campus locations (including 2- and 4-year institutions and historically Black colleges and universities [HBCUs]). Because chapters offer theoretical analyses, narrative storytelling, and practical tools and strategies, the material will resonate with readers with diverse interests and learning styles. This book is an essential resource for anyone who leads, teaches, serves, or studies at institutions of higher education and who seeks to understand and empower Multiracial people on their campuses."—*Belinda P. Biscoe, Interim Senior Associate Vice President for University Outreach/College of Continuing Education, University of Oklahoma, home of NCORE*

"How do Multiracial people navigate a society that prioritizes monoracism? *Multiracial Experiences in Higher Education* beautifully addresses this question. The narratives are the heart of this book, and the contributors underscore the richness and complexities of Multiracial people's experiences. Current doctoral students and recent graduates also contributed chapters, illustrating the importance of having perspectives across various generations. This book restored my faith in story-sharing and vulnerability as vehicles for change, and I applaud the contributors for their courage."—*Stephen John Quaye, Associate Professor, Department of Educational Studies, The Ohio State University*

"This is a beautiful collection of theoretical ideas, personal stories, and examples of praxis; a must-read for scholars and practitioners. I love that the book is grounded in theories about race and (mono)racism while elevating the voices of Multiracial people, scholars, and educators. There are many moments of learning and growth throughout the book."—*Gina A. Garcia; Associate Professor; Educational Foundations, Organizations, and Policy; University of Pittsburgh*

"The editors of this volume have done us a great service. They have compiled one of the most comprehensive, informative, and thought-provoking resources for those hoping to expand their knowledge of mixed-race populations. This collection of excellent scholarly analyses, compelling narratives, and practical implications will surely be a vital asset to researchers and educators seeking to empower and serve Multiracial communities for generations to come."—*Samuel D. Museus, Professor of Education Studies and Founding Director of the National Institute for Transformation and Equity, University of California, San Diego*

D1603327

"*Multiracial Experiences in Higher Education* is an intergenerational journey through the past, present, and future state of Multiraciality in academia. The synthesis of personal counterstories and detailed 'call to action' strategies that challenge monoracism and ultimately white supremacy in higher education make it an important and timely read for all."—*Kelly F. Jackson; Associate Professor, Arizona State University; Vice President of the Critical Mixed Race Studies Association; and coauthor of* Multiracial Cultural Attunement

"*Multiracial Experiences in Higher Education* gives important visibility to a growing segment of the higher education community that is too often rendered invisible by campus policies and cultural practices. The combination of theory, personal narratives, tools, and strategies found in this cutting-edge collection of essays makes it a very useful resource for researchers and practitioners alike."—*Beverly Daniel Tatum, author of* Why Are All the Black Kids Sitting Together in the Cafeteria? and Other Conversations About Race

"This is an essential text for those hoping to understand the experiences of Multiracial individuals in higher education. It is at once general and specific, obvious and nuanced, theoretical and practical, perfect and flawed. The book lives in the in-between of all of those dichotomies, proudly occupying a diunital existence demanding to be seen as real, unique, vital, complex, and essential—very much like the experiences of the Multiracial people explored in the text."— *Raechele L. Pope, Associate Dean and Chief Diversity Officer, University at Buffalo Graduate School of Education*

"This is an important contribution to understanding the challenges facing Multiracial students in a world that resists seeing or understanding their multiracial identity. The book offers reflections on Multiracial identity theory and the voices of students and staff about navigating their Multiracial identities, and it concludes with ideas for improving services for Multiracial students. Readers are provided with a unique view of the evolution of theory and practice on Multiracial identity through the perspectives of foundational theorists and a new generation of scholars who bring new insights questions and challenges to this field."—*Rita Hardiman, Foundational White Racial Identity Theorist and Social Justice Consultant*

MULTIRACIAL EXPERIENCES IN
HIGHER EDUCATION

MULTIRACIAL EXPERIENCES IN HIGHER EDUCATION

Contesting Knowledge, Honoring Voice, and

Innovating Practice

Edited by Marc P. Johnston-Guerrero and

Charmaine L. Wijeyesinghe

Foreword by G. Reginald Daniel

1996-2021 25TH ANNIVERSARY

Stylus
PUBLISHING, LLC.

STERLING, VIRGINIA

Published by Stylus Publishing, LLC.
22883 Quicksilver Drive
Sterling, Virginia 20166-2019

Library of Congress Cataloging-in-Publication Data
Names: Johnston-Guerrero, Marc P., editor. | Wijeyesinghe, Charmaine,
    1958-editor. | Daniel, G. Reginald, 1949- writer of foreword.
Title: Multiracial experiences in higher education : contesting
    knowledge, honoring voice, and innovating practice / edited by Marc
    P. Johnston-Guerrero and Charmaine L. Wijeyesinghe ; foreword by
    G. Reginald Daniel.
Description: First edition. | Sterling, Virginia : Stylus Publishing, LLC,
    2021. | Includes bibliographical references and index. |
Identifiers: LCCN 2021005581 (print) | LCCN 2021005582 (ebook)
    | ISBN 9781642670684 (hardback) | ISBN 9781642670691
    (paperback) | ISBN 9781642670707 (library networkable e-edition)
    | ISBN 9781642670714 (consumer e-edition)
Subjects: LCSH: Racially mixed people--Education (Higher)--United
    States. | Minority college students--United States. | Education,
    Higher--Social aspects--United States. | Multicultural education--
    United States.
Classification: LCC LC3621 .M85 2021 (print) | LCC LC3621
    (ebook) | DDC 378.1/982--dc23
LC record available at https://lccn.loc.gov/2021005581
LC ebook record available at https://lccn.loc.gov/2021005582

13-digit ISBN: 978-1-64267-068-4 (cloth)
13-digit ISBN: 978-1-64267-069-1 (paperback)
13-digit ISBN: 978-1-64267-070-7 (library networkable e-edition)
13-digit ISBN: 978-1-64267-071-4 (consumer e-edition)

Printed in the United States of America

All first editions printed on acid-free paper
that meets the American National Standards Institute
Z39-48 Standard.

Bulk Purchases

Quantity discounts are available for use in workshops and for staff development.

Call 1-800-232-0223

First Edition, 2021

To our families; specifically, Marc to his nieces (Brynna and Keeley) and nephew (Bryson), who will be starting their own multiracial experiences in higher education soon. And Charmaine to Christian, Andreas, and Rebecca Wijeyesinghe Lietzau for their love and support, and wisdom shared at the dinner table over the years.

CONTENTS

FOREWORD

There is increased visibility of multiracials in the media, including websites on the internet, along with other social forums. Support and educational organizations, socials, festivals, and conferences have been devoted to multiracial concerns. Multiracial students have organized groups on college and university campuses. Some of these institutions of higher education offer courses that include the topic of mixed race. There have also been compelling individual studies on multiracial identities and mixed-race experiences in higher education. Some of those publications have been written by the contributors to this volume edited by Marc P. Johnston-Guerrero and Charmaine L. Wijeyesinghe. Yet *Multiracial Experiences in Higher Education: Contesting Knowledge, Honoring Voice, and Innovating Practice* is the first comprehensive study on this topic. It provides guiding themes and an overarching framework in terms of its analysis. This groundbreaking volume includes, among other topics, reflections on the creative resistance to and triumphs over the various challenges experienced by multiracials—including students, staff, faculty, administrators, and others—who increasingly populate college and university campuses.

More important, this compilation suggests "multiracial knowledge" can be a template for engaging in a social praxis that critiques racial essentialism and racial hierarchy as the basis for aspiring toward more inclusive collective subjectivities across the racial spectrum, including multiracials. One should not, however, understand this to posit multiracial identities as the solution, in and of itself, to racism and racial inequality. Rather, this approach is based on the idea that multiraciality—and more broadly, conceptual stances that are "betwixt and between"—can help avoid defensive-aggressive binarisms and polarizations that may be politically counterproductive in terms of collaborating on other issue-based concerns. These offer a basis from which to advance thinking, practices, and policies seeking to ameliorate racism, right racial inequalities, and foster social justice. Consequently, this collection of essays should be required reading for anyone aspiring toward a more just, equitable, and inclusive society.

Multiracial Experiences in Higher Education is a long-overdue publication since Paul Spickard's (1989) *Mixed Blood: Intermarriage and Ethnic Identity in Twentieth-Century America* and Maria P. P. Root's (1992) award-winning anthology *Racially Mixed People in America*. These two books were similarly groundbreaking. Root's edited volume was the first comprehensive examination of multiracial identities and mixed-race phenomena in the United States. Both studies have become canonical publications on this topic and central to establishing foundational discourses in what is now referred to as *mixed race studies*. During this same time period, from 1989 to 1996, I taught my course Betwixt and Between: Multiracial Identity at the University of California, Los Angeles. I also taught the course beginning in 1997 at the University of California, Santa Barbara. I have taught the course and other courses on multiraciality every year since then. Yet my interest in and research on the topic dates back to the racially turbulent late 1960s and early 1970s. At that time, multiracial identities were very much not a topic of conversation, if not unmentionable, in academia and the larger public sphere.

Hypodescent and the Monoracial Imperative

Some of these attitudes can be attributed to long-standing policies and practices informed by hypodescent and the monoracial imperative. These social devices, respectively, categorize multiracials according to their most subdominant racial background and necessitate single-racial identification. This has disallowed and, indeed, repressed the articulation and recognition of multiracial identities—that is, identification with more than one racial background. Consequently, scholars across disciplines failed to comprehend the significance of multiracial identities when they emerged in the United States during the late 1980s and early 1990s.

Of course, the lacuna in analyses on the topic of multiracial identities can be logically attributed, in part, to the fact that hypodescent and the monoracial imperative have prevented their occurrence. Indeed, one could argue multiracial backgrounds are the norm, rather than the exception in the United States, although most individuals display single-racial identities in keeping with hypodescent and the monoracial comportment line. Scholars across the monoracial spectrum, much as the larger society, internalized these tenets of the U.S. racial order. Consequently, monoraciality and hypodescent were so common sense they were taken for granted. Scholars provided little critical examination or questioning of these social forces that prevented multiracial identity formations. Their espoused objectivity blinded them to their own monoracial subjectivity and positionality. The assumed disciplinary value-free ethos was, in fact, imbued with inherent monoracial biases that have historically permeated academia.

English Americans began enforcing hypodescent and the monoracial imperative during the late 17th and early 18th centuries. The objective was to maintain inequitable social divisions between themselves as the dominant "white" group and the subdominant "nonwhite" groups of color, in the interests of property and power. These devices have, thus, buttressed a binary racial order that necessitates identification as either white or nonwhite. Hypodescent was implemented as part of antimiscegenation legislation targeting interracial intimacy, and specifically interracial marriages, as well as the progeny of these relationships. This mechanism sought to sustain the ideology of white supremacy by preserving white racial "purity" as well as maintaining white economic and political power. George Lipsitz (2011) argued it has resulted in grossly inequitable access to education, employment, health care, transportation, and housing, and so on, which perpetuates significant differences in overall quality of life. These regulations reached momentous proportions with the institutionalization of Jim Crow segregation at the turn of the 20th century, which legally sanctioned the unequal treatment of blacks and other communities of color in most aspects of social life.

According to F. James Davis (2001), hypodescent has been applied most stringently to the first-generation offspring of unions between European Americans and people of color. This is less true for people of partial Latinx ancestry. It is less true still for people of partial Asian American descent, and even less true for many people of partial Native American ancestry unless they have connections with Native American reservations. Frequently, these individuals, and successive generations of individuals whose lineage has included a background of color and European ancestry, have been allowed more flexibility in terms of their self-identifications.

Winthrop D. Jordan (2014) maintains this elasticity has not been extended to individuals of African and European descent, whether first generation or later. They have experienced the most restrictive rule of hypodescent—the one-drop rule—which designates as black all individuals of any African ancestry. It requires identification as either white or black, which are the polar extremities of the white-nonwhite binary framework. This mechanism is unique to the United States and is only applied to individuals of African descent. It has historically precluded self-identification and ensured that all future descendants with African ancestry have been designated and have self-identified as solely black. Davis (2001) pointed out the one-drop rule gained currency as the commonsense definition of blackness between the 17th and 19th centuries. It did not become a customary part of the legal apparatus until the early 20th century (circa 1915).

U.S. attitudes toward "dual minority" offspring of unions between African Americans and other groups of color (e.g., Native Americans, Chinese

Americans) have varied. These individuals have generally also been subject to the one-drop rule and monoracial formations. There has been greater ambivalence displayed toward dual minority offspring whose ancestry has combined other backgrounds of color ("Punjabi Mexicans") and Filipino/ Mexican Americans ("Mexipinos") in California. These groups of color occupy a more ambiguous position in the U.S. racial hierarchy compared to that of blacks. Also, membership in these groups has been less clearly defined in U.S. law. And there is no strict or consistent determination of which background is the more subdominant in terms of hypodescent, which can vary situationally. Still, in each of these instances, monoracial norms have historically disallowed the articulation and recognition of multiracial identities.

Accordingly, monoraciality, along with hypodescent, has perpetuated macroaggressions involving state agencies, public policy, and institutional practices that ignore or erase multiracials from the national imaginary. It has also sustained mesoaggressions involving the workplace, community, and schools. These can range from not being able to fill out a form that reflects how one identifies to the absence of material on multiracials in the mass media and school curriculum. Marc P. Johnston and Kevin L. Nadal (2010), along with many contributors to this volume, argued it has also sustained microaggressions in the sphere of interpersonal relations, where individuals are the perpetrators. Microaggressions can involve brief and commonplace daily verbal, behavioral, or environmental indignities that communicate hostile, derogatory, or negative racial slights and insults toward multiracials.

Hypodescent, particularly the one-drop rule, and the monoracial imperative, are the cornerstones of the U.S. binary racial order. George Lipsitz (1998) maintained the resulting "possessive investment" (p. 2) in whiteness has been critical to maintaining white racism and racial privilege, notwithstanding the repudiation of notions of white racial purity that supported the ideology of white supremacy. These are manifested by means of a matrix of practices that leads to significantly different life chances along racial lines. These outcomes are not merely the byproducts of benign neglect. Rather, they are also the accumulation of the purposeful designs of whites that assign people of different racial groups to differential and inequitable social spaces.

The various structures that produce the unearned benefits of whiteness, themselves grounded in hypodescent, are responsible for pervasive and egregious forms of structural oppression perpetuated by white racism against people of color. However, these same social devices also benefit monoracial groups of color. They have the advantage of large numbers of societal outlets and resources—cultural, social, economic, political—for individuals of their groups, also known as "monoracial privilege" (Nadal et al., 2011, p. 43). Although they do not experience anything near the advantages as whites, this may also make it difficult for them to recognize their own monoracial privilege and biases. Whether intentional or unintentional, these discriminatory attitudes and practices form part of what Johnston and Nadal, as well as other contributors to this anthology, refer to as "monoracism" (Johnston & Nadal, 2010, p. 125).

Although monoraciality and hypodescent go hand in hand, they are not necessarily synonymous. The impetus behind support of monoraciality and, by extension, hypodescent among European Americans compared to communities of color differs considerably. European Americans historically formulated hypodescent to sustain monoracial imperatives based on the dichotomous, as well as hierarchical ranking of racial (and cultural), differences in support of white racial exclusivity. The unintended consequences of hypodescent and monoraciality for groups of color, especially blacks, was that the production of exclusionary boundaries around such groups helped forge and legitimate monoracial group identities.

According to Rhett S. Jones (1994), communities of color's possessive investment in hypodescent and monoraciality is grounded in the belief that they are necessary for maintaining community, as well as solidarity in the struggle against the inequities perpetuated by white racism, oppression, and privilege. Communities of color, thus, uphold monoraciality and the accompanying dichotomization of racial differences by *rearticulating* rather than *reproducing* hypodescent. This process involves repetition of hypodescent with a difference in support of racial difference without hierarchy; that is, difference based on equality. Notwithstanding this critical distinction, the outcome in both cases is the same: Individuals reinforce, if only unwittingly, racial designations as if they were mutually exclusive and singular categories of experience, as well as objective phenomena with an independent existence of their own.

Multiracial Identities and Mixed-Race Experiences

The civil rights movement dismantled Jim Crow segregation and achieved the implementation of historic legislation in the 1950s and 1960s that dissolved legal racial discrimination and inequality. The landmark 1967 *Loving v. Virginia* decision, which overturned statutes in the remaining 16 states prohibiting racial intermarriage, was a concomitant outcome of these gains although not specifically part of the civil rights platform. Subsequently, hypodescent was removed from all state laws. The comparatively more fluid social relations in the post–civil rights era led to the growth in the number of interracial marriages. Legalized marriages as consensual relationships include an element of choice, unlike the coercive unions of the past under colonial domination; military occupation; and, particularly, slavery. Moreover, marriage confers equal legal status on both parties and, by extension, equal legitimacy on both parents' identities.

These changes notwithstanding, there was no immediate challenge to hypodescent or the monoracial imperative in terms of racial categories and identifications. It was not until the late 1970s and early 1980s that many interracial couples, particularly individuals in black–white unions, began to counter the one-drop rule and the monoracial imperative by socializing their children to identify with their multiracial backgrounds. They also began forming educational and support organizations addressing the concerns of interracial families and multiracial people, particularly their marginalization and frequently outright erasure and pathologization.

Some of the celebratory, and at times, overenthusiastic images seeking to address and remedy these attitudes, along with those in the mainstream media, have understandably been criticized for reinforcing and perpetuating the notion that interracial marriages would lead to a more tolerant society. There were also imaginings that multiracials are automatically imbued with special temperamental qualities, which make them ideally suited as the solution to racism and racial inequality. Frequently, they have been considered vehicles in the pursuit of a universal humanism that transcends race. Notwithstanding the naïve egalitarianism that has underpinned some of this thinking, it has been an important step toward valorizing the concerns of interracial families and multiracials speaking to institutional and everyday forms of discrimination originating in hypodescent and monoracial imperatives.

By the late 1980s and early 1990s, these educational and support organizations helped mobilize a social movement that began lobbying the racial state to change procedures in collecting official data on race and ethnicity—particularly on the 1990 census—so that multiracial-identified individuals could be enumerated. This multiracial movement was unsuccessful in bringing about changes on the 1990 census. Yet its efforts came to fruition with the 2000 census, which, for the first time, allowed multiracial-identified individuals to check more than one box on the census race question. Consequently, 7 million and 9 million individuals on the 2000 and 2010 census, respectively, took advantage of this option.

This multiracial population includes "first-generation" offspring of interracial marriages in which both parents are socially designated and self-identified as monoracial regardless of the multiple racial backgrounds in their parents' genealogy. It also encompasses "multigenerational" individuals, who have two biracial-identified parents; one parent who is biracial-identified and one whose social designation and means of personal identification is mono-racial. The multigeneration identity is similarly displayed by individuals who have parents, or even generations of ancestors, who have been socially desig-nated as monoracial although they have multiple racial backgrounds.

Previous studies, as well as those conducted by the contributors to this anthology, indicate that multiracial identities are influenced, but not nec-essarily determined, by individuals' phenotypical traits; family, peers, and society also have a significant impact. These data also indicate multiracial-identified individuals have multiple and shifting points of reference, rather than fixed or predictable parameters, which may change over an individual's lifetime. Notwithstanding their illusive parameters, multiracial identities manifest themselves between the boundaries of monoracial groups. They extend outward from that liminal location contingent upon an individual's orientation toward the groups that compose their background. A shared liminality based on identification with more than one racial background is an integral, fundamental part of the self-conception of multiracial-identified individuals. It is a defining component of mixed-race experiences despite myriad backgrounds, experiences, and identities.

Although multiracial identity formations contest the mutually exclusive nature of racial boundaries, they should not be understood as a dismissal of monoracial forms of identification, in and of themselves, as illegitimate. Rather, they question the external ascription of monoracial identifications as the norm against which all other forms of identification are deemed unacceptable. Depending on the circumstances, individuals may manifest different affinities or resonances with specific components of their backgrounds, as well as the groups that embody them. In direct contradiction to hypodescent, they do not privilege any one background over the other in terms of intrinsic value and worth. These identities challenge the hierarchical valuation of racial dif-ferences perpetuated and their inequitable power relations.

Multiracial identities, thus, interrogate monoracial norms supporting European Americans' investment in whiteness and the associated cultural, social, economic, political, and other advantages. They also call into question the equally profound investment communities of color have in preserving monoracial identities in response to those inequities. The latter overlook or outright reject the possibility of multiracial identities formulated on nonhier-archical or antiracist—that is, critical—premises. Consequently, multiracial identity formations were not regarded as a resistance to the core and founda-tional tenets of U.S. racial common sense.

Instead, they have often been conflated with the desire to evade racial stigma and achieve social advantages in the racial hierarchy closer to those of whites. There is no substantive data to support the notion that multiracial identity formations are automatically synonymous with those aspirations. Yet one cannot dismiss the fact that some individuals may identify as multi-racial out of a desire to achieve white adjacency. Moreover, multiracial identi-ties, like all racial identities, continue to be impacted by the constrictions of racist structures of the U.S. social order. Among other things, these structures privilege individuals who more closely approximate the dominant European Americans in terms of physical appearance. Numerous studies, including those in this collection, indicate multiracials display a critical awareness of these inequities. This cognizance can range from informal criticism of every-day manifestations of racist power dynamics to formal engagement in anti-racist work, which centers the role multiracials and multiracial knowledge can perform in the struggle for racial justice.

From Marginality to Liminality

Scholarly studies on the topic of multiraciality and mixed race date back at least several hundred years. Indeed, the original obsession in the United States with miscegenation and multiracial progeny began in the colonial era with a meditation on interracial intimacy between blacks and whites and the offspring resulting from those unions. This thinking fixated on the supposed genetic inferiority of multiracials, supported by scientific racism and theories of hybrid degeneracy. Scientific racist discourse continued to espouse these theories well into the 1940s. By the end of the first half of the 20th century, they had largely been superseded by theories of marginality, as a substitute which focused on the psychological dysfunction purportedly originating in mixed-race experiences.

According to this line of reasoning, marginality was necessarily patho-logical. Individuals stood on the boundary of two mutually exclusive and often antagonistic worlds, not fully a member of either world. This was the source of lifelong personal conflict characterized by divided loyalties, ambiv-alence, and hypersensitivity. Admittedly, such theories emerged when the United States was significantly more hostile to the affirmation of multiracial identities. They rarely critiqued the social forces that made psychological functioning difficult for multiracials. Rather, multiracials were characterized as inherently psychologically dysfunctional. This thinking supported the prevailing ideology that prohibited or discouraged miscegenation, thereby seeking to preserve white racial purity and dominance, and ignored the soci-ological forces that put multiracials psychologically at risk.

These theories of "negative" marginality emphasizing pathology, espe-cially the work of sociologist Everett V. Stonequist (1937), overshadowed the nuances of sociologist Robert E. Park's (1928) original "marginal man" thesis. Park did not dismiss the challenges, psychological ambivalence, and conflict that could accompany marginality. However, Park (1937) believed marginality could also imbue individuals with a broader vision and wider-ranging sympathies. This "positive" marginality might provide them with an ability to help facilitate mutual understanding among individuals from different groups.

Yet prior to the 1980s, identity formation of the offspring of interracial marriages had received limited attention from educators, researchers, social scientists, and mental health professionals. The extant research was outdated, contradictory, or based on small-scale case studies of children who were experiencing "problems" with identity and were referred for psychological counseling. Rather than positing these identity struggles as a sign of alienation in response to the perceived illogics of hypodescent and monoraciality, they were deemed symptomatic of anomie or temporary deviations in an otherwise functioning racial order. In terms of individuals with black and white parentage, professionals stressed the importance of learning to cope as African Americans, because society would view them as such. Their mental health was assessed in terms of how successfully or unsuccessfully they achieved a black identity.

By the 1980s, there had been an important advance in research on multiraciality encompassing a reevaluation of the concept of marginality. A new wave of research finally put to rest theories of negative marginality stressing psychological dysfunction. These and subsequent studies indicated multiracials, generally speaking, are just as psychologically and socially well-adjusted as monoracials notwithstanding the various challenges they may encounter in forming positive identities. The concept of positive marginality (or liminality)—that is, the sense of being betwixt and between—in turn, gained greater acceptance among mental health professionals. More important, this shift also moved the conversation beyond simply thinking about multiraciality in terms of backgrounds or ancestries, which are rather ubiquitous. Instead, the focus was more specifically on examining the formation of multiracial identities originating in mixed-race backgrounds and experiences.

Beginning in the 1980s, the social sciences took the lead in research on mixed-race identities and multiracial experiences. Psychologists, social psychologists, and, to a lesser extent, sociologists conducted the majority of research. A few anthropologists and scholars in social work also made inroads. Demographers grappled with the statistical implications of the growing population of interracial couples as well as the growing population of multiracial children. By 2004, scholarly articles had appeared in all the flagship and high-impact journals in sociology, psychology, anthropology, history, and literature, as well as in other disciplines and fields of study. Since then, the number of articles, book chapters, and monographs published on mixed-race identities and multiracial experiences across disciplines has grown exponentially. Even a partial list would hardly do justice to the volume of publications. Papers, roundtables, sections, and regular sessions on multi-racial identity have increasingly became a component of annual meetings of various academic professional associations. Indeed, the study of this topic has become a distinct interdisciplinary area of scholarly inquiry.

These developments, in turn, were instrumental in the 2010 inaugural biannual Critical Mixed Race Studies Conferences, subsequently incorporated in 2015 as the Critical Mixed Race Studies Association and founding of the *Journal of Critical Mixed Race Studies* in 2011. Yet even with the emergence of mixed race as a field of study, there has been limited attention devoted to scholarly analyses of multiracial identities and mixed-race experiences in academia. *Multiracial Experiences in Higher Education* helps fill in that gap by virtue of its comprehensive, engaging, and thoughtful—not to mention thought-provoking—analyses.

G. Reginald Daniel
Professor, Department of Sociology,
University of California, Santa Barbara, and
Editor in Chief, *Journal of Critical Mixed Race Studies*

References

Davis, F. J. (2001). *Who is Black? One nation's definition.* Pennsylvania State University Press.

Johnston, M. P., & Nadal, K. L. (2010). Multiracial microaggressions: Exposing monoracism in everyday life and clinical practice. In D. W. Sue (Ed.), *Microaggressions and marginality: Manifestation, dynamics, and impact* (pp. 123–144). Wiley.

Jones, R. S. (1994). The end of Africanity?: The bi-racial assault on blackness. *Western Journal of Black Studies, 18*(4), 201–210.

Jordan, W. D. (2014). Historical origins of the one-drop rule in the United States. *Journal of Critical Mixed Race Studies, 1*(1), 98–132. https://escholarship.org/uc/item/91g761b3

Lipsitz, G. (2011). *How racism takes place.* Temple University Press.

Lipsitz, G. (1998). *The possessive investment in Whiteness: How White People profit from identity politics.* Temple University Press.

Nadal, K. L, Wong, Y., Griffin, K., Sriken, J., Vargas, V., Wideman, M., & Kolawole, A. (2011). Microaggressions and the multiracial experience. *International Journal of Humanities and Social Science, 1*(7), 36–44. http://www.ijhssnet.com/journals/Vol._1_No._7_%5BSpecial_Issue_June_2011%5D/6.pdf

Park, R. E. (1928). Human migration and the marginal man. *American Journal of Sociology, 33*(6), 881–893. https://doi.org/10.1086/214592

Park, R. E. (1937). Introduction. In E. V. Stonequist (Ed.), *The marginal man: A study in personality and culture conflict* (pp. xii–xvii). Russel and Russell.

Root, M. P. P. (1992). *Racially mixed people in America.* SAGE.

Spickard, P. R. (1989). *Mixed blood: Intermarriage and ethnic identity in twentieth-century America.* University of Wisconsin Press.

Stonequist, E. V. (1937). *The marginal man: A study in personality and culture conflict.* Russell and Russell.

PREFACE

This book is an intergenerational collaboration—in editorship, content, and contributors. Its pages describe foundations and areas well researched, newer knowledge and practice from which we can further learn, and questions and issues that lie at the horizon of a truly innovative and revolutionary future. To us, the volume follows the arc of theory and practice related to multiracial people—those who claim membership in more than one (mono)racial group and/or identify with a multiracial identity term (e.g., biracial, mixed, Blasian). It is not only topics that evolve but also scholars, concerns, and even language and concepts. Given shifts in culture, politics, systems, and history, we need to constantly consider and wonder about what is known, how we know it, and what we don't know yet.

We offer this book and its chapters as another step in this evolutionary journey of understanding the complexities of *multiracial experiences in higher education*. We approached the creation and cultivation of this volume with an understanding that higher education is a contested space with values pertaining to language, scholarship, voice, methods, and knowledge. All of these concerns come into play when examining the diverse experiences of multiracial people—who live in the racialized landscape of the United States—and their navigation of higher education. In covering an array of multiracial experiences, the book brings together a range of voices, social identities (including race), ages, perspectives, and approaches. The contributors and their words do not support a singular view, because as the book highlights, multiracial people are not a monolithic group, and their needs and knowledge are not universal to all.

Organization of This Book

This volume both expands and challenges traditional frames of what is considered valuable and appropriate academic knowledge. Thus, the book is organized into three interrelated parts. The first part presents literature and theoretical frameworks that help the reader understand multiracial experiences in higher education in general and the material presented in subsequent sections. The second part centers another way of expressing knowledge and offers a range of first-person narratives that highlight navigating to and through higher education from diverse standpoints and positionalities. The third part shares strategies and applied methods that can be used to enhance multiracial inclusion through research, curriculum, and practice. A final, single chapter appears after all of these parts and offers concluding reflections and future recommendations for scholarship and practice.

Part One: Building a Foundation

Part One includes four chapters that address a range of topics related to major aspects of multiracial experiences in higher education. Beginning with specific attention to multiracial experiences on campus, the chapters move from discussions of identity to ever broader circles highlighting the systemic structure and impact of monoracism. Chapter 1 sets the context for the subsequent chapters, where the editors, Charmaine L. Wijeyesinghe and Marc P. Johnston-Guerrero, provide a brief overview of recent statistical information and trends affecting multiracial people on campus, along with their personal accounts of being multiracial people in higher education during different historical eras. Much like the narratives that appear in the second part of this volume, these individual reflections illuminate how the evolution of theories, language, culture, and perspectives on race in America influence identity, sense of belonging, and day-to-day life of multiracial people in higher education.

In chapter 2, Kristen A. Renn illustrates how the increased visibility and political organizing of multiracial communities fueled the push for scholars and educators to understand and address the needs of multiracial students. In her comprehensive overview of research on multiracial students, Renn discusses several areas, including patterns and fluidity of racial identity, perceptions of race and racial categories, sense of belonging and authenticity, and systemic forces on campus and beyond that affect the experiences of these students. Recommendations for future research are also offered, including directions for increasing scholarship on the lives of multiracial faculty and staff.

Charmaine L. Wijeyesinghe employs a reciprocal analysis in chapter 3, investigating how historical representations of identity influence the understanding of Multiracial people, even as the experiences of Multiracial people introduce concepts that require the rethinking of the nature of identity. The chapter explores how four core concepts found within social identity literature—paradigm, context, agency, and salience—are both adopted and stretched by select models of Multiracial identity. Wijeyesinghe then considers key questions that diverse Multiracial experiences raise for future definitions and representations of identity.

In chapter 4, the experiences of Multiracial people on campus are placed within the context of systemic oppression and marginalization as Jessica C. Harris, Marc P. Johnston-Guerrero, and Maxwell Pereyra present a detailed analysis of monoracism. After offering a historical summary of the emergence of the topic, the contributors highlight several areas where previous explorations of monoracism fall short. Through their exploration of three tension points, the contributors present new information on the levels and types of monoracism, how adopting a lens of monoracism increases our understanding of white supremacy and ability to dismantle it, and how monoracism interacts with other systems of oppression to influence the experiences of students on campus. Harris et al. conclude by offering several core tenets of their expanded conceptualization of monoracism to guide future research.

Part Two: Learning From Narratives

Following the conceptual foundation provided in Part One, Part Two presents six chapters based in narrative voices that describe the lives of diverse people of mixed heritage who hold various roles in higher education. As these stories include material from the contributors' early years, they illustrate the lasting influence of precollege experiences on how identity is experienced during time as an undergraduate student and beyond. In chapter 5, Nick Davis shares how his black identity evolved during his early years in California and how he negotiated experiences with his extended family and classmates prior to college. A chance encounter early in his freshman year at Northwestern University introduced Davis to a mixed race student organization, and he goes on to relate his experiences as a member, part of the executive board, and eventually president of this group. Davis's efforts to augment the group's social activities with educational and advocacy efforts around racial issues, particularly those affecting the black community, influence the nature of events offered and responses from the student community. Through his narrative, Davis offers a poignant reflection on his black identity.

Victoria K. Malaney Brown recounts the ways that her experiences as a multiracial person have influenced her paths in higher education as a student, scholar, researcher, and practitioner in chapter 6. After being raised in South Florida, the contributor describes how joining a group for Black/African/Caribbean American students at a liberal arts college in New York led her to attend a national conference on race. This conference, the contributor's experiences with intergroup dialogue, and her involvement with multiracial organizations in national higher education associations have fostered a greater understanding of power, race, and privilege. Malaney Brown describes how her understanding of these concepts continued to grow in her professional work before and during graduate school, guiding her to explore how multiracial students develop a multiracial consciousness that includes taking action to combat systemic forces of monoracism.

In chapter 7 Rebecca Cepeda describes her journey as a Mexipina, recounting experiences of feeling like "an Other" in early environments beyond her home and during her undergraduate years. As a first-year student, the contributor finds that the predominance of White students in her major and questioning of her background by Asian students leaves her frustrated and pondering the lack of acceptance of diverse people and identities. When Cepeda transitions to being a commuter student working multiple jobs, she describes juggling responsibilities without assistance from campus agencies. Enrolling in a master's program in counseling, the contributor engages with faculty and peers of color and finds a sense of belonging and acceptance for her shared identities and cultures. Given her experiences, particularly her work at a community college, Cepeda describes her academic and professional commitment to helping first-generation and low-income students find support and belonging as she pursues her doctoral degree.

In chapter 8 e alexander weaves geography, spirituality, race, and family history in their narrative that covers journeys as an Ancestral orphan across early years in Louisiana and positions at institutions they name as minority-serving institutions (MSIs) and predominantly White institutions (PWIs). Throughout their narrative, the contributor illuminates the effects of white supremacy and colonial history on their sense of identity, the responses of others, and institutions. alexander finds support for exploring Black Indian identity and historical legacies that created false divisions across time and space at MSIs. Moving on to PWIs, the contributor analyzes how the institution retains power over people of color and describes continuing their work to build coalitions and collaborations while combatting colonial legacies, particularly those influencing nonwhite people.

In chapter 9, Naliyah Kaya combines poetry and text to share her stories highlighting the difficulty in finding spaces where all of her identities are accepted, welcomed, and invited. Describing her identities as existing in-between races, religions, and continents, she covers themes of white presenting and passing, sense of belonging, the limitation of categories to capture the experiences of people of Southwest Asian/North African (SWANA) descent, and imposter syndrome. Reflecting on experiences at a community college, a historically Black college or university (HBCU), and a PWI, Kaya's encounters create a unique story that informs the contributor's work on multiracial topics through conference presentations and leadership, professional positions, teaching, and research.

Andrew Jolivétte grounds his narrative in chapter 10 with stories that highlight questions of appearance, background, and identity. The contributor shares how experiences at an HBCU and a small Jesuit university influenced his identity and, at the latter location, his intellectual connection with his Black and Native ancestry. With examples taken from his more than 20-year career as a scholar-activist, Jolivétte discusses his identity, expectations that he serve as a bridge between Black and Native communities, and the weight of multiple expectations. Citing examples of anti-Blackness, anti-Indianness, and anti–Mixed Race/Heritage in higher education, the contributor provides recommendations for disrupting settler violence in the academy.

Part Three: Applying Innovations

Integrating material and insights from the previous sections, Part Three includes chapters that present specific tools and strategies for supporting multiracial students, staff, and faculty; educating others on the experiences and needs of multiracial people; and creating more inclusive environments for these members of their campus communities. In chapter 11, Chelsea Guillermo-Wann and Marc P. Johnston-Guerrero present and discuss their contextualizing multiraciality in campus climate (CMMC) model. This model offers campus leaders, faculty, staff, and students a multilevel tool for incorporating the experiences of multiracial students in efforts to assess and improve the campus climate for diversity. The contributors illustrate how the model is informed by social and community contexts related to racial formation, and how these external contexts influence campus diversity efforts. Six interrelated factors are discussed and demonstrated through examples, and the contributors provide detailed lists of key considerations for institutional leaders, faculty and staff, and researchers and evaluators related to employing the model.

Charlene C. Martinez and Stephanie N. Shippen offer insights and activities based on their Multiracial Aikido program at Oregon State University in chapter 12. This experiential learning retreat, held over a weekend, allows students who identify with more than one racial group to explore identity, build self-awareness, and identify strategies for supporting themselves while on campus. The contributors indicate how the core tenets of respect, recognize, respond, and replenish, as well as the philosophies underlying the practice of the martial art of aikido, inform the structure and activities of the retreat. The chapter provides clear information on the development of the program, descriptions of specific activities, and responses from multiracial participants. Martinez and Shippen close the chapter by highlighting their use of emergent strategies and providing suggestions for people who wish to develop a similar program on their campuses.

In chapter 13, Orkideh Mohajeri and Heather C. Lou present their distinctive approach that brings together art and critique to unveil the impact of four constructs—race ideology, power-blindness, positionality, and multiracial microaggressions—on multiracial student organizations and the faculty and staff who advise them. The goal of their work is to unmask and disrupt hegemonic ideas and norms that inform notions of belonging, identity, and inclusion/exclusion. Drawing on their experiences working with multiracial groups at several campuses, the contributors describe and then demonstrate different activities through the use of drawings, poetry, and performance. After providing additional insight on areas to consider when utilizing the material and activities described in the chapter, Mohajeri and Lou offer material that can be adapted and reproduced by readers.

Nicole Leopardo, Kira Donnell, and Wei Ming Dariotis reveal events and processes related to the establishment of the first critical mixed race studies (CMRS) degree-granting program in the country, founded in 2019 at San Francisco State University, in chapter 14. The contributors describe themes historically shared by ethnic studies and CMRS and their experiences approaching existing departments within the College of Ethnic Studies regarding the placement of the CMRS minor. Leopardo, Donnell, and Dariotis detail the development of the program outcomes and rationale and their gathering and use of data for the proposal for the program. After describing final steps to creating the minor, they provide recommendations for faculty interested in developing CMRS programs at their institutions.

Part Four: Moving Forward

Chapter 15 brings this volume to a close through intergenerational reflections offered by Marc P. Johnston-Guerrero, Charmaine L. Wijeyesinghe, and Lisa Combs. After providing thoughts and reactions on chapters and the volume through individual narratives, the contributors join voices to present several recommendations for students, staff, and faculty who wish to continue to increase their understanding of multiracial experiences in higher education, and to advance theory, knowledge, and practice in several areas related to this population.

Additional Notes to Readers

As readers may have noticed there are differences in grammatical style and format reflected in the abstracts for each chapter. These variations, as well as others, appear throughout the book because of the choices we made as editors and the orientations chosen by the contributors. Thus, instances that may appear as inconsistencies or "accidental grammatical errors" are in fact reflections of the power inherent in language and efforts to disrupt this power. In this last segment, we provide guidance on a few areas related to language and style that appear across the volume.

Terms and Their Form

We understand the importance of contributors being empowered to enact linguistic and/or grammatical changes to disrupt the status quo or subvert power dynamics. Therefore, we did not ask contributors to use a singular or shared definition for terms such as *biracial, multiracial,* or *mixed race.* We also allowed for stylistic variability in capitalization or spellings to align with contributors' personal and political interests. For instance, readers will see that capitalization of terms such as *multiracial* will not be consistent across chapters in the volume. Though reasons vary, some writers may choose to capitalize *Multiracial* for consistency across other identity terms (e.g., African American), whereas others may use lowercase so as to not reify group boundaries. Such differences reflect both the messiness of identities and the contested and evolving nature of language and styles. In addition, some chapters contain wording that, though less familiar to some readers, are integrally related to the history of race in America, such as the term *Turtle Island,* which is used by some Indigenous communities to refer to North America. These words center histories and voices discounted or ignored in dominant representations of language. We invite readers to notice their reactions when encountering terminology that is new to them and to explore the origins and significance of these words in the racialized cultural and linguistic landscapes of the United States.

The Varied Voices That Convey Knowledge

The voice in which knowledge is created and conveyed also differs across chapters and parts of the book. As editors, we believe that this diversity is valuable in furthering the understanding of multiracial experiences in higher education. As a reader we encourage you to note your reactions to each chapter and to consider what those reactions may reveal about the assumptions you may make about what is good and "appropriate" academic writing or knowledge. The varied nature of the voices in this volume offers important entryways to exposing what each of us values or what each of us discounts, particularly in relation to the socialization that occurs in higher education that privileges certain ways of knowing and being while marginalizing others.

Diversity Across Racial Identities

The diversity in voices also aligns with an important understanding that not every person who is considered multiracial or considers themselves multiracial identifies as such. Moreover, some other groups of marginalized people (e.g., transracial adoptees, third-culture kids) might identify similarly with the experiences of multiracial people. Still, we decided to center multiracial lives in this volume. Choice of identity is explored in multiple ways in this book, including through theoretical analysis, narrative, and personal artistic expression. Identity is yet another contested area, and people should not assume that we or the other contributors suggest or represent a singular identity or experience in the book or in the terms that are used.

Source of Contributors

Finally, we want to be transparent that we sought out contributors based on personal networks and access to particular fields of scholarship. As readers might recognize, there are several connections to particular institutions or organizations. These situations happened over time and evolved as contributors originally contacted to write certain chapters withdrew or contributors changed their locations during the production of this book. Multiracial students, staff, faculty, and administrators differ across backgrounds, chosen identities, places of origin, ages, disabilities, genders, sexual orientations, and so on. They reveal so many experiences that can be investigated in so many different ways. Here, we offer you insights into some of those lives and experiences. The chapters in this book represent a sliver of the topics and contributors associated with *Multiracial Experiences in Higher Education*. We welcome the wisdom that will emerge from research and practice that comes after their publication.

Marc P. Johnston-Guerrero, Columbus, Ohio
Charmaine L. Wijeyesinghe, Delmar, New York

ACKNOWLEDGMENTS

This volume would not be possible without the important labor of the contributors featured across the chapters. Thanks also to G. Reginald (Reg) Daniel for his validating and expansive foreword, and to many of our colleagues for their advanced reviews and supportive comments. As editors we cultivated a community of knowledge builders who shared their personal stories, intellectual wisdom, and creative talents (especially Heather C. Lou who designed artwork incorporated into the cover). Together with the fabulous team at Stylus Publishing (especially John von Knorring, Alexandra Hartnett, James Ebersole, and McKenzie Baker), we have demonstrated the power of collaboration for moving our field forward. And honestly, the volume would never have been created without the push from John, who pursued Charmaine as a contributor for several years and generously supported this volume from initial idea to final publication.

Marc

I thank my colleagues and students at The Ohio State University, especially my research lab members: Kristen Mills, Tiffany Steele, e alexander, Jonathan Howe, Victoria Olivo, Wu Xie, and Rebecca Cepeda. These committed mentees provided a validating counterspace for me and also helped review chapters for formatting. I also thank the talented Sam Jacobo of Duotone Creative (www.duotonecreative.com), who contributed graphic design assistance. Over the years, I've benefited greatly from the multiracial community built through the Critical Mixed Race Studies (CMRS) conferences and association, the National Conference on Race and Ethnicity (NCORE), and the American College Personnel Association's (ACPA) MultiRacial Network, where ideas were sparked and identities affirmed. Importantly, the volume would not be possible without the brilliant mind and expert eye of Charmaine. Thanks so much for your guidance and mentorship through my first book project. Finally, I honor family (the Cañedos, Johnstons, and Guerreros), especially my partner Brian, for the constant love and support (and motivation to keep writing).

Charmaine

I thank John for his friendship, guidance, and gentle persistence. And Marc, for all that he brought to this project, including the many contributors whose words are reflected in the pages of this book, his flexibility, and his leadership. Ours has been a rewarding partnership that has both challenged and expanded my thinking. I also acknowledge my friends and colleagues at NCORE who fostered my work for over 25 years. I thank Mary Wilson-Hyde, Georgia Fishburn, Maria Dominitz, Diane Goodman, Jim Bonilla, Liza Ahner, Francie Kendall, Sharon Washington, Susan Jones, MJ Adams, and Mary Ellen Sailer—for always being there to listen and lend support as this book took shape and life went on. Lastly, I wish to acknowledge my siblings Sharon, Rochen, and John, who I remembered fondly as I drafted parts of my introductory narrative, and Christian, Andreas, and Rebecca, who will be there when the next chapters of that story are written.

PART ONE

FRAMING MULTIRACIAL EXPERIENCES IN HIGHER EDUCATION

I

INSIGHTS ON MULTIRACIAL KNOWLEDGE, VOICES, AND PRACTICES

Lessons From Our Lives and Work

Charmaine L. Wijeyesinghe and Marc P. Johnston-Guerrero

From the preceding material, readers know we draw on words such as *complex* and *diverse* when describing Multiracial people in higher education, *contested* and *racialized* when referring to higher education spaces and sites of knowledge, and *innovative* and *revolutionary* when describing the potential of Multiracial lives to transform colleges and universities. Just as the preface noted that the different grammatical styles and forms that appear in the chapters of this book were not employed accidentally, the actual words we and the contributors use reflect purposeful choices. Those choices highlight issues of power, politics, legacy, and possibilities inherent in capturing the experiences of a very diverse group of marginalized people within one of the oldest structures and systems in the United States.

In this chapter, we continue to reflect on some of the topics briefly described in the "Additional Notes to Readers" section of the preface, illustrating the complexities of definitions, categories, and assumptions about identity and belonging, as well as expectations of what is considered real and valued knowledge in the academy. Like the range of perspectives and voices in this volume, we blend types of knowledge here. We begin by sharing stories of our own lives as Multiracial people in higher education. Next we investigate themes that were evident in our narratives and that find space in various chapters in this book, augmenting our analysis with statistics and brief notations of material that readers might refer to for additional insight. Because subsequent chapters provide in-depth literature reviews and significant reference lists, our goal here is to balance presentation of contextual information with efforts to avoid repetition.

Our Personal Stories

In this section of the chapter we offer parts of our own stories of navigating higher education, paths we took to our work on Multiracial topics, and the lessons we learned from these journeys. Because we attended college and worked in higher education in different eras, these stories illustrate the dynamic nature of concepts, institutions, and options for Multiracial people.

Charmaine

In the realm of Multiracial scholarship I've shifted my generational location—from a doctoral candidate searching the (then) limited literature on which to build a study of Multiracial identity and convincing senior scholars that this topic was legitimate and worthy of study to a thinker in her later years who is inspired by the insights of current scholars and practitioners investigating many facets of Multiracial lives. My journey to this point has been neither straight nor planned, much like the path to my identity as a Multiracial person.

My racial identity has changed across the over 6 decades of my life. Looking back, I can't say that I thought about identity, racial or otherwise, until I was in my 20s. That's not to say that now familiar themes from the literature on Multiracial people were absent from my childhood. My family was an anomaly, with my parents and two older siblings immigrating to the United States, from Sri Lanka and settling in a suburban, all-White community north of Boston in 1958. My mother was of Dutch/Portuguese ancestry and my father was Dutch/Sri Lankan. She was thought of as White in the United States, and he was definitely Brown. About a month after they arrived, I became the first American citizen through birth in my family. I am not sure about my siblings, but as I got older I was constantly asked, "What are you?" and was told by my parents that the response to this question was "an American," though I had a nagging sense there was something about my family and me that didn't quite make me "American" in the eyes of our immediate community. Our food, family values, unpronounceable-by-others last name, and range of physical appearances made us different. In the 1960s and 1970s, differences based on race were largely couched in terms of Black and White, and I believe people thought I was Black. I think most people meeting me today do the same. And although I could relay many more stories, given the focus of this book, I turn to identity as I experienced it in higher education.

My environment became much more diverse when I enrolled as an undergraduate at the University of Massachusetts at Amherst (UMass) in 1976. Because of my brown complexion and tight curls, most people assumed I was Black, including the Black students who routinely asked me to join the Black Student Union. I sometimes corrected people, telling them that I was Asian and White, but mostly understood that how I was perceived was how I was labeled. By the time I was a senior, however, several African American staff women were part of my life. I wanted to be like them—confident, assertive, sure of who they were. I began to see that for all intents and purposes, my experiences reflected those of a Black woman, so I thought of myself as Black. Occasionally I encountered situations where I needed to specify my family background. For example, when I became a professional staff member at the university, one of the highest level administrators on campus asked me why I had marked "C" (for Asian) instead of "B" (for Black) on my employment form. In the 1970s and early 1980s, people didn't have the same curiosity they have today with determining whether someone is "mixed." No one would have asked me if I was Multiracial when I was in college. As I moved toward graduate school, race and identity were still in the background of my consciousness, but starting to percolate.

During graduate school at UMass I was still considered Black by just about everyone, and identifying as Black was mostly a matter of convenience. Once enrolled in the doctoral program I began studying foundational literature on social justice, racial identity, and group dynamics. I had incredible opportunities, taking classes with Bailey Jackson, Rita Hardiman, Ken Blanchard, and faculty associated with the National Training Labs (NTL). I once sat within arm's reach of our guest lecturer, Paulo Freire. I began to think of myself as a theorist, but I didn't apply the material, often, to myself. When I did ask which of the theories of racial identity—Black (Jackson, 1976) or White (Hardiman, 1982)—applied to me, I was promptly told I'd fall under the Black one.

As I went through graduate school, I embraced racial identity models and the stage paradigm they adopted. I applied this material in diversity-related work that I did for a consulting collective in the area. Even there my appearance, experiences, and identity had to be negotiated. For example, it was not uncommon for clients to request a Black consultant as part of the team working with their institutions. My colleagues and I often discussed whether I could be that person, and more than once I was. I encountered more dilemmas when language evolved and folks began using the term *African American* instead of *Black*. Although I mostly identified with the broader category of Black, it was inauthentic and just plain wrong for me to identify as African American.

In mulling a dissertation topic, I noted a proverbial gap in the literature. There was no mention of Multiracial people in the material we studied. Given the tradition of stage models produced at UMass, I—let me repeat, I—was supposed to create *the* stage model on Multiracial identity. I was crushed, momentarily, when the biracial models by Poston and Kich were published. Luckily, I found that the experiences that my research participants shared during their interviews did not fit a stage model structure. Instead, certain factors influenced their choices of identity. Even after defending the dissertation, I did not reflect on how "the findings" applied to me. However, one of the postdefense tasks was registering the dissertation in a national database using a paper form, a section of which contained demographic questions about the author, including an item pertaining to race. I checked the boxes for Asian and for White—for the first time and in honor of the people who shared their stories in my research. The paper form was returned to me with a request to include correct information on race. In 1992, checking one box was the only option allowed. After I submitted the form two additional times (it was returned twice) with two boxes marked for race, the form stopped being sent back to me.

I continued to consult on issues of social justice and identity and built a career in higher education and in the not-for-profit sector. In addition to utilizing stage models I offered my "factor-based" work, not realizing that it was part of a growing number of ecological models. My conference sessions were packed, because there were few people speaking about Multiracial identity in the 1990s and at least some higher education faculty and staff noticed the need for information. However, I always had a good number of monoracial parents of Multiracial kids in the sessions. Everyone was hungry for some knowledge, some space to discuss questions and issues.

Almost 2 decades after my defense, I encountered Susan Jones, a professor at Ohio State, at a conference. From Susan's work and knowledge, I became more interested in the idea of intersectionality and how it could help me capture the complex interrelationship between factors and racial identity. A collaboration and new area of interest emerged. Susan and I have gone on to present sessions and write book chapters together. It has been a rewarding, supportive, and invigorating relationship. Through our collaborative work, I've been jostled from my allegiance to stage models and from my allegiance to models at all.

Over the last decade I've focused on larger issues that create the context, knowledge, and questions related to identity, race and, by consequence, Multiracial people. I value the unknown much more than I ever did in my earlier years. I am fascinated by the questions that help me discern what I know, how I know it, and what I have yet to know. In addition, I am

drawn to wrestling with the nature of knowledge itself. What counts as legitimate knowledge, what does not, and who gets to decide? I now understand
more deeply that what I believe about identity reflects the theories I've been
exposed to, the research and teaching I've done, the interactions I've had,
my experiences of the world in light of my social identities and positions,
and the many systems of inequality that have influenced everything from the
start. I am challenged to bring this awareness to my work on identity and
Multiracial people, and I relish the opportunities this book has provided for
me to embrace these challenges.

Marc

I am a multiracial (Filipino and white) man who recognizes my ancestries
go way deeper than these categories actually capture. Born in Pangasinan,
Philippines, my mom immigrated to the United States in the early 1970s as
part of a large wave of nurses and other health care workers. My dad traces
his roots to German American farmers in Wisconsin, though he knows that
his heritage is also made up of Scottish and French ancestry and *not* Native
American ancestry (I grew up hearing those false yet common stories that I
had a great-great-grandmother who was a "Cherokee Princess" and believed
it until undergrad when the president of the North American Indigenous
Student Organization [NAISO] schooled me on it being one of the biggest myths in Indian Country). During my childhood years growing up in
suburban Michigan during the 1980s and 1990s, I didn't have any identity "issues" until other people pointed out that I was different. From the
children on our block making fun of my siblings and me for referring to
our parents as "Nanay" and "Tatay" (*Mom* and *Dad* in Tagalog, which we
stopped using shortly after this teasing) to friends on my high school row-
ing team thinking I was adopted because I didn't seem to match my white
father's skin tone, my multiracial identity only became salient because of
the monoracist system in place that continuously pointed out that I was
different. Of course I didn't have that language back then, but I am able to
articulate those experiences now.

My work in multiracial advocacy began while I was an undergraduate
student at Michigan State University, where in 2001–2002, I founded our
"Hapa" club (before I knew the contested nature of the term, which I no
longer use as I do not wish to perpetuate the co-opting/stealing of Native
Hawaiian language). My rationale was to create a space for Asian American
students of mixed heritage to come together and share experiences and build
community. The Asian connection felt important because mentors at the
institution passed down history lessons to me that there was a previous multiracial student group at the institution that disbanded due to distinctions

between needs of leadership and members, particularly around those who were multiracial Black or not-Black. I felt if we all had some connection to Asian Americanness, that might give our group a better chance at being sustained, not to mention having access to the pan–Asian American associations' resources as an "affiliate group." Little did I know that just a few years after I graduated, this Hapa group would also dissolve.

After several years of working in student affairs and, in particular, multicultural affairs, I felt I had established myself as an advocate for multiracial college students and for infusing multiracial issues into the larger discourse on racial diversity in our practice. I felt confident in who I was and really did feel like my mixed race background allowed me to view problems from multiple perspectives and bridge different communities. This optimistic outlook was disrupted by attending an institute on the increasingly prominent "intergroup dialogues" as a pedagogical and programmatic tool toward educating students to better understand diversity and social justice. I was reminded constantly that I didn't have a "group" to have "intergroup" dialogues with. Worse yet, I was silenced by fellow participants and trainers who did not care to infuse multiraciality into their model, because they had "proven" that their model worked (for monoracial groups).

That experience reminded me of what life might be like for current multiracial college students who are navigating campuses that weren't designed with them in mind. While a master's student and full-time academic adviser on campus, I advised a new student organization focused on the mixed race student experience (aptly named the Multiracial Identity eXperience, or "the MIX"). On this campus, there were four established panracial/ethnic groups (Asian Pacific American Student Association, Black Student Alliance, Culturas de las Razas Unidas, and NAISO) that had fought for many years to secure funding to support these underrepresented populations. When the MIX began, tensions arose over the organization's desire to join a governing body with the other (mono)racial groups. There were suspicions as to why the MIX members could not integrate into the monoracial groups and how its presence might affect the funding available to all groups. Although I didn't realize it at the time, this was about resources and representations; the established groups were worried about losing their share of the small piece of pie they had fought for from the predominantly white institution. It is true that these monoracial groups had a long history of advocating for self-determination, yet in their fight for a more inclusive campus, they were unintentionally (I would like to hope) excluding other marginalized groups—those who didn't fit monoracial categories. Did these established groups not see a benefit in increasing the number of students they could build coalitions with? What happened to strength in numbers? What may have been operating was a feeling that if they (multiracial students) couldn't identify as a part of our (mono)racial group, then they should not benefit from our past fight for resources.

These experiences as an undergraduate student, a graduate student, and a practitioner continue to inform the work that I do now as a faculty member in trying to better understand the dynamics of multiracial identity and monoracism through research, teaching, and service. I owe so much of my career to one of my graduate school professors, Kristen A. Renn, who literally wrote the book on *Mixed Race Students in College* in 2004. Renn opened my eyes to the possibility of becoming a scholar and that my life and experience were worthy of being studied. It was also in her student development theory course during my master's program where my experiences became grounded in a larger context and opened my mind to so many other questions—questions that would continue to propel me in this work and my desire to inspire and provide opportunities for future generations of multiracial scholars and practitioners, like Renn and other mentors (e.g., Kevin Nadal, Rudy Guevarra, Donna Talbot, John Lee) did for me.

Yet I still sometimes struggle with feelings of doubt around the importance of my research topics, particularly those that center my own identities and experiences around multiraciality (not to mention the devastating events highlighting the continued necessity for the Black Lives Matter movement). Those feelings made me decide not to do my dissertation research on multiraciality, opting instead to more broadly explore racial conceptions. I had fears of becoming pigeonholed such that I would only be known for doing multiracial-focused research. In fact, for one of my dissertation studies, I openly excluded multiracial students—engaging in the type of multiracial erasure I would later critique. It is my hope that through this volume I am contributing to the creation of spaces and building of community where emerging and future multiracial scholars (both those who identify as such or are interested in studying multiraciality) do not have the same fears and doubts that I had, toward a future where multiracial faculty, staff, and students can all thrive in higher education.

Interlude and Moving On

Our voices take a more analytical tone in the next section. Before moving on, we invite readers to sit with our stories, to be still with them, and to consider their knowledge contributions without evaluating or analyzing them. Briefly notice how your body and mind are reacting. After a period of time, rejoin us here.

Embedded within our stories are themes such as how appearance affects naming and sense of belonging or ways programs and systems silence or negate Multiracial experiences. Multiracial readers may connect with aspects of our stories, even if they differ in background, age, and so on from us. For the rest of the chapter we focus on five areas that appear in the narratives and resonate throughout the book.

Guiding Themes and Supplemental Information

Chapters in this book use theories, narratives, and applied strategies to highlight the diverse ways that Multiracial students, faculty, and staff navigate campus life. As we noted in the preface, there are so many topics, areas, and themes reflected across the spectrum of Multiracial lives in higher education. Due to limitations of space, we have chosen to discuss five in this section. Although these topics have received attention in previous works on or related to Multiracial experiences, our goal here is to provide readers with some—not all—material to augment ideas and information that appear in the chapters that follow. We also note connections between areas discussed here and specific chapters in the book.

Definitions of Multiraciality and Complexities of Language

When reading this volume, a logical, first question to ask might be "Who are Multiracial people in higher education?" The answer to this question varies based on paradigmatic approaches to identity (see Wijeyesinghe, chapter 3) and data collection and reporting decisions (see Renn, chapter 2), which reflect larger issues and limitations of language and terminology. Are Multiracial people only those individuals who identify as Multiracial? Or is Multiracial identity based on one's background or ancestry (which opens up critiques of biological and genetic essentialism)? Throughout this volume, readers will encounter narratives from people who might be considered Multiracial in terms of background, but who identify monoracially (see Davis, chapter 5; alexander, chapter 8).

Identity labels are both personal and political. For instance, despite the interchangeable use of terms like *biracial, Multiracial,* and *mixed race* in common discourse, we know that these words have their own meanings and may be contested in different spaces and for different people. Individuals and groups often have strong rationales for the specific language they use to name themselves and others who align with shared histories and struggles. Some terms and naming conventions might even be specific to individual families or may look different depending on audience. Thus, we have offered a more inclusive definition of *Multiracial people* in the preface to describe the population we focus on in this book—namely, anyone who claims heritage and membership in two or more (mono)racial groups and/or identifies with Multiracial identity terms, such as the broader *biracial, multiethnic*, and *mixed*, or more specific terms, like *Blasian* and *Mexipino*. Yet we know the definition we adopted for this book still may not capture everyone who identifies with Multiracial experiences, including transracial adoptees (see Combs & Ashlee, 2020). Such broad conceptualizing of multiraciality (a noun used to signify anything related to Multiracial topic) might be open to critique since there is extensive diversity within this category, resulting in very different expressions and experiences of identity. As some authors have argued (e.g., Hamako, 2014), what unites Multiracial people is not necessarily how they identify (i.e., which box or boxes they check or terms they claim) but how they have to navigate monoracism (see Harris, Johnston-Guerrero, & Pereyra, chapter 4).

Multiracial People in Higher Education by the Numbers

Despite the limitations in language and terminology, U.S. higher education generally uses the lens of racial self-identification through "box-checking" to identify those who marked "Two or More Races" as Multiracial. U.S. Census data from 2010 reported that 2.9% of the population (over 9 million people) self-identified with two or more races (Jones & Bullock, 2012). However, the Pew Research Center (2015) has estimated that the Multiracial population may be closer to 6.9% when accounting for parent/grandparent race. With these differences in mind, the following selected statistics on Multiracial people in higher education from *Race and Ethnicity in Higher Education: A Status Report* (Espinosa et al., 2019) and *The Condition of Education* (National Center for Education Statistics, 2020) will help to contextualize the volume:

- In fall 2018, 16.6 million undergraduates were enrolled in degree-granting postsecondary institutions; approximately 647,000 students (3.9%) were two or more races.
- Among all undergraduates enrolled during 2015–2016, the percentage of women (56.5%) was higher than men (43.5%); this gap was higher for students of more than one race (women at 59.4% and men at 40.6%).
- During the 2015–2016 academic year, undergraduates checking more than one box to indicate race attended a range of institutions, including public 4-year (33.8%), private nonprofit 4-year (13.8%), public 2-year (44.8%), and for-profit (7.5%).
- In fall 2018, there were approximately 3 million postbaccalaureate degree program students (i.e., graduate students); approximately 81,300 students (2.7%) were of two or more races.

- During the 2015–2016 academic year, graduate students of more than one race attended a range of institutions, including public 4-year (45.8%), private nonprofit 4-year (39.7%), and for-profit (14.4%); for-profit enrollment outpaced the 10.3% enrollment for graduate students overall.
- In 2016, across all levels of educational attainment, adults (age 25 or older) of more than one race earned less than the national median for all adults; those with a professional degree earned $15,000 less than the national median for adults with professional degrees.
- In fall 2016, people who marked more than one race made up 0.9% of total full-time faculty; of all these faculty, 32.5% held positions as instructors, lecturers, or in faculty positions with no academic rank (compared to 26.7% overall).
- In fall 2016, college presidents were predominantly white (91.9%), with individuals of more than one race comprising 1.4% of all college presidents.

As evidenced in these statistics, the numbers don't tell the whole story; highlighted here is a sample of the contested landscape regarding naming ("two or more races" or "more than one race" may not equal "Multiracial"). Statistics on Multiracial professional staff were not even mentioned. This erasure is just one way Multiracial people might feel included or excluded as they navigate higher education settings.

Issues and Forces Affecting Inclusion and Exclusion

Even with the contested nature of counting and naming, the increasing presence and visibility of Multiracial people across higher education is clear. As Renn (chapter 2) points out and the narratives in this volume embody, there is likely a reciprocal relationship among Multiracial students claiming space, Multiracial staff offering support programs and services, and Multiracial faculty developing research and curriculum, each building off one another to improve Multiracial experiences in higher education. Multiracial student organizations may experience tensions (Davis, chapter 5; Mohajeri & Lou, chapter 13) or turnover, but they still offer important spaces for engagement and leadership development. Often, students themselves are driving educational efforts like Multiracial Heritage Months or Loving Day events (Kaya, chapter 9). Multiracial staff are increasingly finding support networks and professional development through outlets such as the National Conference on Race and Ethnicity (NCORE) and affinity groups within professional associations such as the MultiRacial Network of the American College Personnel Association (ACPA) (Malaney Brown, chapter 6) and the

MultiRacial Knowledge Community of the National Association of Student Personnel Administrators (NASPA). Multiracial faculty (especially those who study multiraciality) are finding outlets like the Critical Mixed Race Studies Association (CMRSA; www.criticalmixedracestudies.com) and its *Journal of Critical Mixed Race Studies* and conferences to legitimize their scholarship. And now, even academic programs (Leopardo, Donnell, & Dariotis, chapter 14) are validating multiraciality within the academy.

Yet alongside increasing inclusion are forces and factors still fostering the marginalization and erasure of Multiracial people in higher education. The limitations and confusion around language and naming point to one area contributing to some people with Multiracial identities feeling seen or unseen. As several chapters in the volume point to (e.g., Guillermo-Wann & Johnston-Guerrero, chapter 11; Harris, Johnston-Guerrero, & Pereyra, chapter 4), these forces stem from larger oppressive structures and systems. These systems have long and winding roots. Thus, the importance of grounding our current understandings in the historical legacies related to exclusion (e.g., slavery, settler colonialism and genocide, imperialism, antimiscegenation laws, rules of hypodescent and blood quantum) cannot be understated as we look to the future.

Sites of Experience

Multiracial people encounter inclusion, exclusion, affirmation, and challenges in many locations within higher education. Several contributors to this volume identify multiple sites that affect personal perceptions of self, belonging, rejection, and resilience, including all of the contributors of the narratives offered in chapters 5 through 10. In addition, Mohajeri and Lou (chapter 13) discuss how student organizations can be improved through reflection, increased awareness, and intentional work of advisers. Enhancing the inclusion of Multiracial people also entails creating new sites for examining, affirming, and nurturing individuals. The Multiracial Aikido retreat featured in chapter 12 by Martinez and Shippen represents one of these innovations. Moving to the future, researchers, scholars, and practitioners are encouraged to look beyond the locations closest to an individual and to consider how larger systems and institutional structures affect outcomes for Multiracial students (Harris, Johnston-Guerrero, & Pereyra, chapter 4; Kellogg & Niskodé, 2008) and the overall climate of inclusion of Multiracial people (Guillermo-Wann & Johnston-Guerrero, chapter 11).

Most of the scholarship on Multiracial people in higher education has focused on students, but some of that research bears relevance to faculty and staff. The complex interwoven nature of these systems is evident in the narratives of faculty (Kaya, chapter 9; Jolivétte, chapter 10) and staff (Malaney

Brown, chapter 6; alexander, chapter 8). The insights provided by these contributors complement scholarship on Multiracial faculty by Harris (e.g., 2020) and Cuyjet (2008), as well as on related topics such as curriculum and teaching methods (Williams et al., 1996). In addition, chapter 14 in this volume (Leopardo, Donnell, & Dariotis) illustrates responses of members of the academic community to Multiracial faculty's efforts to develop a minor on mixed race studies.

Strategies for Surviving and Thriving

Throughout this book, contributors describe multiple strategies that they have utilized to support themselves or other Multiracial people at their institutions. We have chosen to end this chapter by recounting some of those strategies, because they reflect the creativity, resilience, and service of individuals who find and offer strength, community, and wisdom within institutions that are largely ill prepared to welcome and affirm them as full members of the campus community. We believe this list does not detract from the words and experiences of the contributors who follow, and we hope that it makes readers even more eager to read the analyses, narratives, and practices provided in the next chapters. Some of the strategies contributors to this book have used include the following:

- Found faculty and staff mentors who can support and encourage self-exploration and who can assist in skill and academic development; became a mentor for other Multiracial people
- Engaged in spaces that made room for Multiracial people, which can include campus-based organizations, local community groups, and national-level organizations such as CMRSA
- Sought out opportunities to build coalitions with other organizations and people; helped organizations and coalitions develop orientations and activities to further racial justice for Multiracial people, other people of color, and related targeted groups
- Created opportunities for individuals to explore issues of identity, self-care, and navigating campus life; engaged in this critical work personally and continually to be a role model and to remain prepared to help others
- Took, developed, and offered courses and educational programs related to Multiracial topics
- Identified and critiqued knowledge and practices that excluded or contested Multiracial experiences; disseminated new knowledge through research or presentations

- Advocated for the inclusion of Multiracial people in programs offering benefits such as scholarships, internships, or conference programs
- Stayed connected to family and community

Synthesis

As readers will find within the chapters that follow, higher education is a site of discourse, analysis, and knowledge building for subjects that create the contexts in which Multiracial lives are understood, questioned, researched, contested, embraced, and experienced. Almost every aspect of those contexts shifts over time in response to political advocacy and action, evolving cultural and political forces, and insights gained from research and practice. Hence, they require constant assessment and consideration through the knowledge, voices, and practices offered by this book, and in similar volumes that will be produced in the years that follow.

References

Combs, L., & Ashlee, A. A. (2020). *Different like me: Building empathy within multiracial and transracial adoptee communities through identity analogies.* 2020 NASPA Knowledge Community Publication. https://naspa.org/report/2020-knowledge-communities-online-publication

Cuyjet, M. J. (2008). *Bicultural faculty and their professional adaptation* (New Directions for Student Services, no. 123, pp. 73–82). Wiley. http://doi.org/10.1002/ss.288

Espinosa, L. L., Turk, J. M., Taylor, M., & Chessman, H. M. (2019). *Race and ethnicity in higher education: A status report.* American Council on Education. https://www.equityinhighered.org

Hamako, E. (2014). *Improving antiracist education for multiracial students* [Unpublished doctoral dissertation]. University of Massachusetts Amherst.

Hardiman, R. (1982). *White identity development: A process oriented model for describing the racial consciousness of White Americans* [Unpublished doctoral dissertation]. University of Massachusetts Amherst.

Harris, J. C. (2020). Multiracial faculty members' experiences with teaching, research, and service. *Journal of Diversity in Higher Education 13*(3), 228–239. http://doi.org/10.1037/dhe0000123

Jackson, B. W. (1976). *The function of a theory of Black identity development in achieving relevance in education for Black students* [Unpublished doctoral dissertation]. University of Massachusetts Amherst.

Jones, N. A., & Bullock, J. (2012). *The two or more races population: 2010* (2010 Census Briefs). U.S. Census Bureau.

Kellogg, A., & Niskodé, A. S. (2008). *Student affairs and higher education policy issues related to multiracial students* (New Directions for Student Services, no. 123, pp. 93–102). Wiley. http://doi.org/10.1002/ss.290

National Center for Education Statistics. (2020). *The condition of education: Undergraduate enrollment.* https://nces.ed.gov/programs/coe/indicator_cha.asp

Pew Research Center. (2015). *Multiracial in America: Proud, diverse and growing in numbers.* https://www.pewsocialtrends.org/2015/06/11/multiracial-in-america/

Williams, T. K., Nakashima, C. L., Kich, G. K., & Daniel, G. R. (1996). Being different together in the university classroom: Multiracial identity as transgressive education. In M. P. P. Root (Ed.), *The multiracial experience: Racial borders as the new frontier* (pp. 359–379). SAGE.

2

MULTIRACIAL IDENTITY ON CAMPUS

Identities and Experiences of Multiracial People in Higher Education

Kristen A. Renn

T he study of multiracial identities received scant attention prior to the 1980s. Changing social norms and the 1969 *Loving v. Virginia* decision that ended remaining legal bans on mixed race marriages accelerated a multiracial baby boom, which drew attention to relevant and pressing topics for research. By the 1990s a few biracial identity development stage models (Kerwin & Ponterotto, 1995; Kich, 1992; Poston, 1990) and ecological models (Root, 1999; Wijeyesinghe, 2001) emerged to provide guidance for clinical practice. Children of mixed race relationships came of age at a time when racial identity politics created a rhetorical space for narrative accounts of multiracial identities; movements in the 1990s to change the U.S. Census categories from "one race only" categories to a "multiracial" or "check all that apply" format focused on the right of individuals to be able to identify officially as they did privately. This growing political force made up of a critical mass of multiracial people and some parents of multiracial children called for greater awareness of and insight into the multiracial experience (Nakashima, 1996). At the same time, much was made in the media of mixed race celebrities, athletes, and public figures (e.g., Mariah Carey and Tiger Woods), drawing praise from advocates for social progress, while opponents of interracial relationships and holdouts for so-called racial purity attempted to enforce a few remaining bans on, for example, interracial couples attending high school dances (Gross, 1994).

In the course of these developments in the history of race, racialization, and racism in the United States, mixed race college students, faculty, and campus professionals found identities and voice on campus and in emergent digital spaces that allowed for connection on static web resources and then social media. The literature on biracial, multiracial, and mixed race college students follows this history as students and campus professionals relied initially on Poston's and Kich's developmental models, then on the growing body of personal narratives, descriptions of multiracial college students, and ecological models of multiracial identity. Although a number of key areas of experience and identity of mixed race people on campus remain unexplored, a robust base of scholarship on multiracial students is available to guide practice and policy, as well as to form a foundation for multiracial students to find themselves represented in the literature. More recently, scholarship on multiracial faculty and campus professionals has provided a foundation for understanding their experiences and guiding inclusive practice (see Daniel et al., 2014; Harris, 2016). The adoption by some researchers of a critical mixed race studies approach has brought a new perspective to the overall body of literature on multiracial people on campus. In this chapter I provide an overview of literature on multiracial people and multiracial identities in higher education, including students, faculty, and campus professionals. I make recommendations for practice designed to support the identities, identity development, and thriving of mixed race people on campus.

Multiracial People and Multiraciality in Higher Education

A common question about multiracial people in higher education relates to the size of this population. Since the U.S. Department of Education began mandating that institutions report the number of students indicating more than one race, the percentage of this group doubled from 2% in 2010 to 4% in 2016 (National Center for Education Statistics, 2019). U.S. demographics predict an increase in multiracial college students over time (Jones & Bullock, 2013).

Educational institutions (K–12 and postsecondary) are required to collect data from students and employees using the two-step ethnicity and race questions of the U.S. Census (National Center for Education Statistics, n.d.). First, respondents indicate their ethnicity as "Hispanic or Latino" or "Not Hispanic or Latino." Then they indicate as many as apply from five racial categories: American Indian or Alaska Native, Asian, Black or African American, Native Hawaiian or Other Pacific Islander, and White. Institutions report data in seven categories: Hispanic or Latino is one, and then for all respondents who are Not Hispanic or Latino there are six categories (the five racial categories plus Two or More Races for everyone who indicated more than one race). Institutions are permitted to collect additional categories (e.g., Mexican American, Chicano, Puerto Rican, Japanese, Pakistani, Indian) so long as it is clear that they can be rolled up into the seven basic categories. Postsecondary institutions can use two additional categories: Nonresident Alien and Not Reported (Race and Ethnicity Unknown). Because institutional data on race and ethnicity are typically collected at the time of admissions or job application, the Not Reported/Unknown category allows institutions to honor the decision of individuals to self-determine their response. This principle is not followed, however, in the K–12 public school reporting process, in which the federal government requires school personnel to use "observer-identification" to report the race and ethnicity of every pupil, a process that violates self-identification and likely leads to substantial misidentification of multiracial students (Ford, 2019).

The bulk of literature on multiracial people and multiraciality in higher education focuses on college students. Scholarship on multiracial college students took off in earnest in the late 1990s and accelerated into the 2010s. Some university-based researchers conducted studies that used college students as a convenience sample, resulting in literature about multiracial people that was in fact based on a college student population, whereas other researchers purposefully explored the experiences and identities of multiracial college students. A related strand of literature addresses programs and services to support mixed race students, and a burst of research about campus racial data occurred around the time of the 2010 implementation of the Two or More Races mandate in education data. A small but growing body of research addresses multiracial faculty and staff.

Multiracial College Students: Identities and Experiences

Literature on mixed race college students developed similarly to the larger body of literature on minoritized populations in higher education. For a number of social identities, personal narratives, media, and now social media lay a groundwork for visibility of the group. First-person stories, art, images, and media introduce others to the experiences of a previously invisible minoritized group. In the case of multiracial people, books like *Half and Half: Writers on Growing up Biracial + Bicultural* (O'Hearn, 1998), *Black, White, and Jewish: Autobiography of a Shifting Self* (Walker, 2005), and *Dreams From My Father: A Story of Race and Inheritance* (Obama, 1995/2004) provided windows into the mixed race experience in the United States; some volumes highlighted multiracial college students specifically (Garrod et al., 2013). Then quantitative studies, or studies that estimate the size of the population, established an empirical presence, and qualitative studies explored lived experiences and identity development; much of the literature cited in this chapter falls into this qualitative category. As the body of scholarship evolves, it extends into studies of intersecting identities of race, gender, and/or sexuality, such as biracial/bisexual people (King, 2011; Paz Galupo et al., 2019) or multiracial women (Basu, 2010; Harris, 2017c; Rockquemore, 2002; Thompson & Gillem, 2019). The emergence of multiracial scholarship around the same time as the naming of microaggressions as an aspect of campus climate provided another angle through which leaders in the area of mixed race studies (e.g., Jessica Harris and Marc Johnston-Guerrero) explored the experiences of multiracial students.

Three early-stage models of biracial identity development and two ecological models formed a base for later explorations of multiracial college students. Two of the stage models had endpoints that reflected an integration of racial selves within an individual (Kerwin & Ponterotto, 1995; Poston, 1990). Both models posit adolescence as a time when peers and other social factors compel biracial youth to choose one racial group over another; resolving the consequent confusion and guilt is a key step in both models. Integrating racial identities and then further integrating racial identity into other facets of identity mark endpoints of healthy identity development. The third early-stage model (Kich, 1992) proposed that instead of choosing one race over another and then integrating the outcome, biracial people could establish healthy biracial and bicultural identities. This achievement required cognitive flexibility to understand race as a social construction.

Root (1999) and Wijeyesinghe (2001) offered ecological approaches to understanding multiracial identity and the factors that influenced it. Root (1999) located the development of multiracial identity in contexts of interactions among geographic, historical, gender, class, sexual orientation, and generational influences. Wijeyesinghe (2001) offered the factor model of multiracial identity (FMMI), which posited racial ancestry, cultural attachment, early experience and socialization, political awareness and orientation, spirituality, physical appearance, social and historical context, and other social identities as the ecology in which choice of racial identity occurred for multiracial people. For many years higher education professionals relied on these stage model and ecological theories, if they used any theory, to guide practice with mixed race students.

Renn's (2003, 2004) articulation of five patterns of mixed race identities remains a model in wide circulation. The five patterns (monoracial identity, multiple monoracial identities, multiracial identity, extraracial identity, and situational identity) provide a robust description of how mixed race college students experience and express racial identities. Mixed race students with a monoracial identity choose one of their parents' heritage groups and identify as, for example, Black or Asian. Alternatively, in the second pattern, students might choose to identify multiple monoracial identities ("I'm Latino and Native American" or "I'm Black and White"). Students in the third pattern identify as multiracial or another term such as *biracial, mixed race,* or *hapa*, that indicates a mixed identity that forefronts mixedness rather than the component heritage groups. The fourth pattern, an extraracial identity, is one that is not rooted in U.S. racial categories but embraces racelessness, nonracial, or other identity outside racial categorization. Finally, the fifth pattern is situational identity, in which a student chooses to identify differently according to context, perhaps sometimes monoracially ("I'm Asian American"), sometimes multiple monoracially ("I'm Asian and Latina"), sometimes as mixed race, or sometimes extraracially ("I don't subscribe to the categories; I'm just Megan"). Other authors (e.g., King, 2011; Rockquemore & Brunsma, 2002) have found similar, if not identically named, racial identifications among multiracial college students, lending credibility to Renn's findings.

Beyond Renn's work on patterns of identities, scholars have elaborated on the identities and experiences of multiracial students. For example, expanding on Renn's description of contexts and identity fluidity, Casandra Harper (2016) utilized a survey of 1,101 multiracial students from 105 U.S. colleges to examine self-reported race. In this study, 56% of the sample gave different responses at different times, and Harper determined that predictors of senior year students designating a multiracial choice included living on campus, participating in a racial or ethnic student group, taking ethnic studies coursework, participating in a racial awareness workshop, and discussing issues of political or personal importance. These findings align with Renn's (2003, 2004) and Wijeyesinghe's (2001) ecological factors related to multiracial identity and emphasize Root's (1996) claim that multiracial people may define themselves differently over time.

College students have not only racial identities but also ideas about what race is and how it is constructed. In different studies, Johnston-Guerrero explored these ideas. In one, Johnston-Guerrero and Chaudhari (2016) explored how students' awareness of multiraciality might reify the concept of race as a biological concept (to have "mixed race" there must be biological parents of more than one "race" to begin with) and/or lead them to see "multiraciality as the end of racism" (p. 256). Johnston-Guerrero and Chaudhari called these concepts *racial claims*. They found that fewer than half of the 24 study participants (who were from a variety of monoracial and multiracial backgrounds themselves) brought up multiraciality. Among students who did talk about it, multiraciality was used as evidence for two sets of claims: (1) to refute or confirm the biological concept of race, and (2) to argue for a future racial landscape where everyone is mixed (and race and racism no longer matter). (p. 259)

Another study (Johnston-Guerrero & Pecero, 2016) focused on how mixed heritage students' ideas about race, culture, and family interacted with their personal identity construction; the study found that culture and race were both important to identity, and family served as an avenue (and venue) for learning about culture and race. This focus on students' ideas—how they *think about* race, culture, family, and identity—provides evidence for how they make sense of the biological, cultural, social, and familial underpinnings of social identities including race.

In another exploration of students' ideas about race and mixed race, Clayton (2019) examined racial regard (positive and negative feelings about the racial group to which one belongs) of Black–White biracial students at historically Black colleges and universities (HBCUs) and predominantly White institutions (PWIs). She found that exposure to groups of Black peers who had diverse backgrounds (e.g., urban, suburban, rural) and interests (e.g., different majors, extracurricular activities, and career goals), among other factors, improved Black–White biracial students' regard for Blackness. Together, these three studies showed that mixed race students may have sophisticated cognitive understandings of the social construction of race and raciality, though there is variation depending on experience. Exposure to social science knowledge through coursework, media, and discussion with peers provides students a platform from which to construct more complex ideas about race, multiraciality, and racial identification. Today's college students—multiracial and monoracial—have access to a rich theoretical and empirical base for understanding their own identities.

Yet multiracial students still live and learn on campuses where they face racism and systemic beliefs, attitudes, values, and practices reflective of monoracism (Johnston & Nadal, 2010). Monoracism is a specific form of racism predicated on the belief that everyone has one and only one race, and that such a circumstance is superior to being two or more races. Monoracism permeates campuses as it does society and leads to a number of multiracial microaggressions. Johnston and Nadal (2010) defined "multiracial microaggressions, or microaggressions based on multiracial status," as behaviors "which send hostile, derogatory, or negative messages toward multiracial persons" (p. 132). They proposed a taxonomy of five themes, later amended by Nadal et al. (2011) to include a sixth: exclusion and isolation, exoticization and objectification, assumption of a monoracial identity, denial of a multiracial reality, pathologizing of multiracial identity and experiences, and stereotypes. In a qualitative study, Harris (2017b) later confirmed two of these (denial of a multiracial reality and assumption of a monoracial identity) and elaborated an additional microaggression, in which multiracial students receive clear messages from peers that they are "not (monoracial) enough to 'fit in'" (p. 437). One participant, for example, was of Mexican and Black heritage and did not speak Spanish, which she felt "marked her as not enough for her monoracial Mexican classmates" (p. 439).

One manifestation of monoracism, embedded in the larger system of racism and White supremacy, relates to the perception and experience of multiracial college students' physical appearance. Across studies over time, students report that because they look racially ambiguous to others, they are subject to exoticization (Basu, 2010; Harris, 2017c; Museus et al., 2016; Renn, 2003, 2004). If multiracial students have White heritage, they may be lighter skinned than some other people of color and share some of the benefits of being lighter in a society governed by colorism (Ozaki & Parson, 2016). Indeed, their lighter appearance may lead members of some ostensibly monoracial communities to view them as inauthentic or not legitimate representatives of that community.

The issue of authenticity arises frequently in studies of multiracial people in general and carries over to the campus context. A study not specific to higher education found that if multiracial people were seen to engage in social activism on behalf of a community of color, members of that community were more likely to consider them in a positive light (Garay et al., 2019). Yet multiracial college students still face obstacles to this kind of engagement in campus-based communities of color, a finding Renn (2003, 2004) noted among students in the late 1990s that persists today (Harris, 2017b). Investigations using 4 years of data from the National Survey of Student Engagement (NSSE) showed that there are differences in engagement among multiracial students from different racial heritage groups and across institutional types (Harris & BrckaLorenz, 2017; Harris et al., 2018), illuminating diversity among multiracial students and institutional diversity as a factor in student engagement. For example, Harris et al. (2018) found that students with two parents of color tended to be engaged at about the same level as monoracial peers from their respective heritage groups but more likely than their monoracial peers to have engaged in discussions with people who are different from themselves; students with one White parent were also more likely than monoracial peers to engage in such discussions but tended to be less engaged in other ways. In general, American Indian/Asian American and American Indian/Native Hawaiian or Other Pacific Islander students tended to have the highest engagement scores overall on the five NSSE scales.

In addition to considering diversity among multiracial students with different heritages, scholars have extended research on intersections of multiracial identity with other salient identities, most commonly sexual orientation and gender. Bi- and multiracial people, including college students, who are also lesbian, gay, bisexual, or queer have received a fair amount of scholarly attention (Hudson & Mehrotra, 2015; King, 2011; Paz Galupo et al., 2019; Stanley, 2004). This attention is unsurprising given that both mixed race and queer bodies have been subject to legal and social construction by the dominant White settler-colonial agenda in the United States that seeks to preserve White dominance by regulating people's bodies and promoting the reproduction of Whiteness (Stewart, 2019). The intersection of race and gender in bi- and multiracial women's identities (Harris, 2019b; Rockquemore, 2002; Rockquemore & Brunsma, 2004; Thompson & Gillem, 2019) is also located at this embodied juncture, where physical appearance, exoticization, cultural knowledge, and stereotypes about femininity and race converge to influence experiences and identities.

More recently, studies of biracial men have brought forward the specific intersections of masculinity and multiraciality (Joseph-Salisbury, 2019; Sims & Joseph-Salisbury, 2019), particularly in relationship to Blackness and authenticity. Incorporating gender, class, and religion into a large quantitative study (n = 37,000), Davenport (2016) found that gender was the strongest predictor of racial identification, with biracial women more likely than biracial men to identify as multiracial. Davenport also found that White self-identification was predicted by Jewish identity, whereas minority identification was predicted by belonging to a religion more commonly associated with racial minorities (e.g., Baptist for Black–White respondents; Catholicism for Latinx–White respondents; Hinduism, Islam, or Buddhism for Asian–White respondents). Although not all of these studies are specific to college students, there is evidence of a growing interest in understanding multiracial identity across the life span in the context of other identities, as Wijeyesinghe's (2001) FMMI proposed.

Programs and Services for Multiracial Students

Just as research on multiracial students has expanded, literature on how best to support them through campus programs and services has also grown. Ozaki and Johnston (2008) provided early direction in their recommendations for advising multiracial student organizations. Since then, recommendations for engaging multiracial college students (Malaney & Danowski, 2015; Ozaki & Renn, 2015; Ozaki et al., 2020) have promoted creating curriculum, deepening support for student organizations, and auditing all campus policies and practices to identify circumstances that inadvertently treat biracial students differently from their monoracial peers or convey a message that monoraciality is a preferred identity. Best practices include always providing multiple options for self-identification and allowing individuals to change that self-identification over time, as supported by the Harper (2016) finding that 56% of biracial students changed their racial identification during 4 years in college.

College counseling professionals have paid particular attention to the needs of multiracial students. Recommendations based on research include offering multiracial groups in university counseling centers (Narvaez & Kivlighan, 2019; Watson, 2013), developing outreach strategies (Paladino & Davis, 2006), and creating deeper understanding of the complexities of biracial student experiences (West & Maffini, 2019). Here too there is attention to intersecting identities, such as in counseling biracial women (Nishimura, 2004). It is important not to assume that all multiracial students are in need of counseling or seek counseling based on issues of race and identity, but it is also important to recognize that the overall number of students seeking mental health services on college campuses is increasing, and multiracial students are among those in need of support.

Research on Multiracial Professionals and Faculty in Higher Education

Although the bulk of scholarship on multiracial people in higher education focuses on college students, some recent studies have addressed the growing number of multiracial faculty and staff. It makes sense that these studies would emerge as the adult workforce has become increasingly mixed race as a result of the children born during the "multiracial baby boom" reaching midadulthood. Harris (2017a, 2019a, 2020a, 2020b) is by far the leader in producing this line of scholarship, and doing so from a critical mixed race perspective. Based on her related studies of 24 campus professionals and 26 college faculty, Harris has depicted a campus climate for multiracial professionals and faculty that is rife with multiracial microaggressions. Like the students she studied (Harris, 2017b), campus professionals experienced denials of multiracial reality, assumption of monoracial identity, and perceptions that they were not monoracial enough. She found three themes, all related to racial authenticity or the need to demonstrate (or feel) one can legitimately claim identity in relation to monoracial groups: "encountering racial authenticity tests, navigating the authenticity trap, and Black Lives Matter and professionals' internalization of racial authenticity tests" (Harris, 2019a, p. 98). Staff members reported having colleagues ask them to prove their heritage or exclude them from social or professional networks of ostensibly monoracial groups of people of color.

Harris (2020b) found that multiracial faculty members experienced campus a bit differently from their campus professional colleagues, and in some ways more similar to students. They engaged in academic work (research) as a mechanism for social change, though like their staff colleagues they sometimes were invalidated by monoracial peers. One participant, for example, stated that "monoracial colleagues, both White colleagues and Colleagues of Color, were 'suspicious of mixed-race projects'" (p. 6). In spite of this suspicion, some faculty found that their multiraciality made them less threatening to their institutions—a situation that could also lead to additional service as token people of color on committees. Outside these studies, there is little published scholarship on multiracial higher education professionals or faculty. Some recent doctoral dissertations (e.g., Nicholas, 2019; Pannell, 2018) indicate that this area of research may be growing, which would add valuable insight into the identities and experiences of faculty and professionals who work in higher education settings. As the multiracial students who have been the subject of study for 3 decades reach adulthood and diversify academic workplaces, they may have opportunities as faculty and professionals to influence programs, services, curriculum, and policies that in turn influence multiracial students.

Analysis and Future Directions

Thirty years after Poston's (1990) groundbreaking articulation of healthy biracial identity development, what is the state and status of research on multiracial people generally and multiracial people in higher education specifically? As outlined in this chapter and chapter 1, literature on biracial and multiracial people, identities, and experiences has evolved. The introduction of critical mixed race studies has sharpened research on multiracial college students in recent years, and the inclusion of intersectional approaches to identity has built on the tradition of ecological models that incorporated other salient identities with the study of multiraciality. I view all of these developments as positive, and with work coming out through dissertations, narratives, and peer-reviewed studies, it is no longer true that there is a dearth of literature about multiracial college students.

That said, there are a number of topics about which further exploration would enable a more complete understanding of multiracial people on campus, their identities, and their experiences. It has always been true that the study of multiraciality in the United States illuminates regional differences in the proportion of multiracial people and the more common heritage combinations in each region (Nagai, 2016). In the 2000 U.S. Census, the first that instructed respondents to check multiple racial categories in addition to ethnicity (Hispanic/Latino or Not Hispanic/Latino), 2.4% of respondents indicated two or more races. In 2010, that percentage increased to 2.9%, with over 2 million more individuals in this group; of the 9 million total "two or more races" respondents, one third were from just three states: California (1.8 million), Texas (679,000), and New York (586,000) (Jones & Bullock, 2013). The other states in the top 10 in terms of number of multiracial people were Florida, Hawaii, Washington, Illinois, New Jersey, Pennsylvania, and Ohio. Specific heritage combinations are also clustered geographically, with, for example, larger percentages of White and Asian in Hawaii, White and Black in Delaware, and White and American Indian or Alaska Native in Alaska (Jones & Bullock, 2013).

Although there is a nationally mobile group of college students, the average distance a college student travels from home is less than 100 miles (Mattern & Wyatt, 2009). Regional population demographics and attitudes about multiracial people need to be a consideration in studies of multiracial college students, and often they are not discussed in the literature. Some national studies might address this concern through sample selection, but many qualitative studies of multiracial students are single-campus or one region, limiting diversity in factors like institutional type, urbanicity/rurality, and local culture and resources. These geographic constraints limit what can be known about multiracial students more broadly but also afford researchers opportunities to delve into the specifics of a given campus ecology.

Another opportunity to expand the literature lies in the generational shifts to which I have alluded in this chapter. Clearly there were biracial students and researchers in the 1980s and early 1990s; Maria Root and colleagues are evidence. Now a growing wave of biracial students—those who finished college in the mid to late 1990s—has reached adulthood (a student who graduated at age 22 in 1997 reached 45 in 2020), midcareer, and possibly parenthood. They might have their own multiracial offspring in college and could be on the faculty or staff of a postsecondary institution.

Further exploration of the variations in experiences and identities among multiracial people of different birth cohorts could be valuable in understanding experiences of different chronological generations of multiracial people. As an example of this richness, Cathy Tashiro (2015) offered a window into the experiences of 20 mixed race people born between 1902 and 1951. She collected their stories between 1996 and 1998 and heard about a mixed Japanese and White man whose White mother chose to live in a World War II internment camp with him, as well as the discovery that one African American and White man could finally "stand on both feet" (p. 1) when he came to understand the possibility of a mixed race identity. Although some stories—such as the internment camp example—are specific to age cohorts, other stories—like learning one can hold a multiracial identity (both feet)—resonate in studies across decades and social generations. The concept of multiraciality has another meaning of "generation" built in—one is multiracial because of the heritage groups of one's parents and grandparents—and this aspect has not been fully engaged in studies of college students, faculty, or others on campus.

Also somewhat unexplored are the actual effects of campus policy and programs on students. An abundance of literature, empirical and otherwise, makes recommendations for providing space on campus for multiracial students, for eliminating "choose one race only" situations on forms or in programming, and increasing visibility of multiracial people through curriculum, the arts, and staffing. Yet there is scant evidence of the efficacy of these approaches in actually changing campus climate for mixed race people. Indeed, the persistence of multiracial microaggressions over at least 20 years suggests that in spite of increasing the number of multiracial student organizations and improving counseling services, the environments in which multiracial students spend their time with peers, faculty, and others have not actually changed. Although there may be more support for multiracial students to cope with microaggressions, monoracism—the root source of the microaggressions—seemingly prevails.

The collection of choose-all-that-apply racial data on national surveys such as NSSE, the Student Experience at the Research University (SERU), and the Cooperative Institutional Research Program (CIRP) provides opportunities for understanding campus climate for multiracial students through large-scale data collection. SERU, which includes campus climate measures, provides the potential to compare multiracial students' perceptions of campus climate with those of monoracial White students and students of color (see Telles & Mitchell, 2018). They also allow for examination over time of campus climate outcomes of implementing policies and programs designed to support multiracial students. Researchers using these data sets should think carefully about how to treat respondents who do indicate more than one race; selective reassignment of these respondents to monoracial categories, creating (as the census and Integrated Postsecondary Education Data System [IPEDS] do) a Two or More Races category, creating separate categories by racial combinations, or omitting these responses altogether are among the options available, but each has consequences for what can be known about multiracial people and how researchers honor the principle of self-identification. Readers of studies that use these data sets should also be alert to how researchers treated respondents who indicated more than one race.

Advances in technologies create additional opportunities to understand multiracial college students. Students explore and express identities on social media, and social media platforms provide a rich context in which to observe student expression (see Patterson, 2017). Students entering college from high school in 2020 will have spent their entire lives around and engaged in social media, so understanding digital contexts of their lives is as important as the emotional, familial, and physical factors that comprised Wijeyesinghe's (2001) FMMI. Existing in the image-soaked world of smartphones, social media affords new ways of seeing—or not seeing—oneself, for better and for worse in terms of developing multiracial identity and avoiding multiracial microaggressions. Streamable television shows like *Mixed-ish* or podcasts like *Militantly Mixed, Mark All That Apply, Both And,* and *Some Kind of Brown* provide outlets for learning about self and exploring ways of thinking about and being multiracial.

Other technologies also interact with multiracial identities. The prevalence of commercial DNA testing kits, for example, offers a previously unimaginable window into understanding both genetic heritage and how knowledge about genetic heritage influences how people think about and describe their identities. It is important to note, however, that enthusiasm for exploring ancestry through these kits outpaces their accuracy (see Duster, 2016) and risks reinforcing ideas about racial biology and genetic determinism. Though home DNA testing has become popular, it is an inexact technology with potential downsides if the public does not think critically about race, ethnicity, and culture. Lawton and Foeman (2017) conducted interviews before and after 21 multiracial participants took DNA tests and learned the results. They used Renn's (2003, 2004) patterns of identity as a beginning point for understanding how participants described their identities before and after learning DNA results. Results deepened participants' beliefs in the social construction and fluidity of race, and emphasized distinctions between and connections across race and culture. The combination of an advanced technology with a traditional research method (qualitative interviews) represents the kind of new developments that will be possible in the study of multiracial identities.

Application

Even without direct evidence that programs, services, and policies have improved campus climate and quality of life for multiracial students, the literature suggests that it is worthwhile to continue efforts to improve campus climate for students, faculty, and staff. Ozaki and colleagues (Ozaki & Renn, 2015; Ozaki et al., 2020) recommended undertaking an audit of campus policies, programs, and procedures to ensure that mixed race people on campus experience inclusion and equity. An audit might reveal examples of exclusion and inequity that include campus forms and data reporting; provision of programs, services, and professional networks aimed at supporting people of color that assume (or appear to assume) monoraciality; and curriculum and extracurricular educational activities (e.g., lectures, awareness/ pride weeks) that focus only on monoracial groups and identities.

The core principle of the right to self-identify is a central concept in research on multiracial people. Institutional forms should include the opportunity to self-identify in all categories that apply, and guidance should be provided to other campus members who will be asking for racial identity in any context. Researchers should at minimum follow the federal guidelines for data collection and ideally provide response options that reflect local patterns of racial and ethnic identification. Whether for institutional or research purposes, respondents should know how their data will be rolled up into categories for analysis and reporting in institutional data, to IPEDS, or in research. When deciding how to treat more-than-one-category responses, researchers should honor racial self-identification to the extent possible and clearly explain their rationale and procedure for any assignment of multiracial people into monoracial categories.

Reducing monoracism must be a priority on campus (see also chapter 4 of this volume). Improving college counseling and multiracial students' coping skills for dealing with prejudice and discrimination is important (Museus et al., 2015; Narvaez & Kivlighan, 2019); developing support for multiracial faculty and campus professionals lags behind current efforts at student support and should be extended. But given the enduring research findings about encounters with monoracism and multiracial microaggressions, the attention cannot go solely to helping multiracial people build resilience. Building explicit goals for campus learning about multiraciality and multiracial identity into diversity curriculum is one approach; ensuring that training for staff and faculty also includes information on reducing multiracial microaggressions through policy implementation, procedures, and curriculum is also necessary. Just as dealing with racism on campus requires both supporting people of color and implementing changes that will reduce systemic and individual effects of a history of White supremacy in the United States, addressing monoracism requires support, education, and system-level examination and policy change.

Conclusion

From early explorations of biracial and multiracial identity development to today, the literature has grown impressively. Studies of multiracial youth, adolescents, college students, and adults occur in a range of academic disciplines and describe multiraciality and multiracial identity in a range of contexts: home, school, college, work, and community. Large-scale survey studies providing a national perspective have joined a tradition of qualitative studies of mixed race college students; the inclusion of choose-all-that-apply racial self-identification items on existing national surveys such as NSSE, CIRP, and SERU allow for comparisons between multiracial students and their monoracial peers of any race, further deepening the knowledge base on multiracial students. Studies of faculty and staff are emerging, though still very limited, and represent a necessary topic for additional study. What happened to those mixed race college students of the 1990s? What are their lives like on campus today as faculty and staff? Connecting research across geographies and generations will enable new insights and guide emergent policy and practice. The field is rich, and there is more yet to be learned by a new generation of scholars of multiraciality and multiracial identity.

References

Basu, A. M. (2010). The role of gender in the experiences of biracial college students. *Race/Ethnicity: Multidisciplinary Global Contexts*, *4*(1), 97–115. http://doi.org/10.2979/racethmulglocon.2010.4.1.97

Clayton, K. (2019). Black-white biracial students' evaluations of blackness: The role of college in shaping racial regard. *Sociology of Race and Ethnicity*, *5*(1), 70–84. https://doi.org/10.1177/2332649217748427

Daniel, G. R., Kina, L., Dariotis, W. M., & Fojas, C. (2014). Emerging paradigms in critical mixed race studies. *Journal of Critical Mixed Race Studies*, *1*(1), 1–65. https://escholarship.org/uc/item/2db5652b

Davenport, L. D. (2016). The role of gender, class, and religion in biracial Americans' racial labeling decisions. *American Sociological Review*, *81*(1), 57–84. https://doi.org/10.1177/0003122415623286

Duster, T. (2016). Ancestry testing and DNA: Uses, limits—and caveat emptor. In B. Prainsack, S. Schicktanz, & G. Werner-Felmayer (Eds.), *Genetics as social practice: Transdisciplinary views on science and culture* (pp. 75–88). Routledge.

Ford, K. S. (2019). Observer-identification: A potential threat to the validity of self-identified race and ethnicity. *Educational Researcher*, *48*(6), 378–381. https://doi.org/10.3102/0013189X19860803

Garay, M. M., Meyers, C., Remedios, J. D., & Pauker, K. (2019, August 28). Looking like vs. acting like your race: Social activism shapes perceptions of multiracial individuals. *Self and Identity*. Advance online publication. https://doi.org/10.1080/15298868.2019.1659848

Garrod, A., Gómez, C., & Kilkenny, R. (Eds.). (2013). *Mixed: Multiracial college students tell their life stories*. Cornell University Press.

Gross, J. (1994, August 15). In prom dispute, a town's race divisions emerge. *New York Times*. https://www.nytimes.com/1994/08/15/us/in-prom-dispute-a-town-s-race-divisions-emerge.html

Harper, C. E. (2016). Pre-college and college predictors of longitudinal changes in multiracial college students' self-reported race. *Race Ethnicity and Education, 19*(5), 927–949. https://doi.org/10.1080/13613324.2014.911161

Harris, J. C. (2016). Toward a critical multiracial theory in education. *International Journal of Qualitative Studies in Education, 29*(6), 795–813. https://doi.org/10.1080/09518398.2016.1162870

Harris, J. C. (2017a). Multiracial campus professionals' experiences with multiracial microaggressions. *Journal of College Student Development, 58*(7), 1055–1073. https://doi.org/10.1353/csd.2017.0083

Harris, J. C. (2017b). Multiracial college students' experiences with multiracial microaggressions. *Race Ethnicity and Education, 20*(4), 429–445. https://doi.org/10.1080/13613324.2016.1248836

Harris, J. C. (2017c). Multiracial women students and racial stereotypes on the college campus. *Journal of College Student Development, 58*(4), 475–491. https://doi.org/10.1353/csd.2017.0038

Harris, J. C. (2019a). Multiracial campus professionals' experiences with racial authenticity. *Equity & Excellence in Education, 52*(1), 93–107. https://doi.org/10.1080/10665684.2019.1631232

Harris, J. C. (2019b). Whiteness as structuring property: Multiracial women students' social interactions at a historically White institution. *The Review of Higher Education, 42*(3), 1023–1050. https://doi.org/10.1353/rhe.2019.0028

Harris, J. C. (2020a). Multiracial campus professionals' experiences with queering race in U.S. postsecondary contexts. *Race Ethnicity and Education, 23*(4), 509–529. https://doi.org/10.1080/13613324.2018.1511530

Harris, J. C. (2020b). Multiracial faculty members' experiences with teaching, research, and service. *Journal of Diversity in Higher Education, 13*(3), 228–239. http://doi.org/10.1037/dhe0000123

Harris, J. C., & BrckaLorenz, A. (2017). Black, White, and biracial students' engagement at differing institutional types. *Journal of College Student Development, 58*(5), 783–789. https://doi.org/ 10.1353/csd.2017.0061

Harris, J. C., BrckaLorenz, A., & Nelson Laird, T. F. (2018). Engaging in the margins: Exploring differences in biracial students' engagement by racial heritage. *Journal of Student Affairs Research and Practice, 55*(2), 137–154. https://doi.org/10.1080/19496591.2018.1406364

Hudson, K. D., & Mehrotra, G. R. (2015). Locating queer-mixed experiences: Narratives of geography and migration. *Qualitative Social Work, 14*, 651–669. http://doi.org/10.1177/1473325014561250

Johnston, M. P., & Nadal, K. L. (2010). Multiracial microaggressions: Exposing monoracism in everyday life and clinical practice. In D. W. Sue (Ed.), *Microaggressions and marginality: Manifestation, dynamics, and impact* (pp. 123–144). Wiley.

Johnston-Guerrero, M. P., & Chaudhari, P. (2016). "Everyone is just mixed to me": Exploring the role of multiraciality in college students' racial claims. *Equity & Excellence in Education*, *49*(3), 254–266. https://doi.org/10.1080/10665684.2016.1194098

Johnston-Guerrero, M. P., & Pecero, V. (2016). Exploring race, culture, and family in the identities of mixed heritage students. *Journal of Student Affairs Research and Practice*, *53*(3), 281–293. https://doi.org/10.1080/19496591.2016.1165109

Jones, N. A., & Bullock, J. J. (2013). Understanding who reported multiple races in the U.S. decennial census: Results from Census 2000 and the 2010 Census. *Family Relations*, *62*(1), 5–16. https://doi.org/10.1111/j.1741-3729.2012.00759.x

Joseph-Salisbury, R. (2019). Wrangling with the Black monster: Young Black mixed-race men and masculinities. *The British Journal of Sociology*, *70*(5), 1754–1773. https://doi.org/10.1111/1468-4446.12670

Kerwin, C., & Ponterotto, J. G. (1995). Biracial identity development: Theory and research. In J. G. Ponterotto, J. M. Casas, L. A. Suzuki, & C. M. Alexander (Eds.), *Handbook of multicultural counseling* (pp. 199–217). SAGE.

Kich, G. K. (1992). The developmental process of asserting a biracial, bicultural identity. In M. P. P. Root (Ed.), *Racially mixed people in America* (pp. 304–317). SAGE.

King, A. R. (2011). Environmental influences on the development of female college students who identify as multiracial/biracial-bisexual/pansexual. *Journal of College Student Development*, *52*(4), 440–455. http://doi.org/10.1353/csd.2011.0050

Lawton, B., & Foeman, A. (2017). Shifting winds: Using ancestry DNA to explore multiracial individuals' patterns of articulating racial identity. *Identity*, *17*(2), 69–83. https://doi.org/10.1080/15283488.2017.1303383

Malaney, V. K., & Danowski, K. (2015). Mixed foundations: Supporting and empowering multiracial student organizations. *JCSCORE*, *1*(2), 54–85. https://doi.org/10.15763/issn.2642-2387.2015.1.2.54-85

Mattern, K., & Wyatt, J. N. (2009). Student choice of college: How far do students go for an education? *Journal of College Admission*, *203*, 18–29. http://files.eric.ed.gov/fulltext/EJ838811.pdf

Museus, S. D., Sariñana, S. A. L., & Ryan, T. K. (2015). A qualitative examination of multiracial students' coping responses to experiences with prejudice and discrimination in college. *Journal of College Student Development*, *56*(4), 331–348. http://doi.org/10.1353/csd.2015.0041

Museus, S. D., Sariñana, S. A. L., Yee, A. L., & Robinson, T. E. (2016). A qualitative analysis of multiracial students' experiences with prejudice and discrimination in college. *Journal of College Student Development*, *57*(6), 680–697. http://doi.org/10.1353/csd.2016.0068

Nadal, K. L., Wong, Y., Griffin, K., Sriken, J., Vargas, V., Wideman, M., & Kolawole, A. (2011). Microaggressions and the multiracial experience. *International Journal of Humanities and Social Sciences*, *1*(7), 36–44. https://www.ijhssnet.com/journals/Vol._1_No._7_[Special_Issue_June_2011]/6.pdf

Nagai, T. (2016). Multiracial Americans throughout the history of the US. In K. O. Korgen (Ed.), *Race policy and multiracial Americans* (pp. 13–28). Policy Press.

Nakashima, C. L. (1996). Voices from the movement: Approaches to multiraciality. In M. P. P. Root (Ed.), *The multiracial experience: Racial borders as the new frontier* (pp. 79–97). SAGE.

Narvaez, R. C., & Kivlighan, D. M. III. (2019). Third space: The need for multiracial college student groups at university counseling centers. *Journal of College Student Psychotherapy*, 1–15. https://doi.org/10.1080/87568225.2019.1646621

National Center for Education Statistics. (2019). *Indicator 20: Undergraduate enrollment*. https://nces.ed.gov/programs/raceindicators/indicator_REB.asp

National Center for Education Statistics. (n.d.). *Statistical standards: Development of concepts and methods*. https://nces.ed.gov/statprog/2002/std1_5.asp

Nicholas, G. E. (2019). *Understanding the experiences of multiracial faculty members: A phenomenological inquiry* (Publication No. 13887216) [Doctoral dissertation, University of South Florida]. ProQuest Dissertations and Theses.

Nishimura, N. (2004). Counseling biracial women: An intersection of multiculturalism and feminism. *Women & Therapy*, *27*(1–2), 133–145. https://doi.org/10.1300/J015v27n01_09

Obama, B. (2004). *Dreams from my father: A story of race and inheritance*. Random House. (Original work published 1995)

O'Hearn, C. C. (Ed.). (1998). *Half and half: Writers on growing up biracial and bicultural*. Pantheon.

Ozaki, C. C., & Johnston, M. J. (2008). *The space in between: Issues for multiracial student organizations and advising* (New Directions for Student Services, no. 123, pp. 53–61). Wiley. https://doi.org/10.1002/ss.286

Ozaki, C. C., Johnston-Guerrero, M. J., & Renn, K. A. (2020). Engaging multiracial students. In S. R. Harper, S. J. Quaye, & S. Pendakur (Eds.), *Student engagement in higher education: Theoretical perspectives and practical approaches for diverse populations* (3rd ed., pp. 37–54). Routledge.

Ozaki, C. C., & Parson, L. (2016). Multiracial college students and colorism: Oh what a tangled web we weave. In C. Monroe (Ed.), *Race and colorism in education* (pp. 111–126). Routledge.

Ozaki, C. C., & Renn, K. A. (2015). Engaging multiracial college students. In S. J. Quaye & S. R. Harper (Eds.), *Student engagement in higher education: Theoretical perspectives and practical approaches for diverse populations* (2nd ed., pp. 91–104). Routledge.

Paladino, D. A., & Davis, H., Jr. (2006). Counseling and outreach strategies for assisting multiracial college students. *Journal of College Student Psychotherapy*, *20*(3), 19–31. https://doi.org/10.1300/J035v20n03_03

Pannell, J. M. (2018). *The experiences of multiracial and biracial women senior and mid-level administrators in higher education* [Doctoral dissertation, University of Georgia]. http://purl.galileo.usg.edu/uga_etd/pannell_judith_m_201805_edd

Patterson, A. (2017). "I need somebody to hear me": YouTube and identity expression of biracial individuals. *Multicultural Education Review*, *9*(2), 105–116. https://doi.org/10.1080/2005615X.2017.1313020

Paz Galupo, M., Taylor, S. M., & Cole, D., Jr. (2019). "I am double the bi": Positive aspects of being both bisexual and biracial. *Journal of Bisexuality*, *19*(2), 152–168. https://doi.org/10.1080/15299716.2019.1619066

Poston, W. C. (1990). The biracial identity development model: A needed addition. *Journal of Counseling & Development*, *69*(2), 152–155. https://doi .org/10.1002/j.1556-6676.1990.tb01477.x

Renn, K. A. (2003). Understanding the identities of mixed race college students through a developmental ecology lens. *Journal of College Student Development*, *44*, 383–403. http://doi.org/10.1353/csd.2003.0032

Renn, K. A. (2004). *Mixed race college students: The ecology of race, identity, and community.* SUNY Press.

Rockquemore, K. A. (2002). Negotiating the color line: The gendered process of racial identity construction among black/white biracial women. *Gender & Society*, *16*(4), 485–503. https://doi.org/10.1177/0891243202016004005

Rockquemore, K. A., & Brunsma, D. L. (2002). Socially embedded identities: Theories, typologies, and processes of racial identity among Black/White biracials. *Sociological Quarterly*, *43*(3), 335–356. https://doi.org/10.1111/j.1533-8525.2002 .tb00052.x

Rockquemore, K. A., & Brunsma, D. L. (2004). Negotiating racial identity: Biracial women and interactional validation. *Women & Therapy*, *27*(1–2), 85–102. https://doi.org/10.1300/J015v27n01_06

Root, M. P. P. (Ed.). (1996). *The multiracial experience: Racial borders as the new frontier.* SAGE.

Root, M. P. P. (1999). The biracial baby boom: Understanding ecological constructions of racial identity in the 21st century. In R. H. Sheets (Ed.), *Racial and ethnic identity in school practices* (pp. 77–100). Routledge.

Sims, J. P., & Joseph-Salisbury, R. (2019). "We were all just the Black kids": Black mixed-race men and the importance of adolescent peer groups for identity development. *Social Currents*, *6*(1), 51–66. https://doi.org/10.1177/232949651918 7840

Stanley, J. L. (2004). Biracial lesbian and bisexual women: Understanding the unique aspects and interactional processes of multiple minority identities. *Women & Therapy*, *27*(1–2), 159–171. https://doi.org/10.1300/J015v27n01_11

Stewart, D-L. (2019). Envisioning possibilities for innovations in higher education research on race and ethnicity. *JCSCORE*, *5*(1), 6–32. https://doi.org/10.15763/ issn.2642-2387.2019.5.1.6-32

Tashiro, C. J. (2015). *Standing on both feet: Voices of older mixed-race Americans.* Routledge.

Telles, A. B., & Mitchell, T. D. (2018). Much discussion, not much change: Perceptions of campus climate continue to differ along racial lines. In K. Soria (Ed.), *Evaluating campus climate at US research universities* (pp. 395–408). Palgrave Macmillan.

Thompson, C., & Gillem, A. R. (2019). *Biracial women in therapy: Between the rock of gender and the hard place of race.* Routledge.

Walker, R. (2005). *Black, white, and Jewish: Autobiography of a shifting self.* Penguin.

Watson, J. C. (2013). The changing face of college counseling: New services for a new campus population. *Journal of College Counseling, 16*(2), 99–102. https://doi.org/10.1002/j.21611882.2013.00029.x

West, M. T., & Maffini, C. S. (2019). "What are you?" Conceptualizing the complexities of bicultural and biracial college student experiences. *Journal of College Counseling, 22*(2), 164–178. https://doi.org/10.1002/jocc.12128

Wijeyesinghe, C. L. (2001). Racial identity in multiracial people: An alternative paradigm. In C. L. Wijeyesinghe & B. W. Jackson III (Eds.), *New perspectives on racial identity development: A theoretical and practical anthology* (pp. 129–152). NYU Press.

3

THE NAMING AND FRAMING OF IDENTITY

Reflecting on Core Concepts Through the Experiences of Multiracial People

Charmaine L. Wijeyesinghe

In the sphere of identity, one might posit that the willingness to be surprised by what one sees must be retained to balance the homogenizing force of a recognition. If "identity" is not to become a slogan foreclosing on future inquiry, then our capacity to bestow recognition must be prepared with readiness to withdraw it, putting identity back in question. (Evans, 1998, p. 107)

The naming and framing of identity has been influenced by many disciplines, and models derived from these academic fields have informed the work of faculty, staff, counselors, and social justice educators for decades. These models often contain concepts that endure over time and that we recognize and look for in discussions of identity, such as development, salience, and context. However, as Evans's statement implies, identity should be reconsidered, questioned, and reimagined in order to remain relevant. This tension, between what is known and what is yet to be considered, allows identity to remain a core topic through which diverse experiences, lived within evolving social and political environments, can be investigated.

Identity has been a central area of focus in research, theories, and programs related to Multiracial people for more than 35 years, and Multiracial models adopt *and* contest historical representations of identity. This chapter explores how central identity subjects influence the study of Multiracial lives and how these same lives raise tensions, questions, and issues that can inform new understandings of identity. It begins with short vignettes that illustrate how beliefs about identity *and* race (often informed by theory, social and political orientations toward race, and historical contexts) influence perceptions of Multiracial people and their identity. A discussion of four enduring subjects found within identity development literature in general, and student identity in particular, follows. Key questions about identity that arise when the experiences of Multiracial people are centered are offered next. The chapter concludes by encouraging scholars and practitioners to continually reimagine what we recognize about identity, while acknowledging that without concepts that give it shape and meaning, we couldn't discuss identity at all.

True Encounters in Four Parts

Multiracial identity has been a significant area of focus in my work, beginning with the collection and analysis of stories told by the participants in my dissertation research on choice of identity in Multiracial people (Wijeyesinghe, 1992). Over the years I encountered many diverse beliefs about Multiracial people and their identity. Four examples appear in the following segments that, although based on discussions with just a few people, reveal ideas reflected in theories, public policy, educational practices, and general discourse related to Multiracial identity.

Identity Is Based on History and History Hasn't Changed That Much

During my doctoral studies I suggested to a faculty member that I examine the experiences of Multiracial people of Black and White ancestry for my dissertation research. Because my graduate program had already produced models of Black, White, and Asian identity development, I believed work on a Multiracial model would further this tradition. At that time, the faculty member responded by saying that there was "no such thing" as Multiracial identity, noting that identity was constrained by ascribed group membership (if you looked Black, you were Black), societal norms (check only one box for race), and historical precedent (the "one drop rule"). In the late 1980s when I was conducting my research, Multiracial people who lived "in the borderlands" (Root, 1996a, p. xx) of imposed (mono)racial categories were constrained by historical, structural, and cultural dynamics. Although some people would argue this orientation is outdated, it remains a theme in scholarly writing; discussion about social policy; and, in my experience, the current attitudes of many people. In 2020 a 19-year-old Multiracial college student told me that a peer made a statement remarkably similar to the one of the faculty member mentioned previously during a discussion of the Multiracial student's ancestry, identity, and appearance.

It's All About Your DNA

One area of my consulting practice involves working with Multiracial students groups at colleges and universities, where in my experience Multiracial students often express strong positions that people with Multiracial ancestry (indicated by family racial background or what students considered a person's DNA) should identify as Multiracial. Doing so increased the visibility and collective power of Multiracial people both on campus and beyond. This sense of imperative resonates more broadly—many Multiracial people pointedly note that Barack Obama was the nation's first *Multiracial* president of the United States. Although ancestry, genetic material, and identity are often positioned as linked and even conflated concepts (Bolnick et al., 2007; TallBear, 2013), their complexities can be overlooked, evidenced by the name of the company AncestryDNA.

The Times Are a'Changing, but Race Is Not the Only Thing I Think About

A man in his early 20s told me he identified as Multiracial based on the identity assigned to him by his parents and the historical and societal changes that allowed him to claim all of his racial heritages. However, because he was just starting out in his chosen career, he described money and economic issues as the most pressing factors in his life. Living his multiple identities meant he felt some more strongly than others depending on circumstances and needs. Contradicting common assumptions that racial identity is a paramount concern for Multiracial people, this man noted that often the central issues in his life were not associated with his race or racial identity.

My Kid Identifies as Black but Isn't She Really Part White, Too?

A number of White parents of children with Black and White family backgrounds told me they questioned their children's choice to identify as Black. The White parents often recounted how their children grew up in an interracial household and were exposed to "both sides" of the family. They described feeling left out, erased, or being a lesser part of a significant aspect of their children's lives because their children identified with only the racial category associated with the parent of color. When asked whether they discussed their feelings and thoughts about identity with their children, the parents almost universally answered no.

Reflection and Meaning-Making

In their discussion of the sociological construction of race, Telles and Sue (2009) offered that "there is no biological or essentialist basis for race, but rather, race is a concept involving perceptions of reality" (p. 130). The four stories just shared illustrate how different perceptions of reality about Multiracial people and their identity are influenced by positionality, experiences, and evolving social and structural dynamics of race within a given historical period (Daniel, 2014; Johnston-Guerrero, 2016; Rockquemore et al., 2009; Wijeyesinghe, 2001). These dynamics affect individual beliefs and behaviors, as well as larger social, cultural, and institutional orientations toward identity and Multiracial identity. In their recommendations related to Multiracial cultural competencies for social workers, Jackson and Samuels (2011) noted that "theoretical conceptions of racial identity are embedded in dominant and often flawed racial legacies" (p. 243).

Within higher education, knowledge about race and identity is often grounded in scholarly research from academic traditions influenced by dynamics of power (Collins, 2015; Emirbayer & Desmond, 2012). What we, as researchers, practitioners, or members of society, recognize about identity are the concepts and definitions we have been exposed to and use. We know what identity is and how it is experienced through the constructs and processes we have been *taught to see as foundational and valid.* When building identity models, we might easily incorporate orientations and constructs into our work without recognizing and critiquing the histories and dynamics that produced them. The next section of the chapter explores several significant concepts related to identity models.

Central Concepts of Identity and Their Relation to Multiracial Models

Psychology, sociology, human ecology, and student development have contributed language, concepts, and frameworks that allow us to recognize what identity is and how it evolves over a person's lifetime (Collins, 2015; Jones & Abes, 2013; Renn, 2012; Torres et al., 2009). Torres et al. (2009) noted that these fields "share commitments to understanding the individual, his or her social context, the influence of social groups, and various dimensions of identity (e.g., race, ethnicity, gender, sexual orientation)" (p. 578). The disciplines also share central identity concepts. This section discusses some of these concepts in relation to Multiracial identity models. Three overarching paradigms that frame identity models are discussed first, followed by an exploration of context, agency, and salience.

Paradigm

The framework on which a model is constructed, literally, conveys assumptions about what identity is, how and why it changes, and the possible roles

THE NAMING AND FRAMING OF IDENTITY

of people who might apply the model in their work. Collins (2019) characterized paradigms as

> frameworks that describe, interpret, analyze, and in some cases, explain both the knowledge that is being produced as well as the processes that are used to produce it. Paradigmatic thinking involves having a model or provisional explanation in mind, a typical pattern of something, a distinct set of concepts or thought patterns. Such thinking is often difficult to recognize as such, because paradigms are often implicit, assumed, and taken for granted. (pp. 41–42)

Several paradigms have been used to structure racial identity models, including developmental stage, ecological, and intersectional.

Developmental Stage Paradigm

The paradigm of developmental stages is grounded in the psychological and developmental traditions generated from the work of Erikson (1959/1994) and provided the template for the earliest models of Black identity (Cross, 1971; Jackson, 1976), White identity (Hardiman, 1982; Helms, 1984), and Asian identity (Kim, 1981). In general, this paradigm posits identity for members of a social group as a developmental process achieved through somewhat linear movement across a sequence of stages. In addition, "this developmental trajectory is characterized as individuals moving toward increasingly complex ways of making meaning of the issues that they face and in the areas of their concern, which are considered developmental tasks" (Jones, 2019, p. 9). These assumptions reflect the thought patterns referenced by Collins, which can then be operationalized in action patterns when models are applied in practice. For example, the roles of helping agents underscored by stage paradigms include recognizing experiences within a certain stage, assisting in the resolution of tasks or issues that mark that stage, and facilitating movement to a subsequent stage of development. Although the authors of the monoracial stage models did not place value or judgment on individual stages, users of the models may (Wijeyesinghe, 2001). For example, a counselor may assume that a client's position at Stage 1 is less desirable than them being at Stage 2, Stage 3, or Stage 4. Or, a counselor may see somone deemed to be at an earlier stage as less developed and less complex in their self-understanding than a person at a later stage. Unless thought and action patterns are consciously assessed, the impact of underlying bias in understanding and using stage paradigms, or any paradigm, can go unrecognized and, therefore, unaddressed.

The structure and assumptions of the psychological, developmental stage paradigm carried over to some of the earliest models of Multiracial identity, particularly the biracial identity development model (Poston, 1990) and the developmental process of asserting a biracial, bicultural identity (Kich, 1992). In both models, growth in identity was evidenced by advancement toward the final stages of development where individuals claimed identities that reflected all of their racial backgrounds. Like the earlier monoracial identity models, individuals experienced a range of emotions and tasks at each stage, and desires to gain acceptance and reduce internal conflict motivated movement across the stages. Although the Poston and Kich models were structured around identity stages, they included references to environmental factors that influenced the experiences of Multiracial people, such as interactions with family members and peers, and physical appearance.

Ecological Paradigm

Multiracial models were instrumental in advancing an alternate ecological paradigm for racial identity models, one that situated individual development "within the social context and attends to mutual influences of self and context" (Renn, 2012, p. 19). Examples included the factor model of Multiracial identity (Wijeyesinghe, 2001), the ecological framework for understanding Multiracial identity development (Root, 2002), and the ecological approach to Multiracial identity (Renn, 2003). These models depict identity as a complex, evolving interplay between factors and systems surrounding a person and reflective of the meaning a person has made of their experiences within these surroundings. Helping agents could use the models to assist individuals in exploring how they have experienced and made meaning of the ecological factors that support or contradict their sense of identity. When applying ecological models, bias could be assessed by considering personal beliefs as to whether "certain factors are deemed more legitimate indicators of racial identity than others" (Wijeyesinghe, 2001, p. 145) and how those beliefs have influenced a helping agent's ability to work with Multiracial people who claim diverse racial identities. For example, if a counselor felt that ancestry was the primary building block of racial identity, then they may believe that people with multiple racial ancestries should always identify as Multiracial and criticize or judge a Multiracial person who identified as, for example, Asian.

Intersectional Paradigm

Emerging disciplinary perspectives offer new lenses to explore paradigms and their usefulness in framing identity, even if the core tenets of these orientations raise questions as to whether identity can be captured in models at all. For example, intersectionality complicates identity paradigms, because it positions all social identities as mutually constituted and affected by multiple, interconnected systems of social power. Social identity models that incorporated aspects of intersectionality include the reconceptualized model of multiple dimensions of identity (Abes et al., 2007), simultaneity (Holvino, 2012), and the intersectional model of Multiracial identity (Wijeyesinghe, 2012). Although intersectionality has been used to broaden representations of *personal identity*, it centers social locations that people inhabit *as members of groups* and not their individual experiences of identity (Collins & Bilge, 2016; Dill et al., 2007; Wijeyesinghe, 2019; Wijeyesinghe & Jones, 2019). Therefore, it is unclear whether intersectionality can anchor a paradigm for models focused on individual experiences and meaning making.

Although newer disciplinary orientations challenge the structures we have come to recognize in identity models, they don't foreclose reflection about the nature and meaning of identity. For example, intersectionality unsettles what Collins (2019) referred to as "paradigmatic thinking" (p. 41) and raises for reexamination ideas that have endured in the content of models. Intersectionality's core tenets engender a variety of questions. Does identity have meaning outside of the immediate period of its social construction? How does power operate to create, maintain, and enforce social categories upon which models are built? And can a single social identity, such as race, be understood in isolation from other social locations of gender, sexual orientation, age, ability status, and so on? By raising questions relevant to the structuring of identity, intersectionality and other emerging paradigms feed some of the reflection and rethinking needed to ensure that identity remains relevant in light of evolving social, cultural, theoretical, and political dynamics.

Core Concepts Related to Identity

The length of this chapter precludes the discussion of all central subjects related to identity across time, disciplines, and models. Three concepts are discussed here, chosen because of their prominence in identity literature and their relevance to Multiracial identity models. Because the volume in which this chapter appears highlights the experiences of Multiracial people in higher education, the analysis draws more heavily on identity literature within college and university settings where student identity development has garnered the most attention.

Context

Drawing on the identity development work of pioneering psychologist Urie Bronfenbrenner (1979), Renn (2012) described context as representing "levels of interactions an individual has in the immediate setting (microsystem), among/between microsystems (mesosystems), with settings at a distance (exosystems), and within the broader social-historical culture (macrosystems)" (p. 20). These levels highlight how identity is situated within environments that include interpersonal interactions; particular historical, cultural, and political forces; and various settings such as college campuses steeped in their own culture, history, and practices. Context frames where identity derives meaning, shifts and evolves, gains support and affirmation, and faces challenges and contradictions. More recently, scholars and practitioners have noted that evaluating context requires interrogating how power shapes experiences, cultural norms, and institutional practices (Abes et al., 2019; Collins & Bilge, 2016; Stewart & Brown, 2019; Wijeyesinghe & Jones, 2019). Context is also influenced by forces such as social movements that not only change the environments in which identity develops but also create the ability to acknowledge and claim identities that were previously unavailable or discounted. Such was the case when, after much political action by Multiracial communities, procedures changed to allow for the checking of more than one box to indicate race in the 2000 decennial census.

The effects of context figure significantly in discussions of Multiracial identity. The models of Poston (1990) and Kich (1992) indicate that contextual elements influence how individuals might progress through or experience the stages of their respective models. In the works of Root (2002) and Wijeyesinghe (1992, 2001) family socialization, physical appearance, cultural preferences, and larger social approaches to race are some of the environmental factors affecting an individual's choice of racial identity. Renn's (2004) work highlighted levels of contextual influences on Multiracial college students' experiences of campus life.

Models of Multiracial identity expand the understanding of context by offering new examples of how factors such as early socialization and cultural orientations influence identity. In addition, the diverse lives of Multiracial people highlight how evolving social, cultural, and institutional forces related to power and oppression influence the experiences of individuals and members of socially constructed groups. For example, Johnston and Nadal (2010) cited that in addition to microaggressions based on race (structured by monoracial categories), Multiracial people may encounter "daily verbal, behavioral, or environmental indignities, whether intentional or unintentional, enacted by monoracial persons that communicate hostile, derogatory, or negative slights toward multiracial individuals or groups" (p. 126). Because movements to address inequality draw direction and purpose from the issues at hand, the greater, more nuanced understanding of contexts revealed through Multiracial lives can be used to inform social justice efforts.

Agency in Identity Development

The primacy of personal agency in the development of identity is evident in Shields's (2008) observation that "in contemporary society, identity is emphasized as a quality that enables the expression of the *individual's* authentic sense of self" (p. 301, emphasis added). However, theories that center the independent power of an individual may overlook how evolving cultural, institutional, and political structures affect the environment in which agency over identity takes place and the interplay between personal understanding and the systems that influence and give meaning to that understanding (Wijeyesinghe, 2019; Wijeyesinghe & Jones, 2019). For example, a student might identify as a woman and adopt cisgender expectations and behaviors for women without understanding how the category of "woman" is constructed and defined by social systems related to gender, race, sexual orientation, and so on.

Themes related to agency appear in a variety of ways in discussions of Multiracial identity. For example, the second of the three main areas covered in Maria P. P. Root's (1996b) *Bill of Rights for Racially Mixed People* focused on the right to choose identities that differ from the ones imposed by others and that vary across situations. Wijeyesinghe (1992) researched Multiracial people and participants' diverse *choices* of racial identity. Being pressured to choose one identity over another, a situation noted in several models of Multiracial identity (Fhagen-Smith, 2003; Kich, 1992; Poston, 1990; Rockquemore & Brunsma, 2002), illuminates the relationship between identity-chosen-by-self and one's interactions with surrounding environments. Sellers (2016) described meaning-making in identity, race, and ethnicity for African Americans as recognizing "the potential agentic qualities that oppressed people retain and utilize to survive and sometime thrive in the face of oppression" (p. xviii). These agentic qualities reverberate in Root's (1992) declaration that "to name oneself is to validate one's existence and declare visibility" (p. 7). Centering Multiracial lives in discussions of agency highlights how experiences of identity contest social, cultural, and institutional norms about race. For example, choice of identity highlights the complex interplay between identities chosen by an individual and identities ascribed to individuals by other people (López et al., 2018; Rich, 2014; Wijeyesinghe, 1992, 2001). In choosing their racial identities, Multiracial people exert power to contest the larger social, political, and institutional structures that seek to erase or discount their very existence.

Salience

Jones and Abes (2013) defined *salience* as "the prominence or importance attached to a particular experience, idea, feeling, or . . . social identity" (p. 40).

Within discussions of racial identity, salience appeared prominently in the life span perspective on African American identity development offered by Cross and Fhagen-Smith (2001). Here salience referenced the level of attention and exposure to race during a person's preadolescence and early adult years. Emergent low race salience patterns reflected situations where there was little focus or exposure to race, and high race salience patterns represented conscious exposure to race and aspects of Black culture. Cross and Fhagen-Smith indicated that these patterns applied to all "Black children, including those who are Biracial or Multiracial, as well as Black children adopted by White or mixed-race families" (p. 252).

Multiracial models incorporated salience in a number of ways. At the broadest level, all of them presented race and racial identity as integral issues in the lives of Multiracial people. Fhagen-Smith carried over concepts of high and low race salience from the model of Black identity she authored with Cross (2001) to her mixed ancestry racial/ethnic identity development model (2003). In the models by Root (2002) and Wijeyesinghe (1992, 2001) choice of racial identity was associated with the higher salience of various factors that supported identity at a particular time. For example, a Multiracial person might identify as Black based on early socialization by family members and sense of early cultural attachment. After joining a Multiracial student group on campus, this person may change their racial identity to Multiracial in response to feedback from peers and a sense that doing so represents the political act of contesting monoracial social expectations. This example also highlights how salience applies to the various ecosystems surrounding Multiracial students described by Renn (2004). The influence of other social group memberships, such as gender, faith traditions, and economic background, are noted in the models by Root and Wijeyesinghe. However, given that these works appeared when the primary focus of Multiracial research was racial identification, they did not explore how other social identities and social location (as privileged or marginalized position within other social categories) influenced identity in Multiracial people.

Finally, orientations that center power in discussions of identity call for the reexaminiation of salience and for extending the concept to acknowledge larger systems. Multiracial people, like all people, experience social, political, and cultural environments that attribute salience to family background, physical features, nation, and other factors when defining and determining race and racial groups. This extended view of salience appears in the models by Root (2002), Renn (2003), and Wijeyesinghe (1992, 2001, 2012), which note that evolving social and historical dynamics related to race can affect an individual's understanding of their identity.

Synthesis

The impact of power in framing knowledge is unveiled when the experiences of members of social groups, excluded in historical, overarching definitions of identity, move from the margins to the center of analysis (Collins, 2015; Dill & Zambrana, 2009; Jones & Stewart, 2016). Multiracial lives are voices that center "counterhistories and counternarratives to those based primarily on the experiences of social elites" (Dill & Zambrana, 2009, p. 6), on which some of the earliest identity models were built. Models of Multiracial identity provide opportunities to reexamine core components we recognize in identity. They raise questions about the approaches and assumptions grounded in certain disciplines and extrapolated from the experiences of some people to create models of presumed universal experience. Paradigms have structured models without, until recently (Jones, 2019; Jones & Stewart, 2016), being interrogated for how concepts related to identity drew meaning from them. Core concepts such as context, agency, and salience have been embedded in discussions of identity, often without consideration of how these concepts might be experienced differently by Multiracial people or how they would be defined differently if the standpoints of different Multiracial people were considered. Multiracial experiences and efforts to explore Multiracial identity enable identity to remain in question at multiple levels.

Multiracial Identity: Posing Questions Related to the What, How, and Where of Identity

The experiences of Multiracial people are vehicles to examine identity, race, and racial identity through a range of questions. Some of these questions are fed by the content of existing models, such as whether certain racial identities are indicative of a more advanced or healthy development or what other, yet-to-be-identified factors might exert contextual influences on identity. Equally valuable are the broader questions that move discussion beyond the experiences of individuals to areas that focus on the larger environments in and from which these experiences derive meaning. The topics at the heart of these metalevel questions often center power and reflect the persistent and inescapable link between identity formation at the individual level and larger social contexts framed by inequality. The questions posed in this section of the chapter are meant to disrupt the "forces of recognition" (p. 107) that Evans (1998) warned can lead to identity being presented as a static and homogenous construct, and are organized by sections pondering the what, how, and where of identity. Responses to these questions can inform future models and research on identity.

What Is Identity?

Multiracial people's ability to choose and change racial identities reflects the concept of personal agency and is a cornerstone of the Multiracial rights movement and some of the earliest models of Multiracial identity. In relation to race, self-naming and identity questions for further investigation include whether identity (racial and otherwise) is a choice. Can everyone choose their racial identity? If racial identity is a choice that can be made by all individuals (and not just Multiracial people), what are the larger social and political dynamics inherent when, as examples, a person with European ancestry identifies as Black or when a person whose ethnic background reflects Latinx roots identifies as White? Although agency and choice will remain central in discussions of Multiracial identity, exploration of these areas should address the similarities and differences in expressions of power and privilege when these concepts are applied to different socially constructed groups (based on race, gender, economic position, and so on). In addition, agency and choice can be investigated through the experiences within and across Multiracial populations and Multiracial people who differ from each other based on other social positions such as gender, sexual orientation, and age.

Defining identity through socially constructed categories raises a number of questions related to Multiracial people, and the areas raised by these questions might provide new insights on choice, agency, and the influence of larger social factors on individual identity. For example, efforts to construct racial identity models, for any group defined by the racial categories developed and imposed by dominant culture, are influenced by the troubled legacy of the categories themselves. Existing racial identity theories can be critiqued for adopting this system of classification, and future theories will have to contend with the dynamics inherent in it. Jones and Stewart (2016) noted that "to develop a model of racial identity development is to accept *race* as a meaningful and appropriate locus of identity, and thus fails to recognize that the very idea of race was constructed to enforce White supremacy" (p. 22). Thus, one relevant question is, to what extent does a Multiracial identity reify socially constructed racial categories? Put another way, how can we reconcile that Multiracial people, on the one hand, confront "the rigidity of racial lines that are a prerequisite for maintaining the delusion that race is a scientific fact" (Root, 1996b, p. 7), with the perspective that on the other hand "there cannot even be a conception of multiracial identity absent the clear and unequivocal acceptance of biological race [since] we are talking about the biological offspring of (allegedly) different raced parents" (Spencer, 2006, p. 88)?

Exploring the question of whether Multiracial people and Multiracial identity reinforce the myths underlying racial categories might shake loose our recognition of and reliance on these socially and arbitrarily constructed groups. However, equally important is the question posed by Johnston-Guerrero and Chaudhari (2016)—why is responsibility for contesting the fallacy of racial categories laid squarely at the feet of Multiracial people? Wrestling with these complex questions may reveal answers, and possibly more questions, that can feed future understandings of identity within the contexts of larger evolving social systems.

How Does Identity Develop and How Is It Experienced?

The experiences of Multiracial people present alternative ways of understanding the concept of "development." For example, dissonance is a prominent motivator and source of movement in stage-based developmental identity models. Rather than dissonance being tensions between self and environmental influences that can fuel advancement to the next stage of development (as in a number of the monoracial models cited earlier and the Multiracial models by Poston and Kich), Taylor and Reynolds (2019) offered a Black feminist position on dissonance as "the phenomenon of recognizing lies that societal systems and its authorities tell" (p. 103). In turn, what can we learn about dissonance in light of the lies told about identity development when diverse Multiracial experiences are centered? How would allowing Multiracial people to tell their own stories of living within systems of oppression inform the representation of identity "development" and major concepts within identity?

Multiracial lives also introduce new subjects related to how identity is experienced. For example, the concept of liminality appeared in Root's early description of Multiracial people living in borderlands and border crossings (1996a) and in experiences that Turner (1967) described as "betwixt and between" (p. 95). Multiracial lives highlight the rigid, exclusionary nature of racial categories and reframe power by contesting them. Identity in the borderlands or at the margins is not emblematic of experiences that fuel confusion, guilt, and longing, but is "a source of growth, sustenance, and building block[s] for resilience" (Gutierrez, 2019, p. 20). Beyond the individual, liminality fosters a sense of larger connection and community that transcends other differences. As Daniel et al. (2014) noted,

> No matter how porous, fuzzy, and thin the boundary, no matter how soft and illusive the center of that collectivity, the shared liminality based on identification with more than one racial background is an integral, fundamental part of the self-conception of multiracial-identified individuals, and a defining component of the mixed-race experience. (p. 17)

Investigations of liminality can inform how identity is structured in future models and the reimagining of concepts such as resilience and dissonance. Because identity cannot be constrained by boxes or discrete stages, the experiences of Multiracial people require that future models address *and value* the "multiplicity of belonging" (Gaither, 2018, p. 443).

Stewart and Brown (2019) noted "the messy and complex realities of life as a person with multiple minoritized identities defy simple analysis through one ontological or epistemic frame" (p. 117). In considering what identity models, in general, and Multiracial models, in particular, might look like in the future, we must consider whether we are willing to embrace the messiness, complexity, and even confusion that may lay ahead. What language, concepts, frames, or images might be employed to represent an individual's experience of identity over their life span? How might we draw guidance from emerging disciplines that echo the fluidity and complexity of Multiracial lives, such as intersectionality and poststructuralism? And, if these perspectives are utilized, how can students, scholars, and practitioners study Multiracial identity if, as described, the meaning of race is questioned, racial categories are potentially meaningless, and the systems influencing race and the categories are constantly and rapidly changing?

Where Does Identity Develop?

Ecological theories of Multiracial identity offer specific examples of elements and levels of context that researchers, teachers, and counselors can use to explore environmental influences on personal identity. Shifting our view of context from considering solely the immediate, local, and current influences on identity to broader, sometimes spacially and temporally distant environments can move us closer to viewing identity as occurring not "in context" but "through context" (Reyes & Tauala, 2019, p. 49). In addition, Duran and Jones (2019) noted that researchers often allow the individuals they study to define context and describe how it influences their lives. These authors have emphasized that scholars should presume that context is "a significant influence on development, regardless of whether an individual sees it as such" (p. 171) and acknowledge manifestations of inequality and power as contextual features.

The concept of malleability that arises in discussions of Multiracial identity introduces an additional lens for understanding how time and place influence identity. Although the theme of situational identity, or changes of identity in different circumstances, was named over 20 years ago (Renn, 2000), how individuals make meaning of shifts in their identity across contexts has not been heavily studied (Smith et al., 2016). Framing choice of racial identity through malleability and Multiracial experiences demonstrates that race and identity are fluid and influenced by changing dynamics that surround the individual. Such an orientation posits "that race is a dynamic and interactive *process*, rather than a fixed thing that someone *has*" (Pauker et al., 2018, p. 2, emphasis in original).

Several questions can direct future representations of context that center Multiracial people, incorporate larger systems of power, and acknowledge fluid identities. For example, how will evolving conceptualizations of race influence the options available to Multiracial people, and all people, when claiming a racial identity? What impact, if any, will the higher visibility of Multiracial people in the media, arts, and politics have on how people understand race and choose to identify? How might Multiracial people be affected by discussion of race in what some people describe as a "postracial" society, even as race remains a significant and contested marker (Johnston-Guerrero, 2016)?

Closing Thoughts: Or the "Why" of Continuing to Reflect on Identity Through Multiracial Lives

In the introduction to the second edition of *New Perspectives on Racial Identity Development*, an edited volume on racial identity theory and emerging paradigms, Bailey Jackson and I noted that

> given the changing face of America, models of racial identity development must evolve if they are to remain relevant and effective tools. However, the evolution of frameworks is not driven solely by shifts in the racial composition of the country. A greater understanding of how race is lived within a specific context at a particular time, the dynamic nature of the social, cultural, and political climate, and new insights about the nature of racial and social identity are additional forces to be considered. (Wijeyesinghe & Jackson, 2012, p. 3)

The lives of Multiracial people provide central and critical lenses for examining and reexamining identity. Research and theory on diverse Multiracial people reveal insights *and* questions about the effect of evolving political, social, and cultural landscapes on identity. Multiracial identity introduces a level of complexity into everything—definitions of what identity is, representations of how it develops, and an almost mind-boggling number of factors influencing identity that can change over time and space. Even with this complexity, and the surprises we may encounter when we leave ourselves open to new insights about identity, we must still use existing knowledge (however tenuous and temporary) to inform our actions and approaches. Perhaps we can draw awareness, motivation, and challenge from the words of Emirbayer and Desmond (2012), who noted that "racial principles, then, impose themselves as part of the very order of things because they are deeply inscribed in the objective structures of racial domination, which some race analysts take for granted because they largely are formed within them" (p. 278). Examining our disciplines, our theories, and our motives in relation to larger principles of domination will expose what we recognize about identity and what revelations we might reject and embrace as investigations of Multiracial identity continue.

References

Abes, E. S., Jones, S. R., & McEwen, M. K. (2007). Reconceptualizing the Model of Multiple Dimensions of Identity: The role of meaning-making capacity in the construction of multiple identities. *Journal of College Student Development, 48*, 1–22. http://doi.org/10.1353/csd.2007.0000

Bolnick, D. A., Fullwiley, D., Duster, T., Cooper, R. S., Fujimura, J. H., Kahn, J., Kaufman, J. S., Marks, J., Morning, A., Nelson, A., Pilar, O., Reardon, J., Reverby, S. M., & TallBear, K. (2007). The science and business of genetic ancestry testing. *Science, 318*, 399–400. http://doi.org/10.1126/science.1150098

Bronfenbrenner, U. (1979). *The ecology of human development: Experiments by nature and design.* Harvard University Press.

Collins, P. H. (2015). Intersectionality's definitional dilemma. *Annual Review of Sociology, 41*, 1–20. http://doi.org/10.1146/annurev-soc-073014-112142

Collins, P. H. (2019). *Intersectionality as critical social theory.* Duke University Press. http://doi.org/10.1215/9781478007098

Collins, P. H., & Bilge, S. (2016). *Intersectionality.* Polity Press.

Cross, W. E. (1971). Discovering the Black referent: The psychology of Black liberation. In V. J. Dixon & B. G. Foster (Eds.), *Beyond Black and White: An alternative America* (pp. 96–110). Little, Brown.

Cross, W. E., Jr., & Fhagen-Smith, P. (2001). Patterns in African American identity development: A life span perspective. In C. L. Wijeyesinghe & B. W. Jackson III (Eds.), *New perspectives on racial identity development: A theoretical and practical anthology* (pp. 243–270). NYU Press.

Daniel, G. R. (2014). Race and multiraciality: From Barack Obama to Trayvon Martin. In G. R. Daniel & H. V. Williams (Eds.), *Race and the Obama phenomenon: The vision of a more perfect Multiracial union* (pp. 3–40). University Press of Mississippi.

Daniel, G. R., Kina, L., Dariotis, W. M., & Fojas, C. (2014). Emerging paradigms in critical mixed race studies. *Journal of Critical Mixed Race Studies, 1*(1), 6–65. https://escholarship.org/content/qt2db5652b/qt2db5652b_noSplash_95a43d8 677e69babd7473728c3c83a42.pdf

Dill, B. T., McLaughlin, A. E., & Nieves, A. D. (2007). Future directions of feminist research: Intersectionality. In S. N. Hesse-Biber (Ed.), *Handbook of feminist research* (pp. 629–637). SAGE.

Dill, B. T., & Zambrana, R. E. (2009). Critical thinking about inequality: An emerging lens. In B. T. Dill & R. E. Zambrana (Eds.), *Emerging intersections: Race, class, and gender in theory, policy, and practice* (pp. 1–21). Rutgers University Press.

Duran, A., & Jones, S. J. (2019). Context and contextualizing student development using critical theory. In E. S. Abes, S. R. Jones, & D.-L. Stewart (Eds.), *Rethinking college student development theory using critical frameworks* (pp. 171–186). Stylus.

Emirbayer, M., & Desmond, M. (2012). Race and reflexivity. *Ethnic and Racial Studies, 35*(4), 574–599. http://doi.org/10.1080/01419870.2012.648651

Erikson, E. H. (1994). *Identity and the life cycle.* W.W. Norton. (Original work published 1959)

Evans, N. (1998). Identity in question. *Quarterly Journal of Speech, 84*(1), 94–109. https://doi.org/10.1080/00335639809384206

Fhagen-Smith, P. (2003). *The Mixed Ancestry Racial/Ethnic Identity Development (MAREID) Model* (Wellesley Centers for Women Working Paper Series, no. 413). Center for Research on Women. https://www.wcwonline.org/vmfiles/413.pdf

Gaither, S. E. (2018). The multiplicity of belonging: Pushing identity research beyond binary thinking. *Self and Identity, 17*(4), 443–454. http://doi.org/10.4324/9780429331152-8

Gutierrez, R. A. E. (2019). Living liminal: Conceptualizing liminality for undocumented students of color. In D. Mitchell, J. Marie, & T. L. Steele (Eds.), *Intersectionality and higher education: Theory, research, and praxis* (2nd ed., pp. 15–25). Peter Lang.

Hardiman, R. (1982). *White identity development: A process oriented model for describing the racial consciousness of White Americans* [Unpublished doctoral dissertation]. University of Massachusetts Amherst.

Helms, J. E. (1984). Toward a theoretical explanation of the effects of race on counseling: A Black and White model. *The Counseling Psychologist, 17*(2), 227–252. https://doi.org/10.1177%2F0011000084124013

Holvino, E. (2012). The "simultaneity" of identities: Models and skills. In C. L. Wijeyesinghe & B. W. Jackson III (Eds.), *New perspectives on racial identity development* (2nd ed., pp. 161–191). NYU Press.

Jackson, B. W. (1976). *The function of a theory of Black identity development in achieving relevance in education for Black students* [Unpublished doctoral dissertation]. University of Massachusetts Amherst.

Jackson, K. F., & Samuels, G. M. (2011). Multiracial competence in social work: Resources for culturally attuned work with Multiracial people. *Social Work, 56*(3), 236–245. http://doi.org/10.1093/sw/56.3.235

Johnston, M. P., & Nadal, K. L. (2010). Multiracial microaggressions: Exposing monoracism in everyday life and clinical practice. In D. W. Sue (Ed.), *Microaggressions and marginality: Manifestation, dynamics, and impact* (pp. 123–144). Wiley.

Johnston-Guerrero, M. P. (2016). The meanings of race matter: College students learning about race in a not-so-postracial era. *American Educational Research Journal, 53*(4), 819–849. https://doi.org/10.3102%2F0002831216651144

Johnston-Guerrero, M. P., & Chaudhari, P. (2016). "Everyone is just mixed to me": Exploring the role of Multiraciality in college students' racial claims. *Equity and Excellence in Education, 43*(3), 254–266. https://doi.org/10.1080/10665684.2016.1194098

Jones, S. R. (2019). Waves of change: The evolving history of student development theory. In E. S. Abes, S. R. Jones, & D-L Stewart (Eds.), *Rethinking college student development theory using critical frameworks* (pp. 7–16). Stylus.

Jones, S. R., & Abes, E. S. (2013). *Identity development of college students: Advancing frameworks for multiple dimensions of identity*. Jossey-Bass.

Jones, S. R., & Stewart, D-L. (2016). Evolution of student development theory. In E. S. Abes (Ed.), *Critical perspectives on student development theory* (New Directions for Student Services, no. 154, pp. 17–28). Jossey-Bass. https://doi.org/10.1002/ss.20172

Kich, G. K. (1992). The developmental process of asserting a biracial, bicultural identity. In M. P. P. Root (Ed.), *Racially mixed people in America* (pp. 304–317). SAGE.

Kim, J. (1981). *Process of Asian-American identity development: A study of Japanese American women's perceptions of their struggle to achieve positive identities* [Unpublished doctoral dissertation]. University of Massachusetts.

López, N., Vargas, E., Juarez, M., Cacari-Stone, L., & Bettez, S. (2018). What's your "street race": Leveraging multidimensional dimensions of race and intersectionality for examining physical and mental health status among Latinxs. *Sociology of Race and Ethnicity, 4*(1), 49–66. https://doi.org/10.1177%2F2332649217708798

Pauker, K., Meyers, C., Sanchez, D. T., Gaither, S. C., & Young, D. M. (2018). A review of multiracial malleability: Identity, categorization, and shifting racial attitudes. *Social and Personality Psychology Compass, 12*(6), e12392. http://doi.org/10.1111/spc3.12392

Poston, C. (1990). The biracial identity development model: A needed addition. *Journal of Counseling and Development, 69*, 152–155. https://doi.org/10.1002/j.1556-6676.1990.tb01477.x

Renn, K. A. (2000). Patterns of situational identity among biracial and multiracial college students. *Review of Higher Education, 23*, 399–420. http://doi.org/10.1353/rhe.2000.0019

Renn, K. A. (2003). Understanding the identities of mixed race college students through a developmental ecology lens. *Journal of College Student Development, 44*(3), 383–403. http://doi.org/ 10.1353/csd.2003.0032

Renn, K. A. (2004). *Mixed race students in college: The ecology of race, identity, and community on campus*. SUNY Press.

Renn, K. A. (2012). Creating and re-creating race: The emergence of racial identity as a critical element in psychological, sociological, and ecological perspectives on human development. In C. L. Wijeyesinghe & B. W. Jackson III (Eds.), *New perspectives on racial identity development* (2nd ed., pp. 11–32). NYU Press.

Reyes, N. A. S., & Tauala, M. (2019). Indigenous paradigms: Decolonizing college student development theory through centering relationality. In E. S. Abes, S. R. Jones, & D-L Stewart (Eds.), *Rethinking college student development theory using critical frameworks* (pp. 45–54). Stylus.

Rich, C. G. (2014). Elective race: Recognizing race discrimination in an era of racial self-identification. *Georgetown Law Journal, 102,* 1501–1572.

Rockquemore, K. A., & Brunsma, D. L. (2002). *Beyond Black: Biracial identity in America.* SAGE.

Rockquemore, K. A., Brunsma, D. L., & Delgado, D. J. (2009). Racing to theory or retheorizing race. *Journal of Social Issues, 65*(1), 13–34. https://doi.org/10.1111/j.1540-4560.2008.01585.x

Root, M. P. P. (1992). Within, between, and beyond race. In M. P. P. Root (Ed.), *Racially mixed people in America* (pp. 3–11). SAGE.

Root, M. P. P. (1996a). The Multiracial experience: Racial borders as a significant frontier in race relations. In M. P. P. Root (Ed.), *The Multiracial experience: Racial borders at the new frontier* (pp. xiii–xxviii). SAGE.

Root, M. P. P. (1996b). A bill of rights for racially mixed people. In M. P. P. Root (Ed.), *The Multiracial experience: Racial borders at the new frontier* (pp. 3–14). SAGE.

Root, M. P. P. (2002). *Ecological framework for understanding multiracial identity development.* https://www.apa.org/pubs/videos/4310742-framework.pdf

Sellers, R. M. (2016). Foreword. In J. M. Sullivan & W. E. Cross (Eds.), *Meaning-making, internalized racism, and African American identity* (pp. xvii–xix). SUNY Press.

Shields, S. (2008). Gender: An intersectional perspective. *Sex Roles, 59,* 301–311. https://psycnet.apa.org/doi/10.1007/s11199-008-9501-8

Smith, L. E., Kohn-Wood, L., & Nicolas, G. (2016). The "one drop rule": Shifting expressions of racial identity and well-being in Black-Multiracial individuals. In J. M. Sullivan & W. E. Cross (Eds.), *Meaning-making, internalized racism, and African American identity* (pp. 111–125). SUNY Press.

Spencer, R. (2006). *Challenging Multiracial identity.* Lynne Rienner. ·

Stewart, D-L, & Brown, C. (2019). Social construction of identities. In E. S. Abes, S. R. Jones, & D-L Stewart (Eds.), *Rethinking college student development theory using critical frameworks* (pp. 110–125). Stylus.

TallBear, K. (2013). Genomic articulations of indigeneity. *Social Studies of Science, 43*(4), 509–533. https://doi.org/10.1177%2F0306312713483893

Taylor, K. B., & Reynolds, D. J. (2019). Dissonance. In E. S. Abes, S. R. Jones, & D-L Stewart (Eds.), *Rethinking college student development theory using critical frameworks* (pp. 94–110). Stylus.

Telles, E. E., & Sue, C. A. (2009). Race mixture: Boundary crossing in comparative perspective. *Annual Review of Sociology, 35,* 129–146. https://doi.org/10.1146/annurev.soc.34.040507.134657

Torres, V., Jones, S. R., & Renn, K. A. (2009). Identity development theories in student affairs: Origins, current status, and new approaches. *Journal of College Student Development, 50,* 577–596. https://doi.org/10.1353/csd.0.0102

Turner, V. (1967). *The forest of symbols*. Cornell University Press.

Wijeyesinghe, C. (1992). *Towards an understanding of the racial identity of Bi-Racial people: The experience of racial self-identification of African-American/Euro-American adults and the factors affecting their choices of racial identity* [Unpublished doctoral dissertation]. University of Massachusetts Amherst.

Wijeyesinghe, C. L. (2001). Racial identity in multiracial people: An alternative paradigm. In C. L. Wijeyesinghe & B. W. Jackson III (Eds.), *New perspectives on racial identity development: A theoretical and practical anthology* (pp. 129–152). NYU Press.

Wijeyesinghe, C. L. (2012). The intersectional model of multiracial identity: Integrating multiracial identity theories and intersectional perspectives on social identity. In C. L. Wijeyesinghe & B. W. Jackson III (Eds.), *New perspectives on racial identity development* (2nd ed., pp. 81–107). NYU Press.

Wijeyesinghe, C. L. (2019). Intersectionality and student development: Centering power in the process. In E. S. Abes, S. R. Jones, & D-L Stewart (Eds.), *Rethinking college student development theory using critical frameworks* (pp. 26–34). Stylus.

Wijeyesinghe, C. L., & Jackson, B. W. (2012). Introduction. In C. L. Wijeyesinghe & B. W. Jackson III (Eds.), *New perspectives on racial identity development* (2nd ed., pp. 1–10). NYU Press.

Wijeyesinghe, C. L., & Jones, S. R. (2019). Intersectionality, identity, and systems of power and inequality. In D. Mitchell, J. Marie, & T. L. Steele (Eds.), *Intersectionality and higher education: Theory, research, and praxis* (2nd ed., pp. 3–14). Peter Lang.

4

MONORACISM

Identifying and Addressing Structural Oppression of Multiracial People in Higher Education

Jessica C. Harris, Marc P. Johnston-Guerrero, and Maxwell Pereyra

Racism is embedded throughout the fabric of the United States and continues to operate through federal and state-level policies, education, health care, politics, and more (Glenn, 2015; Kendi, 2016; Patton, 2016). For instance, within education, university curriculum excludes racially diverse perspectives, histories, and stories, ensuring that "Whiteness remains embedded, regardless of subject matter" (Patton, 2016, p. 320). Although racism is omnipresent and intricately woven throughout the fabric of U.S. society, white U.S. society has constructed the term *racism* in a narrow manner that rarely, if ever, captures its complexities (Crenshaw et al., 1995; Kim & Sundstrom, 2014). A narrow paradigm of racism often frames "white racism against Blacks as the legitimate scope of racism," which often "leads to the exclusion and marginalization of other racialized people who also suffer from racism" (Perea, 1997, p. 1221).[1]

Recently, some scholars of education have begun to challenge and expand this narrow, often limiting view of racism by exploring the different ways that racism is enacted, or manifests, in educational contexts. For instance, some scholars have explored race-evasive practices that deny or avoid the significance of race (e.g., Annamma et al., 2017), colorblind racism (e.g., Bonilla-Silva, 2010), and internalized racism (e.g., Kohli, 2013). Some have also interrogated the levels through which racism can manifest, such as individual, institutional, and societal (Pérez Huber & Solórzano, 2015). Additionally, various scholars have demonstrated how different forms of racism, such as racist nativism (Pérez Huber, 2010), anti-Blackness (Patton, 2016; Poon et al., 2016), and monoracism (Hamako, 2014; Johnston &

Nadal, 2010) target different racialized communities and manifest in post-secondary contexts.

Although research and theorizing on different forms of racism continues, lingering questions about various forms of racisms and their influence on individuals, institutions, and society remain. Through this chapter, we aim to explore some of these questions, issues, and tension points while expanding the theoretical breadth of one such form of racism in postsecondary education—monoracism. *Monoracism* has been defined as a form of racism built on "a social system of psychological inequality where individuals who do not fit monoracial categories may be oppressed on systemic and interpersonal levels because of underlying assumptions and beliefs in singular, discrete racial categories" (Johnston & Nadal, 2010, p. 125).

Prior to exploring monoracism further, we position ourselves in this work. Jessica is an assistant professor and Black-identified Multiracial cisgender woman, currently working at a historically white institution (HWI). Her research, which often centers Multiraciality and monoracism, is informed by her experiences as a Multiracial woman and is an attempt to explore some of her own questions around the intersections of her racialized and gendered identities. Marc identifies as a mixed race, cisgender, queer Filipino American man and is an associate professor at an HWI. His research has focused on race and Multiraciality in attempts to better contextualize his experiences with white family members and finding home in his identities during college. Maxwell is a PhD student at an HWI who identifies as Filipino, mixed race, cisgender, and gay/queer. His research is informed by his lived experiences of (unknowingly) subverting false binaries of race and sexuality, or, as he would have called it as a child, "not fitting into any of the boxes."

What Is Monoracism in Higher Education?

As monoracism gains some traction in higher education as a relatively "new" concept, we acknowledge that these ideas are not new, just as Multiracial people are not a new phenomenon. Several precursors to describing monoracism in higher education include work outside and within higher education. For instance, in sociology, Daniel (2002) described a type of "psychological oppression imbedded in current methods of data collection, which support and are supported by the one-drop rule" (p. 190) that can negatively affect Multiracial individuals. In higher education, Renn's (2000, 2003, 2004) extensive work on mixed race students documented negative racialized experiences as they negotiated their identities across various ecological systems. Similarly, Chapman-Huls's (2009) dissertation spotlighted the pervasiveness of monoracial systems that Multiracial college women needed to navigate. Despite not using the term *monoracism*, these earlier works clearly articulate larger institutional and cultural forces at play that have structured the negative and oppressive experiences of Multiracial people.

Although the term *monoracism* had been used in social justice trainings and blog posts (e.g., Byrd, 2001), one of the first published articulations of the system of oppression targeting Multiracially identified individuals was a chapter in Sue's (2010) edited volume *Microaggressions and Marginality: Manifestation, Dynamics, and Impact*. In the chapter on Multiracial microaggressions, Johnston and Nadal (2010) defined *monoracism* and mapped their representation of monoracism to ideas from Bilodeau's (2009) definition of *genderism* as the system of oppression targeting transgender and gender-nonconforming students.[2] Johnston and Nadal's (2010) definition of monoracism privileged the psychological (given the fact that the larger volume targeted the field of psychology) and individual perceptions of monoracism (given the focus on interpersonal experiences of microaggressions). The authors did not explore at length what monoracism was, how it related to other forms of racism, and what could be done to resist monoracism as a form of oppression.

In 2014, Hamako took on the challenge of more fully exploring monoracism, or Multiracial oppression, and broadened it beyond the microaggressions framework. Hamako defined *monoracism* as

> the systemic privileging of things, people and practices that are racialized as "single-race" and/or "racially pure" (e.g., "Monoracial") and the oppression of things, people, and practices that are racialized as being of more than one race (e.g., "Multiracial," "Mixed-Race," "Multiethnic," etc.). (p. 81)

To fully illustrate how monoracism is a system of oppression, Hamako used Young's (2000) *Five Faces of Oppression* model to outline how monoracism fitted into the definition of systemic oppression, including how Multiracial people are oppressed through marginalization, cultural imperialism, and violence. Hamako (2014) extended Johnston and Nadal's conceptualization of monoracism that focused mostly on interpersonal dynamics by demonstrating how "monoracism is enacted on institutional, cultural, and intrapersonal or internalized levels of analysis" (p. 82). This broader articulation of the different levels and types of monoracism has been a prime development in scholarship, as described further in the following paragraphs.

Despite the relevance of Hamako's (2014) work in social justice education, there is still limited literature on monoracism with higher education as its focus. Harris's (2016) theorizing of monoracism as part of Multiracial critical theory, or "MultiCrit," was the first article to focus specifically on monoracism in higher education contexts. One tenet of MultiCrit centers how *racism, monoracism,* and *colorism* can interact and influence Multiracial people's racialized experiences. For example, a Black/white Multiracial person may be the target of anti-Black racism (racism), while also feeling a lack of belonging in either Black or white communities (monoracism), all of which is influenced by their skin tone, hair texture, and other aspects of phenotype (colorism). Furthermore, building upon the work of Guillermo-Wann and Johnston (2012), Harris expanded understandings of monoracism to include different types or manifestations, including vertical, horizontal, and internalized monoracism. These three manifestations are explored in a later section of this chapter.

How the Current Literature on Monoracism and Higher Education Falls Short

Although scholars have implemented and described monoracism as a theoretical framework both in empirical research and in theorization (e.g., Ford et al., 2019; Johnston-Guerrero et al., 2020), the existing literature on monoracism falls short in several key ways. First, as scholars who have written about Multiraciality and monoracism in higher education, we continue to receive questions from colleagues, journal reviewers, conference participants, and others in the field about *who* can enact monoracism. Specifically, there exist lingering tension points around whether or not People of Color can be monoracist. Because monoracism is a form of racism, individuals remain skeptical that People of Color can enact mono/racism (both racism and monoracism) because they do not often hold the power to do so (Operario & Fiske, 1998). Yet scholarship suggests that both white individuals and People of Color perpetrate some forms of oppression toward Multiracial students, faculty, and staff (Harris, 2017a, 2017b, 2020a; Kellogg & Liddell, 2012; Literte, 2010; Museus et al., 2016; Renn, 2003). For example, Multiracial student affairs professionals encounter challenges to their racial authenticity, with questions like "Are you sure you are Latinx?" from both white colleagues and Colleagues of Color (Harris, 2017a). Whether or not these behaviors from People of Color are racism or prejudice and discrimination remains contested.

Second, by framing monoracism as a unique form of marginalization that is separate from other forms of racism, scholars may inadvertently create a conceptual binary between monoraciality and Multiraciality. This binary reinforces an unintentional boundary around who can experience monoracism. Even if we aim to disrupt monoracial logics through centering monoracism, we may still support a framework that defines race and racism in discrete and binary terms—one is either monoracial or Multiracial, one either experiences monoracism or does not. Reinforcing this binary unwittingly upholds white supremacy as we are reinscribing, rather than dismantling, a racial hierarchy and a racial binary. Such a mental frame may be convenient for discussion, but it also fails to capture the true complexities of race and racialization as dynamic, temporal, and political systems. These complexities are evident when we explore different questions. Do only individuals who identify as Multiracial experience monoracism? What if those individuals are almost always misperceived by others as monoracial? Furthermore, how does monoracism influence individuals who internally identify as monoracial but may be racialized by others as Multiracial or racially ambiguous?

To address these questions, Hamako (2014) centered his definition of monoracism on racialization, as opposed to race itself. He argued that if something or someone is racialized as more than one race, then it or they are possibly subjected to a monoracist system. Furthermore, Johnston and Nadal (2010) posited that monoracism targeted "individuals who do not fit monoracial categories" (p. 125) instead of "Multiracial people" to allow for a more capacious understanding of the form of racism. However, scholars have yet to interrogate *who* is racialized as more than one race. We contend that whether or not individuals and communities consider themselves Multiracial is not necessarily the lingering issue—it is how they might experience monoracism due to processes of racialization. Racialization is important in understanding "the process through which racial meaning is attached to something that is perceived to be 'unracial' or devoid of racial meaning. Racialization plays a central role in the creation and reproduction of racial meanings" (Gonzalez-Sobrino & Goss, 2019, p. 509), including in the meanings attached to Multiraciality. For example, antimiscegenation laws, which prohibited sex and marriage between white individuals and People of Color, positioned racial mixing, through sex and through birth, as illegal (Pascoe, 2010). These laws racialized Multiracial peoples as tainted, wrong, and inherently unnatural. In this example, we see how racism and monoracism are integrally connected to a false binary between monoraciality and Multiraciality.

Third, another shortcoming of the present scholarship on monoracism is its focus exclusively on race and its failure to consider the interconnectedness of monoracism with other forms of oppression. Although some scholars in the field of higher education (e.g., Harris, 2016) have begun to center the multifaceted experiences of Multiracial students (e.g., Multiracial women and the intersections of racism and sexism), literature of this type is lacking.

By focusing exclusively on monoracism while overlooking its intersections with other systems of domination, scholars obscure the complex lived realities of Multiracial individuals. As an example, some scholars have found that Multiracial women and men experience sexual violence at higher rates than any other racial and/or gender group (Breiding et al., 2014). Yet no scholarship to our knowledge has attempted to unpack Multiracial students' experiences with sexual violence, which may be influenced by monoracism and gender-based discrimination. This may be because the limited literature on sexual violence that centers Students of Color does so through a Black–white binary and monoracial-only paradigm (see Harris et al., 2020). Similarly, on a macro level, little to no scholarship has explored how monoracism (as opposed to Multiracial identity) may intersect with patriarchy (as opposed to gender identity) to condone and perpetuate such violence. Scholars must begin to explore monoracism not as a system of oppression that exists in isolation, but as one of many intersecting systems of domination that shapes the experiences of Multiracial students in complex manners.

Monoracism in Higher Education: Three Tension Points

Our review of monoracism and the ways that literature on monoracism falls short guides us to use the remainder of this chapter to ask and explore three lingering questions, or tension points, that concern monoracism. Aligning with the work of Wijeyesinghe and Jones (2014), we frame our questions as "tension points" that we grapple with as we aim to expand the theoretical breadth of monoracism.

1. Given that racism is often conceptualized as (white) power plus prejudice, how might People of Color, who do not hold (white) power, perpetrate monoracism?
2. How does focusing on monoracism and, subsequently, focusing on Multiraciality, disrupt *and/or* maintain white supremacy and its interlocking systems of domination?
3. How does monoracism intersect with and support multiple systems of domination?

We interrogate these tension points not to offer concrete answers but to expand on existing work and conversations around Multiraciality and monoracism in higher education in an effort to encourage scholars and practitioners to continue to use and advance the theoretical breadth of monoracism and racisms in ways that disrupt white supremacy and its intersecting systems.

First Tension Point: How Might People of Color Be Monoracist?

We first take up the tension point "*How* might People of Color enact mono-racism?" Asking "how" rather than "if" allows for a more capacious, less binary, exploration of this tension point. Although some scholarship (e.g., Barndt, 1991; Hoyt, 2012; Operario & Fiske, 1998) has explored "the frequently accepted notion that, due to power differentials, People of Color cannot be racist" (Cabrera, 2018, p. 226), we argue that People of Color are often complicit in and supportive of systemic monoracism. Although People of Color do not often hold the same power and privileges as white individuals to enact (mono)racism, these power differentials do not preclude People of Color from engaging in (mono)racism (Guillermo-Wann & Johnston, 2012). Furthermore, Ibram X. Kendi (2019) explained "the ubiquity of racism" means "that no one was immune to its seductive power" (quoted in Sanneh, 2019, para. 3). Thus, all persons, including People of Color, who are educated, live, and learn within a society predicated on racism, are not immune to messaging and behaviors of white supremacy and racism (Kendi, 2019; see also Freire, 2014). This line of thinking also guides our claim that, in the United States, People of Color who perpetrate (mono)racism, often unintentionally, are acting within and reproducing the ubiquitous system of white supremacy that they were socialized within.

Monoracism is a form of racism that white people and People of Color can perpetrate to re/construct a monoracial-only paradigm of race, which upholds white supremacy (Guillermo-Wann & Johnston, 2012; Harris, 2016, 2017a; Johnston-Guerrero & Renn, 2016). This paradigm reinforces (mono)race as a biological concept that can be rank ordered into a racial hierarchy wherein white is supreme, pure, and inherently deserving of racial privileges (see Haney Lopez, 2006). Despite a long history of research and reports debunking biological racial hierarchies (e.g., Montagu, 1964; UNESCO, 1978), recent examples of white nationalists using DNA ancestry testing to try to "prove" the extent of their Europeanness (Murphy, 2019) demonstrate how notions of racial purity and white supremacy remain interconnected. The monoracial-only paradigm that is rooted in biological notions of race continues to influence policies and procedures within the academy, but remains "rooted in inaccurate, racist, and pseudo-scientific notions of so-called racial purity that undergirded the US's foundation as slave holding colonies" (Johnston-Guerrero & Renn, 2016, p. 140).

Previous research demonstrates how People of Color can, at times, enact monoracism in education. For instance, Multiracial tenured and tenure-track faculty (Harris, 2020b), Multiracial campus professionals (Harris, 2017a), and Multiracial students (Kellogg & Liddell, 2012; Literte, 2010; Renn,

2003) reported that People of Color on campus challenged their racial identities and questioned if they were "authentic" People of Color. Furthermore, on an organizational level, some Multiracial students, faculty, and staff perceived that racial identity–based organizations often excluded them from membership because they were not enough of a Person of Color (Harris, 2020a; Literte, 2010; Renn, 2003).

Although research suggests that People of Color enact monoracism, some people may remain skeptical, believing that these examples reflect racial prejudice within Communities of Color, but not racism. To address this claim, we assert that People of Color enact monoracism, but, due to power inequities, they may not enact monoracism in the same manners that white individuals enact monoracism. Specifically, monoracism may be *vertically* perpetrated by white communities, *horizontally* perpetrated by People of Color, and *internalized* by Multiracial individuals (Guillermo-Wann & Johnston, 2012; Harris, 2017a, 2020b). All three of these manifestations of mono/racism work to uphold a monoracial-only understanding of race that supports white supremacist assumptions.

Racism, or what we delineate as *vertical racism*, refers to white individuals oppressing People of Color (Wijeyesinghe et al., 1997). Thus, *vertical monoracism* is often enacted by white individuals and works to further subordinate and oppress Multiracial individuals (Guillermo-Wann & Johnston, 2012; Harris, 2017a, 2020b). Vertical, or top-down, monoracism captures how white individuals often hold the power to control societal and institutional systems that embed monoracism into the fabric of individuals' lives. For instance, Multiracial faculty and campus professionals acknowledge that diversity and hiring policies, as well as institutional forms, are monoracist in that they disallow for or punish one's Multiracial identification (Harris, 2017a, 2020b). These policies and procedures, which manifest on institutional and societal levels, are often implemented by white people in positions of power and work to re/create a monoracial-only understanding of race (see Harris, 2017a, 2020b; Johnston-Guerrero & Renn, 2016). (There are exceptions to this statement—e.g., President Barack Obama, Supreme Court Justice Clarence Thomas, and Senator Kamala Harris are People of Color who often have the power and position to enact policies and procedures on a macro level; the nuances of these exceptions are beyond the scope of this chapter.) Subsequently, vertical monoracism informs the world we inhabit and directly influences how and why People of Color enact horizontal and internalized monoracism.

Horizontal racism is "the result of people of targeted racial groups believing, acting on, or enforcing the dominant (white) system of racial discrimination and oppression" (Wijeyesinghe et al., 1997, p. 98). *Horizontal monoracism* captures how People of Color enact monoracism against Multiracial individuals, which works to uphold a monoracial-only paradigm of race that rewards those who do not deviate from a monoracial-only norm. For example, when People of Color question the racial in/authenticity of Multiracial individuals, they are often policing and reifying the boundaries of (mono)race (see Harris, 2017a). Monoracism enacted by People of Color also sends messages to Multiracial individuals that if they deviate from the monoracial norm, there may be repercussions within Communities of Color, such as exclusion from professional organizations that support People of Color (Harris, 2017a). Perhaps due to the lack of power held by People of Color in relation to white individuals, horizontal monoracism often manifests on individual and, at times, organizational levels. Yet horizontal monoracism should not be framed as lesser than vertical monoracism, because it continues to police and uphold the policies, procedures, and discourses put in place by vertical monoracism.

Multiracial people do not escape the omnipresence of racism in U.S. society and may enact monoracism through *internalized monoracism. Internalized racism* is "the result of people of targeted racial groups believing, acting on, or enforcing the dominant system of beliefs about themselves and members of their own racial group" (Wijeyesinghe et al., 1997, p. 98). Internalized monoracism occurs when Multiracial people adopt monoracial-only understandings of race and act in ways that uphold this paradigm. For example, Multiracial campus professionals may police their own racial authenticity, perceiving they are not enough of a Person of Color to support monoracial Students of Color (Harris, 2017a). Similar to horizontal monoracism, internalized racism may not be operationalized in systemic ways, but it continues to uphold systems of oppression that reify a monoracial-only paradigm of race that further supports white supremacy.

Finally, we believe that harm rests in refusing to acknowledge our roles in upholding systems of domination. Kendi (2019) suggested that individuals in the United States stop thinking of *racist* as a pejorative term and start framing racism as a description that applies to all people who are socialized within a nation founded on racism. In naming our racist foundations and behaviors, we are more able to identify the complexities of and our support for these systems. In acknowledging how all individuals might enact mono/racism, there exist more opportunities for healing, cross-community coalition building, and the dismantling of white supremacy. For example, within intergroup dialogue programs that exist at many U.S. institutions of higher education, students examine their identities and the ways these identities may connect to upholding systems of power and domination (Dessel & Rogge, 2008). When students are exposed to more capacious understandings of race, including monoracism, through dialogue, these students often report holding more positive views of conflict, learning more about and from people from other social groups, and valuing new and divergent viewpoints (see Hurtado, 2005; Zúñiga et al., 2007).

Second Tension Point: Monoracism and the Possible Disruption of White Supremacy

Expanding the theoretical breadth of monoracism is necessary to interrogate how processes of racialization, racism, and white supremacy are woven throughout U.S. higher education. In the past, much of the research on Multiracial people in higher education investigated Multiracial students' racial identity development processes (see chapter 2, this volume). Although scholars' focus on Multiracial students' racial identity is important, research centering only Multiracial individuals' experiences can be "disconnected from the larger history of 'race' and the ways in which social, institutional, and structural realities inform racialization" (Osei-Kofi, 2012, p. 253). When scholarship is approached from a micro level, we may perpetuate views of Multiracial students' experiences as reflecting individual choices, attitudes, or behaviors while overlooking the ways systems of domination, such as white supremacy and racialization, structure such experiences (Osei-Kofi, 2012). In addition, the historical focus on Multiraciality in the absence of attention to monoracism contributes to how Multiracial people are often positioned in various, and often contradictory, claims about race and racism (Johnston-Guerrero & Chaudhari, 2016). For example, although some people have cited Multiracial people as evidence of racial progress, many individuals have critiqued advocates of Multiraciality as perpetuating racial hierarchies because of desires to escape Blackness and subsequently increasing the distance between Black communities and white communities (Morning, 2005).

This positioning of Multiracial people is in alignment with what Bonilla-Silva (2004) described as a "tri-racial" system of racial groupings or a "Latin Americanization" (p. 935) of the U.S. model of race relations. The three groupings include "white, honorary white, and the collective black" (p. 935) with most Multiracial people being placed in the "honorary white" category. Even after the election of Barack Obama, Bonilla-Silva (2010) warned of the potential of the Obama presidency to bring the United States closer to what he described as a "Multiracial white supremacy regime" (p. 226), citing similarity to Latin American and Caribbean countries where "'racially mixed' folks are elected to power without that altering the racial order of things" (p. 226). Further, Bonilla-Silva pointed to historical examples of Blacks creating "other classifications such as Multiracial, bi-racial" (p. 271) as an intention to be something other than Black. Some of these critiques seem warranted, particularly as cautions for scholars seeking to further expand on Multiracial identity research. We agree that Multiracial identity may indeed perpetuate the maintenance of white supremacy by providing even further entrenchment in or expansion of racial hierarchies. Yet incorporating an enhanced understanding of monoracism and its relation to other systems of oppression may limit these critiques of Multiracial people by refocusing our attention on the dismantling of white supremacy.

By expanding on monoracism as a system of oppression, and therefore recentering structural manifestations of oppression over much of the current literature's focus on identity, we can more effectively see how monoracism works in concert with white supremacy. If white supremacy is somewhat dependent on maintaining racial divides where communities may be fighting among each other for already small "pieces of the pie," it is not surprising that there might be attacks on Multiracial people. However, given the analysis presented thus far, we raise the following questions for consideration. What if Multiracial people were more fully incorporated into the monoracial communities? What if Multiracial people were not "forced to choose" but rather allowed to do the broader work against white supremacy *in* the community to which they seek belonging?

We argue horizontal monoracism (racism enacted by monoracial People of Color) often manifests in ways that reject Multiracial People of Color who might strengthen antiracist work and ultimately benefits white supremacy. An example of this situation is when Multiracial students seek belonging in monoracial identity-based student organizations. Monoracism polices the borders of the groups and the extent to which someone fits standards or definitions of group membership. An identity-centered lens might focus on the Multiracial students' experiences feeling "forced to choose" or having their particular identities invalidated. These issues are important to highlight, but what a monoracism-centered lens gives us is a broader scope of what might be happening for the groups themselves and the identity policing going on. In some ways, leaders in these organizations are likely mimicking the same oppressive behaviors learned within a white supremacist society. When already marginalized, particularly within predominantly white and elite postsecondary institutions, monoracial identity-based student organizations may seek to hold on to what little space and resources they have, reproducing ideals of individual ownership and excluding those people whose identities do not fit the prototypical membership. By bringing monoracism to the attention of all students involved, this situation can be viewed through a more complex lens, with the potential of monoracial students better understanding how monoracism impedes coalition building and the inclusion of the voices of Multiracial students in creating change.

Highlighting monoracism gives us language and tools to name and then work toward dismantling the interconnected systems of monoracism and racism. Expanding the theoretical breadth of monoracism expands knowledge about other forms of racism. If monoracism is positioned as one of many systems of oppression, then work toward racial justice will be able to incorporate more people (i.e., Multiracial people who have felt excluded from [mono]racial justice efforts). Additionally, this approach will help to more robustly consider the ways the monoracial paradigm of race works in tandem with other racisms to uphold white "racial purity" and white supremacy.

Understanding that monoracism and racism work together to uphold white supremacy provides a more nuanced understanding of how we might move forward together. Monoracism provides a lens for understanding, in new ways, how and why groups draw and police boundaries that limit the potential for fluidity and crossing of those borders. It helps us see why Communities of Color might be skeptical of Multiracial people and use the questions of "What are you?" and "Who are you?" to get at the real question of "Are you with us (in this fight against white supremacy)?" Helping (monoracial) People of Color understand the monoracist undertones of such questioning for Multiracial people can lead to shared learning and coalition building. This learning begins with a common understanding of monoracism, how and why it exists, and its impact on higher education and society as a whole.

Third Tension Point: Monoracism and Intersecting Systems of Domination

In our final tension point, we explore the question "How does monoracism intersect with and support other systems of domination?" We contextualize our discussion on intersecting systems of domination through the concept of intersectionality (Crenshaw, 1989, 1991). Kimberlé Crenshaw (1989) provided a comprehensive description of intersectionality as an analogy to a literal intersection. In discussing employment discrimination against Black women, Crenshaw (1989) argued that Black women's experiences exist at the intersection of multiple systems of domination (namely, racism and sexism). U.S. law fails to recognize this intersection of race and gender—racism and sexism—as legitimate due to a myopic lens that either accounts for gender-based discrimination *or* racial discrimination. This narrow view of a single system of domination instead of systems of domination has obscured the unique discrimination Black women have experienced as a result of their race *and* gender—discrimination greater than the sum of its parts (see also Bowleg, 2008). Crenshaw (1989) posited that "any analysis that does not take intersectionality into account cannot sufficiently address the particular manner in which Black women are subordinated" (p. 140).

Following Crenshaw's work, we assert that a failure to consider the intersections of monoracism with other systems of domination would insufficiently capture the influence of monoracism in educational contexts. Following intersectionality, we understand monoracism as inextricably inter-twined with other forms of oppression, such as patriarchy, heterosexism, ableism, and classism. Previously, we mentioned that monoracism may inter-sect with sexism and patriarchy to influence the experiences of Multiracial students with sexual assault. Harris (2019) also found that sexism, racism, and classism often negatively influenced the social interactions of Multiracial women undergraduate students who attended an HWI. Thus, monoracism interacts with other systems of oppression, such as sexism and classism, to influence Multiracial students' campus experiences.

Some scholars have examined Multiraciality with respect to other identi-ties; however, their analyses have largely focused on individual identity, such as the relationships between gender and Multiraciality (e.g., Basu, 2010; Joseph-Salisbury, 2019) or among gender, Multiraciality, and sexuality (e.g., King, 2011). Although this literature pushes academia to consider Multiraciality in broader terms, most focus on micro-level, identity-based processes, inadvert-ently obscuring the impact of larger systems on racialization. For example, in one study Rockquemore (2002) accounted for the gendered nature of racial identity for 16 Black/white Multiracial women students, but she purposefully circumvented a structural analysis to focus on "microinteractions," because these situations are a "critical terrain where identities and group membership are negotiated" (p. 499). Harris (2019) acknowledged the gap in literature, taking a more structural/system approach, and therefore situated her analysis of Multiracial women within the broader sociohistorical context of whiteness as structuring property and intersectionality.

Although Harris's (2019) research is an important contribution, much more work needs to be done in the realm of examining monoracism in an intersectional context. For example, the intersection of race and (dis)abil-ity status within U.S. education has been well documented. Artiles (2013) expounded on the profound impact these intersecting systems can have on Students of Color, writing, "The racialization of disability is of concern because disability diagnoses for racial minorities often have concomitant negative consequences, such as educational segregation, limited access to the general education curriculum, and a host of negative long-term outcomes" (p. 330).

Thus, the intersections of racism and ableism result in the concurrent maintaining of domination over People of Color and their communities. Although scholarship has sought to understand ableism's relationship to race, it has not examined its relationship to monoracism and/or Multiraciality. This gap is intriguing because Multiracial men and women with disabilities experience some of the highest levels of discrimination and harassment in the workplace (Shaw et al., 2012). Furthermore, in a report by the U.S. Department of Education Office of Civil Rights (2014), Multiracial boys with disabilities and Multiracial girls with disabilities were suspended at higher rates (34% and 27%, respectively) than their peers. This research suggests that Multiracial students' ability status is often intertwined with their racial identities.

The intersections of Multiraciality and ability are not new; the tragic mulatto trope continues to influence the positioning of Multiracial individuals as flawed and riddled with issues because they are caught between two worlds, inherently confused, desperately tragic, and destined to fail (Spencer, 2010). The intersection of Multiraciality with disability oppression, as well as other systems of oppression, combine such that, "as strands of a rope, when these oppressions are woven together, they are stronger and therefore more dangerous" (Annamma, 2017, p. 11). In short, we argue that when scholars and practitioners focus on monoracism, they must do so in ways that also interrogate its relationship to other systems of domination and oppression. This nuanced and complex analysis will better inform work aimed at dismantling all systems of oppression.

Conclusion: Defining Monoracism

Through our discussion of the three tension points, we began to consider a revised definition of *monoracism*. However, our thoughts and efforts were restricted by our collective fear that, by offering a singular definition, we might unnecessarily limit the theoretical breadth and transformative possibilities of monoracism. Individuals and groups who do not fit dominant racial paradigms, including Multiracial peoples and communities, have been and continue to be constrained and policed in relation to their identities and opportunities. It is counterintuitive to reify those borders by restricting who could or could not be impacted by monoracism.

In defining this concept, we caution that we might unintentionally reinscribe and police racial boundaries, which is the antithesis of much of our work and of the goal of expanding monoracism. (Racial) privilege and oppression are clearly linked, yet less clearly understood is how people who experience racism can also enact oppression based on monoracism. These complex dynamics make the construction of a definition for monoracism complicated, if not impossible. The scope of monoracism is difficult to specify, and may benefit from a fluid and evolving process of defining, mirroring the complexity and fluidity of all forms of oppression. Because narrow definitions of racism unintentionally work in complicit ways to uphold white supremacy (see Crenshaw et al., 1995), we believe there is liberation in refusing to confine monoracism to narrow parameters. Yet we also acknowledge that words, definitions, and examples are needed to explicitly label some oppressions. With these tensions in mind, we close this chapter acknowledging that there is still a great deal we do not know about monoracism. Here we offer several tenets to guide future inquiry and continue a perpetual process of defining monoracism.

- Monoracism (re)constructs and maintains the oppression of individuals and communities that deviate from (mono)racial norms.
- Monoracism exists and is enacted on individual, interpersonal, institutional, and societal levels.
- Monoracism influences *all* individuals within U.S. society. Some people are oppressed by, or are the target of monoracism; some people enact monoracism, either consciously or subconsciously; and some people are secondary witnesses to the various levels that monoracism exists within and in which it is enacted.
- Monoracism is one form of many racisms that function to uphold white supremacy. All of U.S. society exists within and plays a part within a framework of racisms, including monoracism.
- Monoracism is inextricably intertwined with other forms of oppression, such as sexism, heterosexism, ableism, genderism, classism, and ageism. Monoracism must be contextualized and analyzed within these intersecting systems of domination.

In this chapter, we reviewed and built upon previous scholars' work to further expand the theoretical breadth of monoracism. Ultimately, we argue for complicating a narrow definition of racism that constricts understanding of lived reality and ultimately contributes to upholding white supremacy. However, scholars, practitioners, and educators must continue to ask questions of monoracism and other forms of racism, engage tensions points, and not settle on one concrete definition because processes of racialization are never fixed or stagnant. In continuing to explore intersecting systems of domination, who and how they oppress, and who and how they privilege, educators may work toward educational and social transformation.

Notes

1. Guided by the works of Lindsay Pérez Huber (2010), we capitalize *Asian, Black*, and other minoritized groups, including *People of Color*, as a form of linguistic empowerment. We do not capitalize *white* to challenge hegemonic grammatical norms and "reject the grammatical representation of power capitalization brings to the term 'white'" (Pérez Huber, 2010, p. 93).
2. For reflections on this analogizing of oppressions, see Tran and Johnston-Guerrero (2016).

References

Annamma, S. A. (2017). *The pedagogy of pathologization: Dis/abled girls of color in the school-prison nexus.* Routledge. https://doi.org/10.4324/9781315523057

Annamma, S. A., Jackson, D. D., & Morrison, D. (2017). Conceptualizing color-evasiveness: Using dis/ability critical race theory to expand a color-blind racial ideology in education and society. *Race Ethnicity and Education, 20*(2), 147–162. https://doi.org/ 10.1080/13613324.2016.1248837

Artiles, A. (2013). Untangling the racialization of disabilities: An intersectionality critique across disability models. *Du Bois Review, 10*(2), 329–347. https://doi.org/10.1017/S1742058X13000271

Barndt, J. R. (1991). *Dismantling racism: The continuing challenge to white America.* Augsburg Fortress.

Basu, A. M. (2010). The role of gender in the experiences of biracial college students. *Race/Ethnicity: Multidisciplinary Global Contexts, 4*(1), 97–115. https://doi.org/ 10.2979/racethmulglocon.2010.4.1.97

Bilodeau, B. L. (2009). *Genderism: Transgender students, binary systems and higher education.* VDM Verlag.

Bonilla-Silva, E. (2004). From bi-racial to tri-racial: Towards a new system of racial stratification in the USA. *Ethnic and Racial Studies, 27*(6), 931–950. https://doi.org/ 10.1080/0141987042000268530

Bonilla-Silva, E. (2010). *Racism without racists: Color-blind racism and the persistence of racial inequality in the United States* (3rd ed.). Rowman & Littlefield.

Bowleg, L. (2008). When Black + lesbian + woman ≠ Black lesbian woman: The methodological challenges of qualitative and quantitative intersectionality research. *Sex roles, 59*(5–6), 312–325. https://doi.org/10.1007/s11199-008-9400-z

Breiding, M. J., Smith, S. G., Basile, K. C., Walters, M. L., Chen, J., & Merrick, M. T. (2014). Prevalence and characteristics of sexual violence, stalking, and intimate partner violence victimization (National Intimate Partner and Sexual Violence Survey, United States, 2011). *American Journal of Public Health, 105*(4), 1–18. https://doi.org/10.2105/AJPH.2015.302634

Byrd, C. M. (2001). *Editorial: The political color continuum.* Interracial Voice. http://www.interracialvoice.com/editor12.html

Cabrera, N. L. (2018). Where is the racial theory in Critical Race Theory?: A constructive criticism of the Crits. *The Review of Higher Education, 42*(1), 209–233. https://doi.org/10.1353/rhe.2018.0038

Chapman-Huls, M. M. (2009). *Strategies multiracial college women use to navigate monoracial systems* [Unpublished doctoral dissertation]. University of Nebraska.

Crenshaw, K. (1989). Demarginalizing the intersection of race and sex: Black feminist critique of antidiscrimination doctrine, feminist theory and antiracist politics. *University of Chicago Legal Forum, 1989*(1), 139–168. http://chicagounbound.uchicago.edu/uclf/vol1989/iss1/8

Crenshaw, K. (1991). Mapping the margins: Intersectionality, identity politics, and violence against Women of Color. *Stanford Law Review, 43*(6), 1241–1299. https://doi.org/ 10.2307/1229039

Crenshaw, K. W., Gotanda, N., Peller, G., & Thomas, K. (1995). Introduction. In K. W. Crenshaw, N. Gotanda, G. Peller, & K. Thomas (Eds.), *Critical race theory: The key writings that formed the movement* (pp. xiii–xxxii). The New Press.

Daniel, G. R. (2002). *More than Black: Multiracial identity and the new racial order.* Temple University Press.

Dessel, A., & Rogge, M. E. (2008). Evaluation of intergroup dialogue: Review of the empirical literature. *Conflict Resolution Quarterly, 26*(2), 199–238. https://doi.org/10.1002/crq.230

Ford, K. S., Patterson, A. N., & Johnston-Guerrero, M. P. (2019). Monoracial normativity in university websites: Systematic erasure and selective reclassification of multiracial students. *Journal of Diversity in Higher Education.* Advance online publication. https://doi.org/10.1037/dhe0000154

Freire, P. (2014). *Pedagogy of the oppressed.* Bloomsbury.

Glenn, E. N. (2015). Settler colonialism as structure: A framework for comparative studies of U.S. race and gender formation. *Sociology of Race and Ethnicity, 1*(1), 54–74. https://doi.org/10.1177/2332649214560440

Gonzalez-Sobrino, B., & Goss, D. R. (2019). Exploring the mechanisms of racialization beyond the black–white binary. *Ethnic and Racial Studies, 42*(4), 505–510. https://doi.org/10.1080/01419870.2018.1444781

Guillermo-Wann, C., & Johnston, M. P. (2012, November). *Rethinking research on multiracial college students: Toward an integrative model of Multiraciality for campus climate.* Paper presented at the Second Biannual Critical Mixed Race Studies Conference, Chicago, IL, United States. https://eric.ed.gov/?id=ED538027

Hamako, E. (2014). *Improving antiracist education for multiracial students* [Unpublished doctoral dissertation, University of Massachusetts Amherst]. ScholarWorks. https://scholarworks.umass.edu/dissertations_2/90

Haney Lopez, I. (2006). *White by law: The legal construction of race.* University Press.

Harris, J. C. (2016). Toward a critical multiracial theory in education. *International Journal of Qualitative Studies in Education, 29*, 795–813. https://doi.org/10.1080/09518398.2016.1162870

Harris, J. C. (2017a). Multiracial campus professionals' experiences with multiracial microaggressions. *Journal of College Student Development, 58*(7), 1055–1073. https://doi.org/10.1353/csd.2017.0083

Harris, J. C. (2017b). Multiracial college students' experiences with multiracial microaggressions. *Race Ethnicity and Education, 20*(4), 429–445. https://doi.org/10.1080/13613324.2016.1248836

Harris, J. C. (2019). Whiteness as structuring property: Multiracial women students' social interactions at a historically white institution. *The Review of Higher Education, 42*(3), 1023–1050. https://doi.org/10.1353/rhe.2019.0028

Harris, J. C. (2020a). Multiracial campus professionals' experiences with queering race in US postsecondary contexts. *Race Ethnicity and Education, 23*(4), 509–529. https://doi.org/10.1080/13613324.2018.1511530

Harris, J. C. (2020b). Multiracial faculty members' experiences with teaching, research, and service. *Journal of Diversity in Higher Education 13*(3), 228–239. https://doi.org/10.1037/dhe0000123

Harris, J. C., Cobian, K., & Karunaratne, N. (2020). Reimagining the study of campus sexual assault. *Higher Education: Handbook of Theory and Research, 35,* 1–47. https://doi.org/10.1007/978-3-030-11743-6_12-1

Hoyt, C. (2012). The pedagogy of the meaning of racism: Reconciling a discordant discourse. *Social Work, 57*(3), 225–234. https://doi.org/10.1093/sw/sws009

Hurtado, S. (2005). The next generation of diversity and intergroup relations. *Journal of Social Issues, 61*(3), 593–610. https://doi.org/10.1111/j.1540-4560.2005.00422.x

Johnston, M. P., & Nadal, K. L. (2010). Multiracial microaggressions: Exposing monoracism in everyday life and clinical practice. In D. W. Sue (Ed.), *Microaggressions and marginality: Manifestation, dynamics, and impact* (pp. 123–144). Wiley.

Johnston-Guerrero, M. P., & Chaudhari, P. (2016). "Everyone is just mixed to me": Exploring the role of Multiraciality in college students' racial claims. *Equity & Excellence in Education, 49*(3), 254–266. https://doi.org/10.1080/10665684.2016.1194098

Johnston-Guerrero, M. P., & Renn, K. A. (2016). Multiracial Americans in college. In K. O. Korgen (Ed.), *Race policy and multiracial Americans* (pp. 139–154). Policy Press. https://doi.org/10.1332/policypress/9781447316459.003.0009

Johnston-Guerrero, M. P., Tran, V. T., & Combs, L. (2020). Multiracial identities and monoracism: Examining the influence of oppression. *Journal of College Student Development, 61*(1), 18–33. http://doi.org/10.1353/csd.2020.0001

Joseph-Salisbury, R. (2019). Wrangling with the Black monster: Young Black mixed-race men and masculinities. *The British Journal of Sociology, 70*(5), 1754–1773. https://doi.org/10.1111/1468-4446.12670

Kellogg, A. H., & Liddell, D. L. (2012). "Not half, but double": Exploring critical incidents in the racial identity of multiracial college students. *Journal of College Student Development, 53*(4), 524–541. https://doi.org/10.1353/csd.2012.0054

Kendi, I. X. (2016). *Stamped from the beginning: The definitive history of racist ideas in America.* Bold Type Books. https://doi.org/10.14296/RiH/2014/2165

Kendi, I. X. (2019). *How to be an antiracist.* Random House.

Kim, D. H., & Sundstrom, R. R. (2014). Xenophobia and racism. *Critical Philosophy of Race, 2,* 20–45. https://doi.org/ 10.5325/critphilrace.2.1.0020

King, A. R. (2011). Environmental influences on the development of female college students who identify as multiracial/biracial-bisexual/pansexual. *Journal of College Student Development, 52*(4), 440–445. https://doi.org/10.1353/csd.2011.0050

Kohli, R. (2013). Unpacking internalized racism: Teachers of color striving for racially just classrooms. *Race Ethnicity and Education, 17*(3), 367–387. https://doi.org/10.1080/13613324.2013.832935

Literte, P. E. (2010). Revising race: How biracial students are changing and challenging student services. *Journal of College Student Development, 51*(2), 115–134. https://doi.org/10.1353/csd.0.0122

Montagu, A. (Ed.). (1964). *The concept of race.* Free Press of Glencoe.

Morning, A. (2005). Multiracial classification on the United States census. *Revue Européenne Des Migrations Internationales, 21*(2), 1–20. https://doi.org/10.4000/remi.2495

Murphy, H. (2019, July 12). How white nationalists see what they want to see in DNA tests. *New York Times.* https://www.nytimes.com/2019/07/12/us/white-nationalists-dna-tests.html

Museus, S. D., Lambe Sariñana, S. A., Yee, A. L., & Robinson, T. (2016). An qualitative examination of multiracial students' experiences with prejudice and discrimination in college. *Journal of College Student Development, 57*(6), 680–697. https://doi.org/10.1353/csd.2015.0041

Operario, D., & Fiske, S. T. (1998). Racism equals power plus prejudice: A social psychological equation for racial oppression. In J. L. Eberhardt & S. T. Fiske (Eds.), *Confronting racism: The problem and the response* (pp. 33–53). SAGE.

Osei-Kofi, N. (2012). Identity, fluidity, and groupism: The construction of multiraciality in education discourse. *Review of Education, Pedagogy, and Cultural Studies, 34*(5), 245–257. https://doi.org/10.1080/10714413.2012.732782

Pascoe, P. (2010). *What comes naturally: Miscegenation law and the making of race in America.* Oxford University Press.

Patton, L. D. (2016). Disrupting postsecondary prose: Toward a critical race theory of higher education. *Urban Education, 51*(3), 315–342. https://doi.org/10.1177/0042085915602542

Perea, J. F. (1997). The Black/White binary paradigm of race: The normal science of American racial thought. *California Law Review, 85*(5), 1213–1258. https://doi.org/10.2307/3481059

Pérez Huber, L. (2010). Using Latina/o critical race theory (LatCrit) and racist nativism to explore intersectionality in the educational experiences of undocumented Chicana college students. *Educational Foundations, 24*(1–2), 77–96. https://eric.ed.gov/?id=EJ885982

Pérez Huber, L., & Solórzano, D. G. (2015). Racial microaggressions as a tool for critical race research. *Race Ethnicity and Education, 18*, 297–320. https://doi.org/10.1080/13613324.2014.994173

Poon, O., Squire, D., Kodama, C., Byrd, A., Chan, J., Manzano, L., Furr, S., & Bishundat, D. (2016). A critical review of the model minority myth in selected literature on Asian Americans and Pacific Islanders in higher education. *Review of Educational Research, 86*(2), 469–502. https://doi.org/10.3102/0034654315612205

Renn, K. A. (2000). Patterns of situational identity among biracial and multiracial college students. *Review of Higher Education, 23*(4), 399–421. https://doi.org/10.1353/rhe.2000.0019

Renn, K. A. (2003). Understanding the identities of mixed race college students through a developmental ecology lens. *Journal of College Student Development, 44*(3), 383–403. https://doi.org/10.1353/csd.2003.0032

Renn, K. A. (2004). *Mixed race students in college: The ecology of race, identity, and community.* SUNY Press.

Rockquemore, K. A. (2002). Negotiating the color line: The gendered process of racial identity construction among black/white biracial women. *Gender & Society, 16*(4), 485–503. http://doi.org/10.1177/0891243202016004005

Sanneh, K. (2019, August 12). The fight to redefine racism. *The New Yorker.* https://www.newyorker.com/magazine/2019/08/19/the-fight-to-redefine-racism

Shaw, L., Chan, F., & McMahon, B. (2012). Intersectionality and disability harassment: The interactive effects of disability, race, age, and gender. *Rehabilitation Counseling Bulletin, 55*(2), 82–91. https://doi.org/10.1177/0034355211431167

Spencer, R. (2010). *Reproducing race: The paradox of generation mix.* Lynne Rienner.

Sue, D. W. (Ed.). (2010). *Microaggressions and marginality: Manifestation, dynamics, and impact.* Wiley.

Tran, V. T., & Johnston-Guerrero, M. P. (2016). Is transracial the same as transgender? The utility and limitations of identity analogies in multicultural education. *Multicultural Perspectives, 18*(3), 134–139. https://doi.org/10.1080/15210960.2016.1186548

United Nations Educational Scientific and Cultural Organization (UNESCO). (1978). *Declaration on race and racial prejudice.* http://portal.unesco.org/en/ev.php-URL_ID=13161&URL_DO=DO_TOPIC&URL_SECTION=201.html

United States Department of Education Office of Civil Rights. (2014). *Office of civil rights data collection, data snapshot: School discipline* (Issue Brief 1). https://eric.ed.gov/?id=ED577231

Wijeyesinghe, C. L., Griffin, P., and Love, B. (1997). Racism curriculum design. In M. Adams, L. A. Bell, & P. Griffin (Eds.), *Teaching for diversity and social justice: A sourcebook* (pp. 82–109). Routledge.

Wijeyesinghe, C. L., & Jones, S. R. (2014). Intersectionality, identity, and systems of power and inequality. In D. Mitchell Jr., C. Y. Simmons, & L. A. Greyerbiehl (Eds.), *Intersectionality & higher education: Theory, research, & praxis* (pp. 9–19). Peter Lang.

Young, I. M. (2000). Five faces of oppression. In M. Adams, W. J. Blumenfeld, R. Castañeda, H. W. Hackman, M. L. Peters, & X. Zúñiga (Eds.), *Readings for diversity and social justice* (pp. 35–49). Routledge.

Zúñiga, X., Nagda, B. A., Chesler, M., & Cytron-Walker, A. (2007). Intergroup dialogue in higher education: Meaningful learning about social justice. *ASHE-ERIC Higher Education Report, 32*, 1–128. https://doi.org/10.1002/aehe.3204

PART TWO

MULTIRACIAL NARRATIVES
ACROSS THE HIGHER
EDUCATION LANDSCAPE

5

BACK TO BLACK

Nick Davis

I was born in the summer of 1995 at the Ronald Reagan Medical Center at the University of California, Los Angeles (UCLA), to a black father and a white mother, the first of three children to come. My parents were both resident directors, so my family had to live on UCLA's campus, steeping me in the diversity of the students and staff. My parents made a concerted effort to keep our friend groups diverse and were a notoriously kind and justice-oriented couple, both well loved in their respective fields and positions on campus.

Black?

Learning and Questioning My Identity

I first experienced racial segregation when traveling to visit extended family, my mother's white family in the suburbs of Minneapolis and my father's black family in Philadelphia. I treated the process of acclimating to the respective social environments as if it were an experiment or a game, dipping my toe into both worlds. I felt like I was balancing on the partition between two pools of water, playfully and precariously lowering my leg into one pool, then lifting it out and sinking it in the other. I was reveling in the shock of the changing temperatures, living in the moments of adjustment and tension.

When I was around age 7 my family moved to a neighborhood in Inglewood, California, that was predominantly black. It was there in elementary school that I was first asked "What are you?" directly. It came without maliciousness, from a young black boy who knew well where he stood, and was wondering the same of me. The question threw me off in a way he couldn't have understood—I had never felt like I had to articulate what I

79

was. I'd never asked myself that question. At UCLA either nobody cared or everyone seemed to have me figured out, and in my family it wasn't a conversation I remember having. Either way, I felt underprepared. But I would get used to the question.

As a little brown boy with short hair I was mistaken for every nonwhite racial group under the sun. A white woman once approached my mother and asked her, without an ounce of shame, if "the father was Mexican," while my black father was sitting right next to me. White women would exclaim, grab my cheeks, and declare how cute I was to my mother. I couldn't imagine why this was happening, I rarely if ever saw such egregious violations of personal space happening to white children. But I observed and learned.

I went to a black high school, and there were shades and personalities of black people that ran the gamut. I came into myself more there, grew to be more ostensibly black, but was still in a precarious position in terms of my confidence in my identity. There was plenty of room for the diversities of blackness to thrive, but the situation was also ripe for those who believed themselves gatekeepers of the black identity to police who was and who wasn't black enough. I did a lot to prove my blackness—a stint on the football team; 4 years of basketball; and, eventually, becoming the vice president of the school while getting the vast majority of the black vote. I had to study blackness, observe my own ways of moving through the school, and adjust accordingly. I didn't feel totally comfortable in my blackness, and I certainly was not aware of a mixed race option.

At the same time I knew on some immovable level that I was black. In the wake of Trayvon Martin's murder, my dad sat me down and talked to me about how important it was that I knew how to talk to police, kept my hood down while walking home at night, paid attention to my surroundings at all times. How I walked, talked, looked was life or death. I knew I was black because there are consequences to being black that only black people need be aware of.

During the college application process I (only) checked the black box. I received some letters welcoming me into the black community at Northwestern and sharing some of the resources black students had access to. But when I got to campus I was still in fighting mode, expecting to have to either prove my blackness or avoid it being called into question altogether. I somehow missed the memo for joining the black student Facebook group, and so I didn't see the announcement of the new black student dinner. The following week I felt like the eyes of black students I passed on the street were all accusing me: "Why weren't you there?" and "Do you think you're too good for us?" My undiagnosed anxiety was creating the illusion of exclusion and authenticity politics, and I felt like I had botched my entry into the community.

The next experience was a bit of a blur, but here is generally what happened. I was walking around the new student club fair looking for the club volleyball team. I certainly wasn't expecting, then, to hear from my 8 o'clock: "Sorry if this is presumptuous but are you mixed race?"

This was at once the most alarming and affirming question I'd been asked since I stepped on campus. There was a moment of panic. Was I being exposed as nonblack or was I being affirmed in a new identity?

The inquiry came from a bubbly sophomore, and one glance told me she had no intention to play gatekeeper to my black identity. She introduced herself as Elana, the copresident of the brand-new club created that quarter called "MIXED: Northwestern's Mixed Race Student Union," and she was recruiting, shamelessly, on a speculating glance. Her criteria was shaky but I let her corral me into MIXED's booth. I was greeted by a rainbow coalition of smiles, all welcoming me with an enthusiasm that made me empathize with folks roped into cults. They touted grey shirts with "100% MIXED" in bold white and yellow block text across their chests. They explained their club was a space to talk about being mixed race and for "mixed kids" to be themselves.

I was shocked by the whole encounter and vaguely committed to attend a meeting and sign up for their mailing list, as is customary with every club a freshman is coerced into interfacing with. Were these people performing the same balancing act as I was? I didn't know what to think.

In the meantime I was shopping around other clubs and organizations, trying to figure out where I fit in. The perceived authenticity politics of black student groups began to fall away bit by bit as I was introduced to the diversity of black students on campus.

After a well-respected black senior took me under his wing, I was introduced to a lot of black leaders on campus who helped me get involved in other organizations like For Members Only (FMO), the premier black student alliance on campus. I got to know some of the same individuals who I felt were skeptical of me around campus and I found they were kind, generous, and fun. My perception of my blackness being under assault was a myth and, as I'd later discover, a side effect of my own insecurity and proximity to whiteness.

My blackness was never called into question, but my politics were. The early 2010s were a tumultuous time on Northwestern's campus, and there was a lot of momentum for action. If you were not willing to engage politically with the black student agenda, most prominently informed and guided by FMO, it was difficult to be taken seriously. I learned then that I had a lot of listening and learning to do before I could feel like an active member—another case of insecurity and adverseness to vulnerability on my part. I loved the black community at Northwestern, but I was still clunkily navigating their cultural and political field. I was scared to jump in.

All the while I was experiencing the simultaneous exclusion and fetishization of black students that white students engaged in. I had an insatiable social appetite, and white students loved it. I was tall, laid back, athletic, gullible, and black, a ripe combination for white people who were looking to borrow a black card to rap "Gold Digger" *word* for *word*, show off a signed Waka Flocka mixtape from high school, or ask if I was homies with Nipsey Hustle. I realized that I had been tossed off the opposite deep end to the one in Inglewood and experienced a degree of culture shock. I even dipped my toe into the white Greek system, which, to put lightly, was a horrifying experience. But the theme was that I was seeking validation from all around campus, learning about how power moved through the school, and flailing a bit. Classes were astronomically more difficult than I was expecting or prepared for, and I was looking for outlets. I still hadn't felt like I found my people.

Mixed Race

Searching for My People on Campus

One night around week 7, hunkered with some friends over some midterm review guide or chemistry lab write-up, I was making no progress. Naturally I checked Facebook to engage in some mindless scrolling, where there was a notification for a MIXED general member meeting happening that night, in 5 minutes. And for the first time I felt compelled to go to a student group event. The thought kept running through my head—*this is a meeting for mixed race people, right? And I guess I'm mixed race . . . isn't it my responsibility to check it out?* It was a moment where I knew I needed to be there, but not fully why.

The classroom was one of those ruthless designs where the door is at the front of the room, so when you fly in 10 minutes late you're greeted by a whole classroom of eyes and the professor's incredulous about-face. And there were a lot of eyes: the room, meant to fit 40, was far over capacity. People were sitting on window ledges, leaning on chalkboards, and sitting cross-legged in front of chairs. The copresidents, Elana and Cory, were giving a well-rehearsed introduction to the club. They paused to welcome me and told me to sit anywhere, which was crueler a request than they knew. I was herded to the last chair available, awkwardly wading through my peers.

As I looked around, it was objectively the most diverse space I had been in at Northwestern. I was surprised to see many faces I identified as white. As I met the people around me I was getting giddy—these were some of the coolest people I'd ever met. They were from all over the world, had incredibly diverse talents and interests, and were at Northwestern for a litany of reasons. But one thing was clear. Everyone was here because they felt they were riding the margins, walking the same partition I was. They hadn't found their people either.

We spent the hour commiserating over our "mixed race experiences" and debating what a Cheerios commercial with a mixed race family and the ensuing media flurry meant for racial progress in America. It was a light conversation, but people were deeply engaged, and it was the most fun I had had in a group discussion on campus up until that point. More than anything it felt like people wanted me to be there, to belong. And I needed that.

I began attending more and more meetings and parties and informal gatherings. After some time I decided I wanted to be more involved, and I approached Elana to ask her if I might be able to contribute some ideas. She invited me to come talk to the executive (exec) board the following week.

I was surprised to see the exec board had 14 members on it, bigger than any other exec board I knew about on campus. Once I was given the floor, I expressed that, as much as we had enriching and fun conversations about our identities and the problems that sometimes came with them, we never addressed the root of the issues, spoke of them critically, or thought of the power we were gathering on campus. I thought we could do huge things, find ways to help members develop their racial identities, host education and health initiatives, and begin collecting data on multiracial students to better advocate for their needs. The ideas seemed to be refreshing, and after the meeting I was approached by an exec member and offered a position as administrative chair on the board, which I immediately accepted.

Multiracial Black

Complicating My Definition of Multiraciality

At the tail end of my freshman year in the spring of 2014, on my way to an on-campus concert, I ran into one of the other exec members for MIXED. After some light conversation he got bold.

"I've noticed you've been hanging out with a lot of black people lately; what's that about?"

I might have literally spit out my water. I can't remember my response or how I got out of that awful conversation, but I remember his reasoning. He claimed that it was a bad look for exec members to hang out with only a select group of people on campus, that "self-segregating" based on only one facet of my identity didn't align with MIXED's mission. This member was black as well.

It's probably unnecessary to explain that I had a remarkable diversity of friends and that he knew next to nothing about my social life outside of MIXED. But it really stood out that this guy was one of the people defining the culture of MIXED, and it was beginning to dawn on me why many of my friends of color were leery of the group. How could an organization that claimed to help unify cultural groups on campus also contain members who thought like this? I knew that I was in for an uphill battle if I wanted to change this culture.

. . .

The night of December 3rd, 2014, in the aftermath of the nonindictment of Eric Garner's murderer, black students at Northwestern were reeling. Within 8 hours a petition was circulating to leaders of color condemning the nonindictment, articulating the pain of black students, and demanding that students and administration alike respond in a meaningful way.

The letter was signed by an incredible diversity of students, including leaders of Latinx, feminist, low-income, Asian, Palestinian, and LGBTQIA groups. Friends of mine at FMO sent it my way and asked if MIXED would be willing to sign the petition in solidarity.

I reached out to Elana immediately and laid out the importance of being a part of this response, what it would mean for black members of MIXED, and how it could be a signal to other groups around campus that we had their backs.

In retrospect it was also crucial that MIXED throw their support behind this because it meant something momentous for me. I could imagine myself in the shoes of Eric Garner and the litany of other black people murdered by police, and if MIXED refused to support them then, they were refusing to acknowledge the significance of my own life. It would signal that if I was killed unjustly, they wouldn't take to the streets for me.

Elana refused to sign the petition, stating that it was too politically charged and that MIXED was a nonpolitical space. I was furious. I began to question, again, if these were my people.

I messaged another black exec member who I had been in conversation with, pushing to mobilize around the issue. We decided we would ignore Elana's wish to not implicate the group—we each signed the petition, with our MIXED credentials.

My accomplice then reached out to two other "political" (read: radical) black women on the board, and the four of us decided we would construct a letter to the MIXED exec board that asserted our concerns, funneling our rage and frustration in a way that might convince them to act. We sent it to MIXED executives the night before our next exec board meeting.

The response was nothing short of explosive.

People fell on one side or the other—it was impossible to ride the fence. One half insisted we were a social group and should keep our noses out of politics. The other urged that we had black members who needed our support and that it was a crucial opportunity to show *their* lives mattered and that inaction is as political as action. It was, to us, an issue of condemning racial oppression or standing idly by.

Our anger was broadly dismissed and misunderstood by the other half, and it was difficult to ignore the rift it was causing in the group. We didn't know how to move forward, so the meeting ended without resolution. The next day I met with Elana one on one. She agreed to letting MIXED host a space for black members to speak their mind and engage in healing in response to the nonindictment. I decided to facilitate.

Dozens of black students and nonblack supporters showed up, contributing to a heart-wrenching and compelling discussion about what it means to be black in a primarily white institution. A majority of the people who showed up were new faces. They felt as if they weren't sure of whether MIXED was for them—some of them had only heard about MIXED because they saw a couple of exec members sign the aforementioned petition. The group that showed up that night would become some of the core constituency of MIXED in the years to come.

The event was a massive success, but the bigger problem was the hoops that we black exec members had to jump through to make it happen. In the following weeks the conversation around this series of events was so tense and frustrating that it compelled two of my coconspirators to leave the group. One of them, Audre, decided to stick around. The two of us decided to run for the presidency and vice presidency in the elections that spring.

. . .

Looking back, my bid for the presidency was not just an attempt to right the course of MIXED but also to grab the helm of my own racial identity and justify my emotional investment in MIXED. It was exhausting having to explain to other black leaders why I was continuing to throw my weight behind a group that time and time again refused to support the causes that would protect my black identity and the interests of other black students. At the same time as my bid for the MIXED presidency I was approached by members of FMO to run for their exec board, prompting a fair amount of soul-searching. In the months since the healing event we hosted, I had been steeped in black activist culture and was really feeling supported by and at home in the black community at Northwestern. It was a grueling decision, but I decided I could have a bigger impact helping MIXED articulate a new vision and was elected president of MIXED in spring of 2015.

My platform was to focus the group more on advocacy and education, and help students to find their place on campus. To break down barriers of perceived authenticity politics we hosted mixers with several cultural student organizations in the hopes that our members would feel more comfortable navigating those groups. I wanted other students to feel as at home in their respective cultural identities as I was learning to be in my black identity.

But we ran into some major problems. One was that there was a major drop in membership, by some measures up to 70%. This could be attributed to a couple of things. First, many had joined the group on the pretense that it was a purely social group that didn't require them to engage "politically" with their multiracial identities. Second, we dove right into a course of political action that was not supplemented by an educational campaign to help members understand the inherent political nature of their identities and connect that to their everyday lives. In a survey sent out shortly after we noticed this decline, members cited that they felt some of the programming didn't speak to them anymore.

In spite of some of the feedback we got, the remaining 30% of members showed up, often and strong. We catered a lot of the programming to these students, building on concepts from years past and diving into theoretical texts on multiracial identity development. For many of us, MIXED was the first time we had ever had a chance to discuss race in a comfortable setting with people who were at the same stage of identity development, and we wanted to go deeper.

Black

Returning to and Affirming My Blackness

Although the group was making progress in a lot of ways, we ran into issues with recruitment. We spent a lot of time thinking of how to have deeper, sequential conversations about identity with regular members while also welcoming new students into the fold, no matter their experience discussing issues of identity. We wanted to meet everyone where they were at, but meetings were only an hour long.

At first we were stumped, trying to figure out the best ways to get younger students up to speed and at times rushing conversations that they weren't ready for or didn't have the context to engage in meaningfully. So we slowed it down. Every meeting, we would start with someone sharing their experience navigating life as a mixed race person, pick a discussion question to facilitate an exploration of our identities, and spend a lot more time bonding. Numbers started to rise again. But the more we catered to our younger members, the more experienced members began looking for advocacy or deeper identity explorations—to books, classes, and other student organizations.

For my cohort of MIXED members, the attempt to explore history, politics, and identity was all in order to transition ourselves to a position where we would no longer feel the tension within ourselves we felt while navigating campus. Once we felt this tension released and found our own ways forward, it was time for transition. I, and many other exec members, felt that the conversations were not serving us in the same way.

MIXED slowly evolved into a sort of stepping stone for identity development. For some, it was a path to exploring the barriers to feeling more comfortable in another group that we really longed to feel comfortable identifying with, to find our people. Others simply wanted to have foundational conversations about race they weren't having elsewhere. We realized the importance of the space being a landing pad for students who were feeling lost in the cultural seams of campus and decided that was where we would put the most focus.

MIXED was a crucial space for me to have the conversations I needed to figure out what compelled me to doubt my blackness in the first place. It's hard to put my finger on the actual cause, but the process of helping other people navigate their identities unlocked something inside me. I no longer felt any tension between myself and a black identity. The internal mechanisms working to make me insecure about identifying fully as black were gone. I realized that positioning myself as multiracial was doing little, anymore, to make me feel more whole.

I was taking African American studies classes, reading books, and sharing space with people who were arming me with a new vocabulary and set of theories around my identity that were invaluable. I learned the history of my people, that there had always been black people with mixed heritage, but that they all were a part of a long black tradition. I no longer felt as if I was balancing precariously on a partition, but I was able to tap back into my childish wonder from when I lived at UCLA, this time swimming eagerly through the waters I'm now comfortably acclimated to.

. . .

I know who I am, where I come from, and that my particular amalgamation of stardust is unique and mystical and complex. To the world I would face outside of Northwestern I was black, and this was an important thing to internalize. Identifying as multiracial would not protect me from violence against black people. My identifying as black was not a new identity; it was an affirmation, a return. And I'm as black as they come.

6

ON THE PATH TO
MULTIRACIAL
CONSCIOUSNESS

Reflections on My Scholar-Practitioner
Journey in Higher Education

Victoria K. Malaney Brown

Outside of the Box

I live a fractured existence
Being asked to prove my race
Questions from strangers, peers, and classmates constantly
Interrogating.
Asking me to prove what I already know is true
Sometimes I feel as though my voice is muted
Sometimes I feel as though I cannot break out of this
structural border that pressures me to stay inside
one race box.
But when I reflect and remember who my family is
I fight to live outside of the race box as my roots grow from my multiracial
heritages.
And I am proud to be me—whole;
not pieces or fractionalized parts.[1]

W hen I was a little girl growing up in South Florida, I remember hearing these recurring questions from my peers in elementary school. "No, that can't be your real hair." "Is that really your Dad?" "Where are you *really* from?" "Where is Trinidad?!" These interrogations eventually started to fragment my views of the world. Being asked these questions made me self-reflect about my own bicultural heritage growing up in a Trinidadian and American household. The poem with which I began this chapter, "Outside of the Box," was written when I was a third-year doctoral student at the University of Massachusetts Amherst. This poem, written through an assignment from my qualitative data analysis course, in some ways represents my own path to better understanding my racial identity while also strengthening my racial consciousness. My racial identities as a multiracial cisgender woman of Irish and Trinidadian American (Indo-Caribbean, Spanish, White) descent has always shaped the way that I view myself and the world around me. Before sharing more about my identity, I provide more context about my family. My mother immigrated to the United States from the Caribbean islands of Trinidad and Tobago when she was in her early 20s. She came to the United States to help out a cousin with the care of her young children. Although she did not initially imagine settling in the United States to live, it was in South Florida where she met my father, a boat captain and White Irish man hailing from Boston, Massachusetts. Their love and union "quietly revolutionized" (Root, 1996, p. 9) their families and their friends around them.

I later learned from reading the work of Maria P. P. Root (1996) that "everyone who enters into an interracial relationship or is born of racially different heritages is conscripted into a quiet revolution" (p. 9). My mother and father were the first in their families to marry interracially in the 1980s. A couple of years into their relationship, my older brother was born, followed by my fraternal twin sister and me. Last but not least, my younger sister arrived about 6 years later. In our home community we were known as the Malaney family. Growing up in South Florida was a happy place for me, but I was always observing and taking note in school that I was considered "the other" and "different" from my monoracial peers and their families. While growing up, I often was met with confusion from peers, particularly when they realized that my father was White and that my mother was Caribbean, but then I was this ambiguous brown-skinned girl. Most times my classmates would not often believe that my White father could be my dad because his White skin color contrasted my darker skin features and brown eye color. In contrast, having a mother from the Caribbean, many times teachers and peers would assume that my mother was African American based on her skin color. But my mother does not identify as African American because she is Trinidadian and also has mixed heritage.

My Multiracial Journey

As a young person in South Florida, I did not have the language to voice or analyze my lived experiences that I was noticing around me. In particular,

I could not see how these personal experiences (e.g., "Where are you really from?") actually were reactions to multiracial microaggressions to how my physical appearance intersected with Whiteness and racial privilege. I remember a specific instance in elementary school, when my family had just returned from a trip to Trinidad to visit my maternal grandparents. During my trip to Trinidad my twin sister and I got our hair braided. When we returned to school with our hair still braided in cornrows, I was told that my hair could not be my "real" hair from Black girls in my school. I remember feeling upset because I told the girls that this was my real hair, but they would not believe me. Because of these early life experiences, I began to have a heightened awareness of my racial backgrounds in different environmental spaces (e.g., in school or when meeting new kids) which generally showed up for me in how I was treated by my peers. I continued to grapple with understanding who I was against the backdrop of an overarching monoracial society. My reflections on my mixed race background continued for me, especially when I transitioned into college, far away from Florida.

My College Journey Begins

Even though I grew up in an interracial and loving family that both shared and taught me about my bicultural heritages, it was not until I went to college that I began my own journey in becoming a multiracially conscious individual. However, I can now say that my development of what I will call being multiracially conscious began when I entered college at Skidmore College (a predominantly White private liberal arts institution in upstate New York) as a first-year student in 2006. At Skidmore, I faced a contrasting racialized reality that forced me to contend with learning how to navigate the predominantly White and monoracial student community around me. Even though my high school in Florida was racially diverse, as I spent more time at Skidmore, I realized that I was beginning to question whether I "fit in" with my college peers. I believe this was because the majority of my peers were White, and I really longed to meet students of color and mixed students who were like me, searching for community at college. So I connected with a cultural student organization during the spring semester of my freshman year that spoke to my lived experiences based on my bicultural Trinidadian heritage and I joined Ujima (a Black/African/Caribbean American) student organization as a first-year student. I was only a member of the club for a semester when Tiffany, the club president and a junior, encouraged me to apply for the treasurer position on the executive board for the upcoming academic year. I was surprised that I was approached to take on a leadership role, but this special recognition made me feel seen and like I belonged in my new school. After being elected as the treasurer of Ujima in spring

2007, I was encouraged to apply to the National Conference on Race and Ethnicity (NCORE) by the director of diversity programs. Skidmore funded my travel along with a group of faculty, administrators, and two other students to attend the conference in San Francisco, California, over the summer. Flying from Florida to attend NCORE at age 19 was my first time going to a national conference and to the West Coast. At the conference, I decided to participate in a workshop on multiracial identity where I met one of the facilitators, Charmaine L. Wijeyesinghe. During the workshop, I learned about the different stages of multiracial identity and that there were researchers who sought to answer questions about the multiracial population. This conference experience catalyzed my awareness of multiraciality, because it made me realize that I was not the only person who had a multiracial or mixed background. To my knowledge, I was the only mixed person in Ujima. However, it was in this session at NCORE that I found other mixed people and heard personal stories that resonated with me and made me feel as though I finally belonged. In an exercise facilitated by Wijeyesinghe, I was even asked to share with conference participants how I lived my social identities and mixed race heritages in the world around me. I remember sharing what it was like growing up in Florida, with interracial parents, and how my parents shaped my understanding of my multiracial identity. Suffice to say, participating in NCORE workshops and meeting the facilitators and scholars who study race in the United States helped me self-reflect on my mixed heritages and my social identities in a way that I had not been asked to do before.

Racial Awakening With Intergroup Dialogue

NCORE was important in another way because it was at this conference that I also met Professor Kristie A. Ford, who at the time was an assistant professor in sociology at Skidmore. She is now a full professor in sociology at Skidmore and is the director of the Center for Leadership, Teaching, and Learning. Meeting Professor Ford directed me on a path toward becoming her student research assistant when I returned to my sophomore year at Skidmore. Simultaneously, working for Professor Ford introduced me to the Program on Intergroup Relations (IGR), an educational pedagogical program that teaches about social justice. Intergroup dialogue is a form of social justice education that began at the University of Michigan in 1988, addressing social identities such as race, gender, sexuality, social class, religion, and nationality.

By taking two courses in intergroup dialogue pedagogy on People of Color/White People and leading a dialogue with my cofacilitator, Megan (a White woman), I learned to self-reflect, empathize, and truly hear other perspectives through deep dialogues with peers and faculty about the history of race in the United States. It was during my experience being trained as a peer-facilitator and being an intergroup dialogue participant that I learned important racial constructs and terminology such as "White privilege" and I began to recognize my own privileges in my social identities. Because of Professor Ford, I embarked on my own journey of becoming a social justice advocate and I was later able to write about how transformative IGR was for me (see Malaney, 2018). Being an active participant in the IGR program at Skidmore left an indelible mark on me as a young adult. For instance, with the IGR training, I began to be more consciously aware of oppression occurring around me (i.e., racial injustice, religious oppression, resistance to some forms of gender identity and expression).

Before IGR, I was not noticing how I was privileged or oppressed by my social identities. Ultimately, being involved with IGR challenged me to see how race and power are connected in the U.S. context. At the time, I didn't know as much about multiracial history or that interracial marriage was actually illegal in the United States because of previous racial miscegenation laws. As my college years ended, I was becoming more aware of the racial oppression that surrounded me—including monoracism. My newfound understanding of my racial backgrounds and social identities again directed me on a path toward becoming a social justice advocate.

Postcollege Exploration

When I graduated from Skidmore in May 2010, I took the time to explore working full time before applying to graduate school. However, when I really think back, it was my experience as an intergroup dialogue peer-facilitator and my first summer research experience with Ford that subsequently transformed the kind of professional jobs that I began searching for. I applied for a variety of postcollege positions, but I ultimately found employment through the AmeriCorps Volunteer in Service to America (VISTA) program and served 2 years in the program. AmeriCorps VISTA is a national service program designed to alleviate domestic poverty through service members' commitment to serve a 1-year term for a nonprofit organization (AmeriCorps, 2020). My involvement with AmeriCorps allowed me to work with women who were incarcerated in the New York State correctional system. I was tasked with developing a mentoring program for incarcerated women, many of whom were much older than me. The privilege I held to freely enter and exit the county jail system to visit with the inmates about the mentoring program gave me cause for reflection. I was learning about the criminal justice system and the struggles that women faced when incarcerated (i.e., loss of connection to family, children, community), but I found myself yearning to find a deeper connection to understanding my multiracial background in relation to my professional work as I began a second year of service as a VISTA leader.

Around this time in 2011, I stumbled upon the American College Personnel Association's (ACPA) Multiracial Network (MRN, 2020). Through a serendipitous Google search about multiracial identity, I connected with the leadership team of MRN. My connection to MRN coincided with the conclusion of my second year of AmeriCorps VISTA and right when I was starting a full-time position at my alma mater, Skidmore. In this role, I was a fellow in the Office of Student Diversity Programs (OSDP). Even though I was only 3 years postgraduation from Skidmore, coming back as an administrator in higher education and working for a diversity programs office was challenging and exciting. It was during my fellowship position when I became more aware of the conscious need to create a multiracial student organization at Skidmore. Thus, I used my role and growing self-awareness of my mixed race identity to create a new initiative to bring awareness to the multiracial student population and inspire undergraduate students to build their own collective agency on campus (see Malaney & Danowski, 2015).

During my year working professionally at Skidmore, I was able to facilitate student focus groups on multiraciality. These conversations ended up igniting interest among students to create their own mixed race student organization on campus. All the while, I continued to participate with MRN, and I expanded my knowledge of multiracial student programming. Being present at another key professional conference called the Critical Mixed Race Studies Conference (CMRS) in Chicago was also influential in building my network of multiracial community and scholars. Going to CMRS in 2012 opened my eyes to the greater multiracial community and attending a professional conference that explicitly centered the mixed race experience solidified my desire to continue to study and also contribute to the scholarship of the multiracial community. This conference represented the very first time that I was surrounded by so many mixed people who were consciously invested in and affirmed what it meant to be a proud multiracial individual. Until this experience, throughout my life, I sometimes felt unheard and at times invisible in conversations about race. CMRS allowed me to see that I could become a member of the community and therefore become part of a larger multiracial scholar-practitioner community.

Transition to Graduate School at the University of Massachusetts Amherst

When I made the decision to apply to graduate school, I knew that earning a master's degree would allow me the opportunity to continue to learn more and progress my career forward in understanding social justice and diversity and inclusion initiatives in higher education. I made the intentional

choice to attend the University of Massachusetts Amherst (UMass) in western Massachusetts because I connected with the most brilliant faculty. I truly
felt that the faculty were committed to my learning. They helped me deepen
my social justice values, and they were genuinely invested in my personal
and professional development as a future scholar-practitioner-activist in the
field of higher education. Additionally, securing a graduate assistantship at
UMass in the Dean of Students Office (DOSO) helped to offset the cost of
my out-of-state tuition and fees. In the DOSO, I worked as the special assistant to the deans to identify and advise students to connect with university
resources, while assessing and responding to students in crisis using a case
management model. My ability to connect with students with empathy and
critical thinking helped me understand the challenges they were facing with
medical issues, including their mental health and wellness concerns.

Throughout my time at UMass in the master's program, my work experience gained in DOSO encouraged me to think more expansively about the
interlocking systems of power and privilege within higher education campuses. In my role, I was privileged to be able to create a safe space in meetings
for undergraduate and graduate students to share the struggles that they were
facing at the university, which included topics such as mental health, financial issues, disability, and how these issues intersected, and involved students
sharing how their real lives were impacted by challenges both inside and
outside of the classroom.

My participation as the scholarship and resources coordinator with ACPA
MRN continued to shape my professional service and involvement in the
field of higher education. I wrote blog posts about our national conference
and started to develop my own voice as a multiracial graduate student and
aspiring higher education professional. It was during my involvement with
MRN that I met Marc P. Johnston-Guerrero, who encouraged me to present with him at several subsequent ACPA conferences and NCORE. These
professional opportunities continued to transpire for me, which affirmed
my journey and further influenced my awareness of racial consciousness.
So, when the time came to complete my master's in education program,
I knew that I was not done or ready to leave UMass Amherst. Therefore, I
applied to UMass's PhD program in higher education because I desired to
learn how to become a researcher to study student experiences and provide
a much-needed voice to multiracial student experiences in higher education.
I realized that as I completed my first program of graduate study, I often
questioned and reflected on the effectiveness of higher education systems and
practices. Over that 2-year time span, much of my self-reflection was based
on my years of observation prior to attending my master's program. I also
noticed during my program that higher education institutions do very little

to prioritize their undergraduate students' development of racial and ethnic identity development.

Developing a Multiracial Scholar-Practitioner Identity

My research, teaching, service, and practitioner work have been driven by my experiences as a multiracial person. I truly believe that being a multiracial cisgender woman has allowed me to view the world from multiple intersecting perspectives. Being in academia has often meant for me that I made the conscious choice to use my privilege in the academy to make a difference in the lives of college students. I have also sought out ways to connect with the multiracial community and have been involved in developing intentional educational initiatives, engaging in critical dialogue and community building, and supporting institutional change through advocacy on our campuses.

Throughout my doctoral program, I often found myself having to defend my position of studying multiraciality to other graduate students because of their belief that virtually "everyone is mixed." I also at times felt other scholars studying monoracial groups of color discounted my focus on the voices and racialized experiences of multiracial people. In the first stages of my dissertation work, initially I struggled a bit when I was developing my dissertation proposal topic. However, I knew that I had to further study multiraciality and the college student experience, because our racialized experiences needed to be validated and written into existence. I was often motivated by my own multiracial family members—the youngest being my 8-year-old niece and 5-year-old nephew. Now more recently, as I become a parent my own development of racial consciousness will be pushed further when I meet my own multiracial son, who I will coparent with my White husband. My dissertation study resulted in a new theoretical framework that I called "multiracial consciousness" (MC). My qualitative dissertation critically interrogates the narratives of 15 multiracial collegians at one predominantly White institution in New England, which I named North University. The definition of MC was created based on narrative inquiry analysis and centers the voices of the students interviewed.

As I found out in my dissertation study, becoming multiracially conscious compels a multiracial person to take action to use their voice to influence people around them. In taking action as a multiracial person against the structural social forces of monoracism and Whiteness, a resistance builds to counter the societal normalization of being White and monoracial (Malaney Brown, 2020).

Although in some ways my dissertation was a culminating experience for me as a scholar-practitioner, I also think of my experience dissertating as an opportunity to take the time to be more self-reflective of my own voice and power as a multiracial doctoral candidate. As I continue in my higher education career, I hope to further develop my own multiracial consciousness and to contribute to the field of higher education as both scholar-practitioner and a faculty member who interrupts the narratives on monoraciality and racial oppression.

Professional Experiences in Higher Education: Pathways to Take Action

In my work as a scholar-practitioner, I often draw on my experiences from intergroup dialogue and the diverse positions I have held to unpack conversations about multiracial identity, integrity, and the courage it takes to be an authentic person and professional. For over 2 years, I have worked at Columbia University for Columbia College and Columbia Engineering as the inaugural director of academic integrity. During this time, I have developed a preventative education curriculum, which includes an online preorientation tutorial, an in-person orientation program, and a follow-up case management program where I meet individually with students who were found responsible for violating the honor code and pledge. I have the ability to create deeper moments of self-reflection for students because I challenge them to understand the importance of ethics and integrity and because my multiracial background affords me a unique ability to view complicated issues from multiple perspectives. I can make sense of different ways of meaning-making. I use motivational interviewing skills to understand the students' perspective. However, because my current administrative role does not directly intersect with diversity and inclusion initiatives, I asked my supervisor if there were opportunities where I could support our undergraduate student life community. Last year, I became a staff member on the Multicultural Affairs Students of Color Advisory Board. I am one of three professional staff on the advisory board who identifies as multiracial. In this position, I advocate both for multiracial students *and* students of color. Sharing more about my multiracial background with students and colleagues has created a broader community, where I am conscious of my White privilege and the ways that I view the world from a monoracial and a multiracial lens. As a multiracial person with White heritage, I do feel as though I experience some White privilege, but mainly through interactions with White folks because I always acknowledge that being mixed or multiracial is complicated. Even though my current administrative role does not center race in my programming initiatives, I continue to self-reflect daily on my racial identity and how I can focus on increasing multiracial consciousness in my everyday work with students, faculty, and staff in academia.

Concluding Thoughts: The Path to Multiracial Consciousness

As far as I have come in my own journey as a scholar-practitioner, I know there is still so much work left to do. Contemplating my racial identity and ongoing goals as a multiracial scholar-practitioner is an iterative process for me because I am constantly reevaluating my personal growth, as well as time and context influences on my awareness of multiraciality. To that end, I will need to create spaces for my own self-reflection and work to deepen my connections to community spaces (i.e., family narratives, professional support through ACPA). I am dedicated to being a lifelong learner in order to continue on my path toward multiracial consciousness and becoming authentically me—I am complete because *"I am proud to be me—whole; not pieces or fractionalized parts."*

Note

1. Copyright © 2016, Victoria K. Malaney Brown, "Outside of the Box." Reproduced with permission.

References

AmeriCorps. (2020). *AmeriCorps VISTA.* https://www.nationalservice.gov/programs/americorps/americorps-programs/americorps-vista

Malaney, V. K. (2018). On becoming a social justice advocate. In K. A. Ford (Ed.), *Facilitating change through intergroup dialogue* (pp. 36–46). Routledge.

Malaney, V. K., & Danowski, K. (2015). Mixed foundations: Supporting and empowering multiracial student organizations. *Journal Committed to Social Change on Race and Ethnicity, 1*(2), 55–85. https://doi.org/10.15763/issn.2642-2387.2015.1.2.54-85

Malaney Brown, V. K. (2020). *Exploring multiracial consciousness: Voices of multiracial students at a predominately White institution* [Doctoral dissertation, University of Massachusetts Amherst]. Scholar Works. https://scholarworks.umass.edu/dissertations_2/1852

Multiracial Network. (2020). *About MRN.* https://multiracialnetwork.wordpress.com/about/

Root, M. P. P. (1996). *The multiracial experience: Racial borders as the new frontier.* SAGE.

7

BEING MEXIPINA IN
HIGHER EDUCATION

Rebecca Cepeda

I raised my hand and asked the proctor for clarity on the race and ethnicity section of the state exam. "It says to bubble in one option. What if I identify with two of them?" He responded, "You can bubble in the option that says *Other*." Everyone in the classroom laughed. My heart sunk, and I felt a strong sense of embarrassment.

My Beautiful Family, *Mi Preciosa Familia,*
Ang Maganda Kong Pamilya

My *inay* (mother) was born and raised in Lian, Batangas, Philippines. She left her family in the Philippines and immigrated to the United States in hopes of finding a stable career to financially support them. She knew her family was living in poverty and wanted to alleviate some of their financial stress. My *papi* (father) was born in Monterrey, Nuevo León, Mexico. When he was 12, his family immigrated to the United States to find better opportunities. While crossing the U.S.–Mexico border, my father was separated from his family and had to find his way to Los Angeles on his own to reunite with them. My parents have different immigration narratives, but they immigrated to this country in hopes of pursuing the American Dream they had always heard of.

"*Wait. Your mom is from the Philippines, and your dad is from Mexico . . . how did they even meet?*" This question never fails to get asked when I tell people I am biracial.

My parents met at Metropolitan Hospital in Los Angeles. Papi was a dishwasher, and Inay was a registered nurse. When they began dating, their families had concerns about how different they were, including their racial differences. Disagreements continued to develop about their relationship. My parents ignored their family's concerns and eloped.

My parents created a family with a beautiful blend of cultures. Growing up, I looked forward to weekends because they were dedicated to spending time with family. On Saturdays, I woke up to the smell of *chorizo con papas y tortillas de harina hechas a mano* (chorizo with potatoes and handmade flour tortillas) cooking on the stove. I was always excited that Inay learned how to make *tortillas de harina* just like my *abuelita* (grandmother). Homemade flour tortillas were Abuelita's specialty, and she encouraged my *inay* to practice every day until she perfected the recipe. I would always run to the kitchen to steal a tortilla straight from the *comal* (griddle) when Inay wasn't looking. After breakfast, Inay cleaned the house while she listened to Selena and Patsy Cline on her portable radio. Papi typically went to Home Depot to buy supplies to repair something in the house or the backyard. My siblings and I helped with chores, wrestled in the living room, and glued our eyes on a book until my parents told us it was time for dinner. I remember going out for dinner when my parents were exhausted from cleaning and wanted to spend time outside of the house. We usually went to Pinoy Pinay, a Filipino chain restaurant, and ordered white rice, *pancit* (Filipino noodles), and *dinuguan* (pork blood stew). Some days, we even had *halo halo* (Filipino shaved ice) for dessert. These were our favorite Filipino dishes—they still are.

Within my household, I loved my cultures. I listened to my parents call each other nicknames of endearment, such as *mahal* and *mi amor,* in both of their native languages. Although I was not fluent in either language, I loved listening to my family speak in Spanish and Tagalog. I loved eating Filipino and Mexican food every day. I loved watching telenovelas like *Yo soy Betty, la fea* or Filipino shows like *Eat Bulaga!* I thought it was beautiful how my parents tried to teach us about their own cultures. It made me appreciate who I was. Unfortunately, I later realized not everyone understood my biracial identity.

"What Are You?": Recognizing Racial
Differences and Feeling Like an "Other"

I was raised in the city of Lynwood, California, a predominantly Latinx community in South East Los Angeles. During my K–12 experience, I was surrounded by Latinx and Black students. When I started school was when I began to notice how different I was compared to other people around me. I looked Asian but had a Spanish last name. People were always so confused about what I "was." I encountered experiences in my K–12 education that made me become embarrassed about my racial identity.

The security guard at my middle school greeted me every morning and said, *"Hola Chinita!"* I always responded saying, "I'm not a *Chinita*. I'm half Mexican and half Filipino." He never stopped calling me *Chinita*.

My 10th-grade English teacher was Filipina. I was so excited because she was the first Filipina teacher I ever had. Students teased me and said I looked like her and insisted we were related because we had the same flat nose. I started to hate my Filipino nose.

My Advanced Placement Statistics teacher in high school was a Latinx man who constantly told me I must have eaten dog because I was Asian. When I tried to defend myself and explain how his statement was racist, he'd just laugh at me.

It became challenging for me to navigate my racial identity outside of my home. I felt like an *"Other"* because I was different than the people around me. At the same time, I was repressing a traumatic experience I had suffered years prior. I felt like no one really understood what I was going through or cared about how I was feeling. So I just pretended like everything was okay.

I buried myself in extracurricular activities at my high school to distract myself from my problems. Through college access programs, I learned about higher education. I wanted to get away from my problems. Therefore, I made it my mission to go off to college and leave my hometown. Fortunately, I was admitted to my dream school, the University of California, Los Angeles (UCLA). It was one of the three colleges I ever visited in high school and by far my favorite because my older brother and sister attended. I always looked up to my siblings and wanted to be just like them. I saw UCLA as a way to follow their footsteps. We became a family of Bruins.

Not Smart Enough, Not Rich Enough, Not Asian Enough, Not Chicana Enough

As a first-generation student and Mexipina, I struggled to navigate higher education. I majored in political science, in which all of my classes were filled with White men. I experienced culture shock because I was so used to being surrounded by Brown and Black folks, so I felt like a minority. I was a minority.

During my first year, I had a teacher's assistant for my political science lower division course explain that the course was going to be writing intensive, and they did not want us writing like students from Compton because those students did not know how to write. I looked around the discussion session in search for any and all of the students of color in that section. There were a few of us in a room of about 20 students. No one said anything. I raised my hand with a knot in my throat, ready to burst into tears as I tried to explain how I grew up down the street from Compton. I spoke about the inequities of resources from students in low-income neighborhoods compared to students in wealthier neighborhoods. I told my teaching assistant that it was their job to support us academically, if needed, and they should not be making assumptions about students based on where they are from or the color of their skin. They ended our class discussion. We never spoke again throughout the rest of the quarter.

As a first-year college student, I was very timid and afraid to introduce myself to new people on campus. What if people didn't accept me for who I was or where I came from? I wanted to avoid being made fun of like I was in high school for my racial identity. One of my friends introduced me to a group of students who identified as Asian American. I was excited to meet new people who shared a part of my racial identity. However, when I shared that I was half-Filipino and half-Mexican, they said I wasn't "really" Asian. I felt confused as to why Filipinos weren't "really" Asian, and it made me feel like I wasn't Asian enough to exist in Asian spaces.

Through my first-year experiences, I became frustrated with the fact that the institution I attended lacked representation and acceptance for people's identities. As a Mexipina, I couldn't find a space on campus where I felt accepted. I also felt like I was academically unprepared. I was battling the imposter syndrome, and it was winning. I felt like I didn't belong.

Before I began my 2nd year of college, my family couldn't keep up with the mortgage. We received a notice that we were losing our home, and we had to move out within a certain time frame. My parents insisted I drop out of UCLA and work full time to help them financially. As much as I knew they needed help, I didn't want to stop going to school and give up. Therefore, I decided to commute 2 hours in Los Angeles traffic to and from UCLA. I worked countless hours at fast food restaurants like Chipotle and Wing Stop to help with school-related costs and support my parents. I had no knowledge about the resources available on campus. I never sought out help from a counselor or the financial aid office. I didn't think anyone could have helped me throughout this financial challenge. I tried to figure it out on my own.

As I commuted to school, I carefully crafted my class schedule to fit into 2 days; that way, I would be able to work 5 days a week. One quarter, I signed up for an introductory Chicana/o studies course to meet a general education requirement, because it fit perfectly into my schedule. I was inspired by the course, because it provided me with the opportunity to learn about Mexican American history. The classroom was also filled with students of color who were familiar with the foods I ate and the city I grew up in. I found a sense of belonging on campus that I was yearning for. I even decided to minor in Chicana/o studies. However, I still felt like a part of my identity was unfulfilled. Even though I was glad to be learning about my Chicana identity, I also did not feel Chicana enough. My peers often questioned why I was not fluent in Spanish or why I "looked" Asian. I wondered about my Filipina identity and when I would have the opportunity to really learn about that part of my history. Because I felt so overwhelmed with classes and work, I brushed off trying to find a space in academia to learn about my Filipino roots. However, reflecting back now, I realize there was never really a space on campus where my biracial identity was fully acknowledged or accepted.

I spent most of my undergraduate career working, commuting to school, and going to class. When I graduated, I thought about the people I knew who left college because they didn't find a sense of belonging on campus, their financial aid was insufficient, or they were afraid they were not academically prepared. I often thought about why higher education was "weeding out" students of color from low-income communities. Why were these students dropping out or going to a community college but not transferring? Why didn't I see more people from my community obtaining college degrees?

These thoughts about the racial inequities within higher education stayed with me as I tried to figure out what I wanted to pursue. I began my college career convinced I wanted to go to law school, specifically to learn about immigration law. Once I graduated, I felt discouraged from applying; I assumed I wouldn't get accepted into law school because of my lack of professional experience interning at a law firm. I was too embarrassed to explain that I worked in the food industry because I had to have an income to survive. I convinced myself that no law school would want to accept someone who was good at making buttermilk ranch by hand or rolling burritos.

Pursuing Graduate School, Feeling Accepted, and Learning About Multiraciality

Struggling to find a job I was interested in, I applied to every posting I came across. After finally finding a job and working at a start-up company, I felt displeased with my life. I was making phone calls 8 hours a day and speaking to dentists across the country; however, I knew that was not my passion or calling for life. I found myself in a predominantly White space, where I felt I could not speak freely about my racial experiences or cultures. I knew I wasn't growing or learning. Then one night, I had a dream about my K–12 counselor, who supported me after my trauma. During my sessions with him, he taught me a valuable lesson: Learn one new thing every day. I dreamt that he was telling me to continue my journey into education. When I woke up, I realized he planted a seed into my mind. He taught me to keep learning, no matter the circumstance. Regardless of the obstacles I faced in K–12 or college, I continued to pursue education as a pathway toward freedom. I learned that no one could take away my knowledge and no one should discount my experiences as a first-generation college student and a Mexipina.

That dream inspired me to pursue graduate school and help students. I wanted to be a counselor just like him and help students of color succeed in higher education. I did not want students to feel isolated because of their identity. I wanted to encourage students to keep learning something new every day. I wanted to plant that seed into their minds.

I decided to apply to a master's program less than 2 months before applications were due. Due to financial reasons, I couldn't apply to more than one program. Because I was applying so late, I signed up to take the GRE a week before the exam. I even emailed my former Chicana/o professors from UCLA to beg them for letters of recommendation. The application process made me feel anxious because I was unsure about whether I was completing it correctly and doubting whether I would even be accepted. I was too embarrassed to reach out to the program's office and ask for help. I didn't know anyone who went through the graduate school application process. So I tried to navigate that journey on my own. I mentally prepared myself for a rejection letter and told myself if I didn't get accepted, I would try again the following year. Fortunately, I was accepted.

I began the master's of educational counseling program at the University of Southern California. Because of the discomforting experiences I faced in the classroom throughout my undergraduate career, I was afraid I would fail in graduate school. I had no idea what I was doing. No one in my family pursued graduate school or even knew what a master's program was. Fortunately, I felt supported by my program, faculty members, and my cohort. Most of my professors were people of color who shared they knew what it was like being a student of color in predominantly White spaces or being a first-generation college student. Additionally, the cohort I was in comprised predominantly students of color, and my peers listened and supported me when I needed them most. I found people that I could connect to who identified as Latinx and people that I could connect to who identified as Filipino. I even became friends with folks who also identified as multiracial or multiethnic. My shared identities and cultures with the students and faculty members within my program was different from my undergraduate experience. I became proud of my Mexipina identity because I felt accepted, and I felt like I belonged.

During my program, I was privileged enough to take student development and race in higher education courses throughout the same semester.

These classes introduced me to readings about multiracial students in higher education. I read Kristen A. Renn's multiracial student development theory and Samuel D. Museus's research on multiracial students and the discrimination they face on college campuses. Before these courses, I had never heard of academic literature highlighting multiracial students. I had never thought of searching for it, because multiraciality had never been discussed in any of my courses throughout my entire educational journey. I remember reading these works and being astonished that there was research on something I deeply resonated with. I engaged in dialogue with peers who also identified as multiracial and shared experiences about our racial identities within familial and educational contexts. I also began to question why my other classes didn't assign readings on this topic and why there was a lack of discussion about multiracial students when talking about race. The two readings assigned weren't enough for me. Therefore, I met with one of my professors, Kristan Venegas, to discuss my professional goals and research interests. I knew I was passionate about wanting to conduct research and teach others about multiracial student identities. She asked if I would be interested in pursuing a doctoral degree; I was unsure about what doctoral programs entailed. I questioned if I was even capable of pursuing a doctoral degree. She took time to sit down with me and thoroughly explain the differences between a PhD and an EdD, demonstrated how to research various programs and institutions, and recommended I attend in-person or online informational sessions. Most importantly, she reminded me that I was capable of pursuing any degree I was interested in and has continued to support and mentor me since.

My Professional Journey as a Mexipina . . . and Beyond

My personal journey in higher education informed my professional journey. Throughout my graduate program, I worked for the University of Southern California's TRiO Educational Talent Search program, where I supported first-generation and/or low-income high school students throughout different high schools around South Central Los Angeles. I educated students about the systems of higher education and college application processes through one-on-one meetings, academic workshops, or campus field trips. Through my work, I shared my narrative as a first-generation college student and a Mexipina in higher education. It was heartwarming connecting with students who were excited to share that they also identified as Mexipina/o/x or multiracial. They expressed to me that they had never seen people in their high schools who understood what it was like to be multiracial, and I was the first staff member who could relate to their racial identities or experiences.

Throughout my graduate career, I aspired to gain professional experience at a California community college. Many of my family members and closest friends attended a community college and didn't finish or transfer within 2 years. I noticed many of the people I knew attending community colleges were enrolled in school for 6 or more years. I didn't understand the inconsistencies with the marketing of community colleges as 2-year institutions, yet students were not transferring within 2 years. Fortunately, I was offered a part-time position as a student success coach at Rio Hondo College, a California community college located in Whittier, California. Rio Hondo College is a Hispanic-serving institution and predominantly Latinx. I was assigned to work in the Guardian Scholars department, which serves former or current foster youth students. Initially, I felt nervous about being assigned to work with this specific program because I didn't know much about the population. However, I was determined and willing to learn from this opportunity.

As a student success coach, I managed a caseload of first-time former or current foster youth community college students to support them through their transition, cotaught a counseling course, and coordinated program events and field trips. I was privileged to have been paired up with the counselor/coordinator of the Guardian Scholars program. We were a two-person team serving approximately 150 students in the program. As my supervisor, she ensured I learned about the population of students we were serving before really meeting with students. She sent me to numerous conferences where I was able to learn about legal and financial information that impacts students. I learned how to fill out the FAFSA for former or current foster youth students and what the eligibility requirements were for students to receive the Chafee Grant. I learned that students can call the California ombudsman to find a student's Ward of the Court letter to prove they were in the foster care system for educational program purposes. I learned about independent living program coordinators and how they can support students with transitional housing or expenses for school and work. Most importantly, I listened to former or current foster youth students' narratives on higher education.

Through the conferences I attended and the students I met during my time there, I developed an admiration for the students I worked with and the program I worked for. At first, I was concerned I would listen to narratives of trauma, thinking it would trigger strong emotions from the trauma I experienced. However, I deeply connected with students because of their willingness to persist regardless of the challenges they faced. I often found myself reflecting on the encouraging words my middle school counselor instilled in my mind about learning one new thing every day. So I also tried to encourage students I worked with to learn one new thing every day to continue their paths toward their educational goals.

Although I was working with majority Latinx students at Rio Hondo College, each student's narrative was unique and inspiring in so many different ways. For example, there were students I worked with who did not identify as Latinx and observed a lack of representation of their racial identity on campus. Some students were adopted by foster parents who were Latinx and were uncertain about their racial and cultural backgrounds from their biological parents. The students I worked with were continuing to make meaning of their identities in higher education and navigating what identities were most salient to them. When students expressed their feelings of not fitting in because of their identities, I shared my narrative of being Mexipina and not feeling Mexican or Filipino enough in certain spaces in hopes of connecting with them and letting them know they were not alone. I encouraged them to be proud of their identities and reminded them that they belonged in educational spaces, even if they didn't see a strong representation of themselves within the campus. Students were surprised when they learned I was Mexipina because they recognized that the majority of staff, faculty, and administrators were Latinx. Although the students I worked with did not identify as multiracial, they were interested in learning about my experiences being Mexipina in higher education. Engaging in dialogues about social identities and learning about each other's personal narratives was meaningful for me. I developed a strong connection with students and learned so much from them.

My personal and professional experiences in education reinforced my desire to continue learning. The racial inequities I witnessed as a student have motivated me to continue to work and support minoritized students. My professional experiences have inspired me to learn about student narratives in education and practices to best support them.

Currently, I am a first-year PhD student in higher education and student affairs at The Ohio State University. My narrative as a Mexipina has motivated me to aspire to learn about multiracial students in higher education and how they make meaning of their racial identities on campus. Students shouldn't feel like they don't belong on campus or feel like an *"Other."* I desire to create awareness and dialogue for inclusive practices and environments for students of color. During the next 4 years of this doctoral program, I hope to learn one new thing every day that will support my career goals. As a first-generation doctoral student and a Mexipina, I know I will encounter challenges along the way, but I am also excited to embark on a new educational and personal journey, not only for my future but for my family's, too. Inay and Papi, this is for you. I love you. *Te quiero. Mahal kita.*

8

REMEMBERING TO RESIST RACIST COLONIAL FORGETTING ON CAMPUS

e alexander

For Mattie, Vera Mae, Armelia, Geneva, and Teresa

In my master's studies, I had the honor of taking the class Multiculturalism in Planning and Policy with an esteemed ethnic studies scholar. As someone with roots in Louisiana (Creole) and Appalachia (Melungeon), I felt that the course's assignments provided perfect opportunities to explore how policy and shared space shaped racial identity formation for people who descended from both West Africa and Southeast Turtle Island—sometimes known as Black Indians—during Amerikkkan slavery and Reconstruction. I argued that the settler government attempted to use policies (e.g., allotment, blood quantum, one drop rule) to curtail collaboration and coexistence among Africans, Choctaws, Creeks, Cherokees, and Seminoles. In the concluding excerpt of the course's final assignment, I said I felt like an Ancestral orphan—unable to find one parent and unwelcomed to grow with and learn from the other. Seemingly, the colonizer had won.

As a scholar, I am interested in ways that white supremacy manifests in academe to cause racialized harms that are analogous to those of Amerikkka's Antebellum South and Reconstruction periods. Through my experiences as both student and administrator in higher education, I interrogate here how nonwhite groups' remembering or forgetting of their colonial pasts have encouraged or prohibited my intersectional self-actualization as a multicultural multiethnic Black queer femme. I tell my story of prohibition through the composite of a predominantly white institution, in a majority-white region of Amerikkka (PWI). I provide context for my positioning through a second composite that preceded my time there: a predominantly nonwhite institution in an anticolonial nonwhite region of the world (MSI), which encouraged me.

As part of my story, I acknowledge that cousins beyond those with origins in West Africa and Turtle Island have been subjected to Amerikkkan colonial violence—many times, through forms of military presence that have caused irreversible damage that is invisible to Westerners (e.g., global displacement of peoples, sex tourism, and refugee crises). Although my story centers peoples with origins in West Africa and Turtle Island, I consider us all to have a transnational bond through western imperialist violence that makes us anticolonialist allies.

Race, Place, Family, and Spirit

Through Elders' stories, historical documents, and geographies from my mother's family, I am Choctaw, Muskogee, French, Irish, and Congolese and/or Senegalese by way of Haiti. Through Elders' stories and geographies from my father's family, I am Cherokee, likely Lumbee, and Scotch-Irish; our African ancestry is not yet known. My families' customs are multicultural yet Black, reflecting their ties to land on which they live and ways of the ethnic groups that created us. Members of both families also phenotypically belong to various racial groups. Depending on where they are in the world, my kin have been read as Black, white, Native, Creole, Yellow, Redbone, Mixed, Latinx, Mediterranean, and Polynesian. Some members of my mother's family identify as Creole; all identify as Black while acknowledging "having some Indian in them." My father's family does not discuss their racial identity often. They acknowledge their social statuses as nonwhite discursively when (a) discussing anti-Blackness and (b) coveting Black–white romantic relationships. They also differentiate themselves from local Native community members by having neither known blood quantum nor connections to Indian Country. To my knowledge, neither family has tried to enroll in any Tribe that is Indigenous to Turtle Island for four generations.

My mother's family is matrilineal, so I claim it as mine and tell its story. We carry oral histories, place names, Dawes Rolls and other public records, and decades-old handwritten notes—all of which we have cobbled together to better understand our lineage. Like many others in Amerikkka who descend from African slaves, we have conflicting accounts of origins and relations by both blood and geography. However, we are immediately tied to rural Louisiana by land: Elders have near century-old dwellings and livestock there, and our family church and cemetery are there. My mother, who has been read as many racial descriptions, groomed me to be pro-Black. I grew up consuming Black media, participating in Black community events through a Black church, and socializing with other Black families. Our Elders, who have now walked on, shared stories and customs of the Old Ways with me whenever I was around them. During those times, I learned that my family's blood, customs, and knowledges—like those of other Louisianan families— were spliced together from descendants of West Africa, Southeast Turtle Island, and Western Europe.

Where and How Can I Practice My Self?

As an educator, a creative, an activist, and a therapeutic professional, I understand that the physical realm of Creation manifests from the Spirit one. The challenge for me, as an Ancestral orphan, is that Spiritual practice is necessarily tied to one's connections with land: an ability to know that one's grandparents' grandparents' grandparents were there before, that we are there now because of them, that they are with us through that place, that we all were/are/will be with our children's children's children in that place, and so on. As a descendant of stolen and displaced peoples, my ability to engage Spiritual practice is (arguably) undercut by geographic displacement and racialized social structures that historically pitted Blacks and Natives against each other through government restriction of access to resources—following a shared history of survivance throughout the Southeast. Hence, I also frame my racial identity in terms of what I am *not*: someone who grew up either (a) steeped in philosophies, beliefs, customs, or visions for the future from my Tribes in either Turtle Island or West Africa or (b) beholden to genocidal settler/colonial policies that target Tribes in either region. I have not had to navigate legal liminalities with western governments to access resources or protect my peoples' sovereignty; contextually, I am monoracial; I have not engaged Tribal life in Turtle Island; I am only now finding West African cultural knowledge. I am Black Amerikkkan not by choice. But I wonder: Will Tribes anywhere ever claim their descendants who have been removed and displaced by no choice of their own, and whose connections to Home have been systemically erased?

Let me be clear: No one is entitled to someone else's spaces, (home) lands, or resources based on genetics or geography. However, with each passing generation, peoples across my two racialized groups, who used to coexist under violent colonial circumstances, forgot that they once were intertwined through coalitions and progenies. This chasm and forgetting permits multiethnic Blacks to live in relative peace, particularly those who are content with western lives as settler byproducts. But it leaves descendants of the intertwining who cannot forget—descendants like me—in a state of *felt* orphanage.

My racial journey is inherently Spiritual and geographic: I/we exist because our Ancestors—brought together through many forms of violence—made forced geographies their own and created new life there. The Amerikkkan South is my proxy Ancestral land: there, I tended crops, played with animals, received multigenerational nurturing, and learned about Creation. I plan to return and nurture younger generations there, until I walk on and rejoin the Earth there.

Finding Cultivation at MSI

My statement of positionality reflects learning and guidance that I received at MSI with regard to illuminating the complexity of Black Amerikkkan existence as ascending from settler violence. Because of my time there, I can (a) articulate my racial, ethnic, national, geographic, and Ancestral identities as manifestations of my Spirit self and (b) understand my own existence as multicultural, multiethnic, monoracial, anticolonial, queer, and pro-Black.

MSI lives in one of the most diverse regions of the world. Virtually all my peers, faculty, and community connections were of color and well versed in their colonial histories. Daily life reflects cultural values and customs of the ethnic groups that are now prominent there, of which Blacks and whites are not; the people who are Indigenous to the region are highly visible and asserting in their presence. Guests learned to respect our social positions as such and to prioritize internalized decolonization as a requisite process toward peaceful coexistence—or leave. I moved there after college: Indigenous cousins there welcomed me when cousins from Turtle Island did not. At the time, I was grappling with tensions between Black Capitalist Ideology and a desire to discard it as vestiges of colonization.

As a Black Amerikkkan student in a therapeutic field, my time in MSI—the beginning of a lifelong journey—was one of great (un)doing. It was painful, scary, frustrating, confusing, and sometimes invalidating and lonely. All but three of my mentors were Indigenous; they supported me in charting a journey toward nonwestern self-affirmation—a journey that included Ancestral displacement and confusion as a part of my narrative. It was these mentors who pushed me to take on scholarship about Black Indians. They put me in situations to help me realize how western my life was—despite my expressed desire for it not to be. These Elders helped me to see Creation from a decolonial perspective: I was forced to examine how I made sense of the world, related to and shared space with others, (de)constructed knowledge and authority, engaged power, and so on. With time, I shifted into wanting to more deeply explore Creation with nonwestern cousins. My mission became confronting historical traumas as part of collectively healing harms—starting with how I existed within myself, and with the rest of Creation as an Ancestral orphan.

Integral to my (un)doing was how I came to understand converging identities. More than half the people in this region are multiethnic or multiracial. When self-identifying, locals list the ethnic groups to which each of their parents belongs, but no race; Indigenous peoples also name their kin group. Most locals considered western documentation, such as U.S. Census or other categorical data, to be regressive for its limitations in capturing the complexity of human life. With local friends and colleagues, I explored the roles of colonial violence in simultaneously making us hate ourselves and denying us entry to white spaces despite our forced assimilation. On mountaintops, in boats under the stars, in classrooms, and over midnight bonfires, we cried with each other about trying to change our speech and appearances, never being "smart enough" or "good enough," and feeling conflicted about loving folkways that our Elders taught us while being made to feel as though those folkways were backward.

It was during these conversations that I shared about Antebellum interracial relations, Black Indians, and my known family history. Peers and mentors understood the complexities of Black Indian identity—including disconnect from Ancestral communities. As Indigenous peoples, they considered Black Amerikkkans to also be Indigenous peoples . . . but whose separation from our homelands and folkways was the root of our modern-day malaise. They understood how western policies and institutions created divisions between Africans and Tribes of Turtle Island to result in necessary protectionism by many groups, which reproduced itself over generations until we all forgot that we have a shared past. They encouraged me to cultivate community with cousins in West Africa and Turtle Island whenever I encountered open minds and hearts for doing so and support the decolonization journeys of other Black Amerikkkans.

Some locals connected my desire to reconcile the past and present across groups and geographies with my identity as queer. Queerness was generally not stigmatized in the region. Elders saw it as an asset through which to understand Creation's "both-and" and "in-between": masculine/feminine, de/colonized, displacement/belonging, and so on. Further, because non-whiteness and multiethnicity were normalized, I had space to explore and develop more complex understandings of myself beyond race—namely, my identities as queer, multicultural, Southern, upwardly mobile, and westernized with a desire to undo internalized colonization.

As I completed my studies at MSI, I felt compelled to return to Turtle Island and support other Blacks in their own decolonial journeys. I departed my cousins' homelands, eager to take on work as a campus professional with a critical lens. However, I found myself in PWI. There, multifaceted and inter-sectional lives that included many intertwining identities were erased and flattened—such that individuals were reduced to only what campus power-holders valued about them. I felt that by leaving no space for multiraciality, multiculturality, multiethnicity, or intersectionality, PWI was robbing me of parts of myself that I had worked for years to reclaim at MSI. I later realized that, as was the case in the Antebellum South and Reconstruction Amerikkka, white supremacy was working to undermine interracial coexist-ence and collaboration in academia.

Race, Space, and Colonial Campuses

Here I share how white and nonwhite peoples enact the racist settler tool of forgetting at PWI, my current campus setting, to advocate for their own well-being—and in doing so, perpetuate white supremacy. PWI represents three institution types and proclaims itself diverse, inclusive, progressive, and affirming. I explore how it politicizes race to exercise power and how I have worked to locate myself on campus after transitioning there from MSI.

Observations: Politicizing Race to Exercise Power

PWI preserves its power over people of color through three strategies that are also meant to facilitate the forgetting of its settler colonial past and present.

Weaponizing Place and Time
The institution legitimizes itself as progressive, wherein *progressive* means "postracial" or "race-neutral," to insulate itself from national discourses of racialized unrest. Although PWI acknowledges its lack of racial diversity, it also denies its racial disharmonies by forgetting or minimizing its violent racial past. In turn, PWI deflects by (a) discussing race as an antiquated social construct that undermines collective advancement of the campus com-munity and (b) ascribing disharmony to regions of Turtle Island that have been explicitly known in historical discourse as racist (namely, my home, the "Deep South"). By framing racial difference as a foil to progress, powerhold-ers seek to absolve themselves of responsibilities to account for or respond to racial aggression at PWI. Further, leaders demonize race-related justice movements (e.g., Black Lives Matter, North Dakota Pipeline protests, and DREAMers advocacy) as inciting discontent among students of color (and discomfort among white students, who avoid racial discourses). Blame is ascribed passively through an expressed desire for postracial harmony.

Defining and Policing

A major motivation for characterizing racial difference as regressive is to delegitimize stories of campus racism. Keeping conversations of race out of PWI's consciousness has denied peoples of color opportunities to (a) self-author how they experience and relate to whiteness therein through western policies, funding structures, decision-making processes, and so on and (b) define their own understandings of life as nonwhite peoples in a white settler space that was not created by or for them. PWI's denial of how racial differences shape lived realities extends in group-specific ways to people of color with origins in every continent. This fosters widespread forgetting of each group's history on campus, including their efforts for racial justice, such that they give minimal attention to addressing institutional violence altogether.

PWI's racial denial and erasure of nonwhite people's nonwhiteness renders multiethnic collegians invisible. Although nonwhite peoples tell their stories of survivance, they are only "allowed" to publicly share those that PWI approves of without facing any consequences. Institution-sanctioned stories are those in which nonwhites are tokenized as present at PWI but without racial or ethnic discontent or difference that the institution must accommodate through restructuring. This policing of nonwhite storytelling confirms whites' ideas about nonwhite people's beliefs, localities, needs, behaviors, and so on without engaging their pasts. Consequences for people of color who tell stories of survivance that problematize PWI include ostracization and losing access to compensation, funding, networks, and recognition of labor.

Dividing to Conquer

Grassroots interracial coalitions are not present at PWI, among students or professionals, resulting in a lack of intergroup dialogue to discover shared norms, values, histories, needs, goals, barriers, and so on. Racialized siloing keeps groups apart, discouraging multiracial/multiethnic people from finding a sense of place on campus. The siloing also leads to competition among peoples of color for attention and resources from PWI leadership; each group works to prove itself more deserving of both than their cousins. Such disharmonies call back to race-based legacy policies that forced nonwhite groups to positions wherein they are reliant on white governments—whose goal is to maintain their subservience—for their livelihoods.

Locating Myself in PWI

My time in PWI has been demarcated by three stages: experiencing a bait-and-switch, talking back to the institution existentially and politically through my multiraciality, and simultaneously being "too" and "incorrectly" Black.

Bait-and-Switch

During my recruitment to PWI, members of the department that I eventually joined told me that they were looking to bring in more nonwhite members whose knowledge and skills could support PWI's larger mission of better serving a diversifying student population. I was told that I would be encouraged to bring my critical perspectives and practical knowledge into the program. However, what I found upon entering PWI was that unit leaders—who were almost entirely white and self-identifying as "progressive"— did not understand that part of their foundational work in serving a wider array of collegians was interrogating (and where possible, working to reduce) their own biases manifest in policies, protocols, presumed cultural norms, physical spaces, and discourses around specific groups. Further, while comfortable with discussing gender, leaders were afraid to talk about race and hated naming themselves as white. Discursively, they expected nonwhite people to exist in alignment with Eurocentric beliefs, priorities, values, and imaginations—especially about us as being acquiescent to them.

Early on, my naiveté as a newcomer caused me to interpret the department's cognitive dissonance and lack of introspection as blind spots of blissful ignorance in leadership. Armed with knowledge from MSI, I inquired about plans to interrogate structural biases and racism. I was met with indignant proclamations such as, "There's no way I could discriminate against others! I'm a womxn!" or "I'm queer!" and "I work in this field because I value social justice!" I also progressively received evasion from white colleagues who were previously friendly and warnings to not "rock the boat" or "burn bridges." This period of time prompted my first feelings of emotional unsafety at PWI: I had been courted there under certain pretenses and was then chastised for doing work that aligned with them!

Talking Back Through Multiculturality

After realizing that my department claimed a desire to do social justice work while still operating through hegemonic white cultural norms, I sought to identify unmet needs therein. I asked colleagues of color, across races and campus levels, "How are you doing?" and "Do you have any unmet needs?" Those who spoke with me were very honest about grievances. I affirmed people's stories across racial groups and encouraged dialogue among them.

These grassroots efforts have slowly grown into assessments and programming that are student-advised and meant to address group-specific needs. Initiatives have coincided with rises in national race-based justice movements: the temporal alignment has encouraged student leaders to advocate for better treatment across campus, specific to their racial and other groups, while citing historical and contemporary discourses that PWI "forgets" (read: denies).

PWI's leaders have sometimes taken actionable steps to address specific incidents and needs but still express desire for "postracial" harmony that ideally makes racial discourse obsolete. They are also still resistant to organizational changes that would create substantive structural equity across social groups.

Lessons from Louisiana and MSI inform my approach to campus research and supporting others in their advocacy efforts. In both places, historical interracial convergences yielded new customs and means of communication. Consequently, people in both places have a great deal of empathy and patience in locating anyone they meet within the larger mélange of their respective regional populace. Two people can be of the same race but be any combination of ethnicities that then interact with their geographies—yielding different but related folkways. Hence, getting to know someone for who they are—and locating them relative to one's self—takes time, goodwill, and openness; peoples in both regions have plenty of all three. My therapeutic training amplifies these tendencies within me, which family and mentors have also nurtured.

These ways of building community have led me to reach out to as many nonwhite peoples at PWI as possible—to share stories with them and find common ground. My approach encourages students from different backgrounds who have not conversed previously or in a long time to (re)connect and find mutual understanding—while respecting each other's histories, values, and customs and sometimes discovering a shared past of mutual advocacy. I have supported the forging of many relationships, if only by encouraging two people to meet.

Being Too Black

For multiethnic people who identified as Native, there is a social reward for presenting as white and aligning with whiteness at PWI—as a way to gain power and/or not be targets of powerholders. Inversely, there is consequence for either presenting as Black or not aligning with whiteness. White-presenting colleagues who identify as Native have been permitted to practice white hegemonic cultural norms (i.e., ways of relating to others, decision-making, etc.) in their daily lives, while claiming Indianness and receiving legitimacy from local Elders. Some have documentation of Tribal citizenship, but others simply claim a desire to nonharmfully engage their Indigenous pasts. When I have expressed the same desires and explained the politico-historical complexities of my lineage (including family attempts in Tribal enrollment), I have not received the same openness or welcome into spaces as white-presenting folks. Where they receive messages of "Welcome, cousin!" I receive "You're a guest—you can enter at our discretion, but you must stay at a distance." Sometimes, I also receive open hostility.

My conversations with others who identify as Black and Native have revealed a pattern in raced differences of openness from various Indigenous communities, based on Amerikkka's Black–white racial hierarchy, despite Indianness existing outside of it. The contrast from MSI, and lessons from Elders therein about openness, signaled that I should respect boundaries and not attempt to participate in PWI's Indigenous community life. Though not surprised, I have felt disappointed and incomplete. I also long for MSI: a place where Indigenous peoples intentionally remember the intertwining of histories that white supremacy works to erase, in order to reclaim control of nonwhite narratives. By remembering my history, MSI acknowledged my full existence.

Being Black Incorrectly

PWI's Black community only welcomes forms of Blackness that adhere to specific performances of it. Foremost, "doing" Blackness does not entail interracial collaboration because past coalition attempts resulted in other racialized groups (a) stealing ideas from Blacks to adapt and promote as their own; (b) advocating that PWI expand and dilute Black-specific initiatives into "people of color" ones, then minimizing attention to Black issues therein; and (c) demonizing Blacks as requiring relatively more labor from PWI's leadership, due to higher demands for structural equity. PWI's Black community also functions through Civil Rights Era respectability that is heteronormative, androcentric, Christian-normative, and working class with aspirations for middle-class life through meritocracy myths.

Individuals who are racially ambiguous, and therefore assumed multiracial, are pressured to perform Blackness aggressively to receive community acceptance. Those who refuse to relinquish other racial parts of themselves, who do not perform Blackness "correctly," or who have multicultural perspectives, are not trusted as "safe" in PWI's Black spaces. Some multiracial Black collegians find welcome from their other racialized communities, depending on physical markers of multiraciality and their cultural knowledge as currencies. Other racially ambiguous Blacks relinquish their other ethnoracial identities to be accepted among PWI's Blacks. The community does not socially locate PWI's non-Amerikkkan Blacks, or Blacks of non-Christian or no faiths.

My multicultural approach to coalition building has been seen by most Blacks on campus as suspicious or odd; my anticolonial, anticapitalist feminist sentiments have been treated as incompatible with Christianity and aspirations of upward mobility. Contrary to MSI, many Blacks ascribe my "different" views to my queerness, which I have also been socially reprimanded for "doing." The pressure to minimize my multiethnicity, multiculturality, and queerness in Black spaces has been exhausting and invalidating—leading me to disassociate from PWI's Black community collectively while associating individually with open-minded members. Given the Black community's global role in interracial coalitions throughout recent history, I am disappointed in its closed-mindedness to them now; however, I understand the need for self-protection amid anti-Blackness on campus.

Resisting Limited Colonial Imaginations

Multiraciality, multiculturalism, and multiethnicity are unintelligible at PWI, and consequently they are liabilities that most nonwhite groups currently will not accommodate. White supremacy discourages us from remembering and telling stories about how our histories and present lives are more multifaceted than colonial narratives allow them to be. I am saddened that people of color oppress each other by adopting PWI's practices of forgetting (or denying) our complex shared pasts and present. Still, campuses such as MSI give me hope. They reject colonial sentiments of exclusivity, acknowledge humanity's complexities, and reaffirm multiethnic and multiracial lives by honoring the paths that our Ancestors forged for us. They encourage us to tell stories of our existence as survivance that transcend the colonial imagination—which is why I am telling mine.

9

EXISTING IN-BETWEEN

Embodying the Synergy of My Ancestors

Naliyah Kaya

We are
cross-cultural babies
border straddling youth
intercontinental adults

We are infants formed out of true
sometimes forbidden
love, tours of duty and pleasure travels
brought back like souvenirs

We are the children that have hidden our cultures and stories
inside diaries and memory boxes[1]

I racially identify as mixed. To be more specific, I have family from Southwest Asia and Europe, but I do not identify strongly with a singular racial or ethnic identity—although I have begun feeling more comfortable identifying as Middle Eastern/Southwest Asian[2] with the movement toward disaggregating our communities from the White racial category. I would describe my life as being a transnational mixed experience—perhaps more similar to the existence of a transnational adoptee—than resembling the life experiences of most biracial Americans. I am the first American-born member of my father's family, raised in the United States by my White American mother and stepdad with my brother, their biological son. In my mid-20s I reconnected with my dad for the first time since I was a toddler and flew thousands of miles to meet paternal family members in Türkiye who speak another language, claim a different religion, and live in a country

118

and culture very different from the ones I'd known. This trip occurred during my early years of graduate school and played a pivotal role in how I identify. Throughout this chapter I will share experiences that have influenced my racial identity; the importance of including, representing, and recognizing multiracial populations; and how I've navigated feelings of isolation and alienation throughout my academic career—attending and working at predominantly White institutions (PWIs), historically Black colleges and universities (HBCUs), and majority "minority"-serving institutions (MSIs).

I was raised in spaces that reflected my mom's background—predominantly White, middle class, and Christian. Out of fear my father would take me out of the United States my mom did not give me his last name. Instead, she chose a European last name that was also unrelated to her ancestry (Kaya, 2015).When I turned 18, I changed my name in its entirety. I was tired of being defined by a name to which I had no connection. Although it may seem like a patriarchal practice, taking my father's surname was my choice and I've never regretted it. It feels like home. To say my identity is complex is an understatement. Like many of my mixed peers raised by White families, I was treated with colorblindness. My family often denied that there was anything different about me as their way of demonstrating acceptance. They brushed off racial comments as family members "not meaning anything by them"—such as my grandmother asking about my skin color after I was born. When I attempt to have direct conversations about experiences with racism or prejudice, my mother wavers between acknowledgment and emphasizing my proximity to Whiteness. My differences are discussed as mere spices, small and exotic, before reminding me that we are all the same without seasoning.

I've always had anxiety when answering curious and prying questions meant to uncover what is "not quite White" about me or when asserting my racial identity to those who derive their conclusion about it from my light complexion. Too often I find myself rambling, hoping that I'm giving an acceptable explanation and leave the interaction upset that I tried to explain and justify who I am. These conversations often go something like "You said you are mixed. What *exactly* are you?" The question usually comes across in an accusatory way as if I must prove my "claim." I then attempt to explain my mixedness in a way that will satisfy them, at times supported by data (e.g., providing photos of my dad). For mixed people who have White ancestry and are White presenting there is frequently a tension between how we identify and how others identify us. Trying to be inclusive, our well-meaning White family members and community tend to deny our differences and experiences. Simultaneously, because of the political nature of race and our ability to pass as White, the communities of color we strongly identify with may not fully embrace us either, leaving us somewhere between, not quite White and not quite a person of color (POC).

What *exactly* are you? | *100% mixed.*
You don't look like the ones I've met. | *We come in a wide variety.*
How do you pronounce your name? | *Correctly.*
Is it Arabic? | *Kind of.*
Are you a Muslim or Christian? | *May I have my beef & broccoli now?*[3]

My monolingual tongue has been a constant hindrance to passing cultural authenticity tests. Multiple attempts at learning Turkish have resulted in an appreciation for the translate button on social media and the gradual realization that my ancestry does not have a bilingual prerequisite. The most difficult thing about my identity is explaining to others that the U.S. Census is not the authority on racial categories and experiences. In high school and college I started challenging dominant racial definitions and narratives as I began to realize the part of Asia my paternal family most recently originates from is erased in U.S. discourse by refusing to disaggregate us (as well as North Africans) from the White population—thereby ignoring the racialized experiences of Southwest Asian/North African (SWANA) people while boosting the White population count. What seemed like a victory historically, Middle Eastern people successfully arguing their performance of Whiteness before U.S. courts in order to immigrate and become citizens (when Asian immigration was severely restricted and at times completely blocked), has come back to haunt us in a post-9/11 era (Tehranian, 2009). Even now, I occasionally find myself questioning my "Asianness." When I received an invitation to write a review for an Asian American journal I pondered if they confused my surname with being from East Asia and if I was "Asian enough" to accept it. In these moments I'm reminded that unlearning is an ongoing process.

Existing In-Between

I've always existed in-between: in-between races (White and Asian), in-between continents (Asia, North America, Europe), in-between religions (Islam and Christianity)—fully all of them and simultaneously none of them. I am a fringer. What seemed like a deficit in my youth—being unable to fully fit in with a particular culture, race, or religion—has proven to be a gift. By existing in peripheral spaces, I've learned to navigate and appreciate cultural similarities and differences and to have empathy for those who challenge definitions of what their culture, race, belief system, or language "should" look, sound, or act like. We are the synergy of our ancestors and at the same time something completely unique and indefinable.

We will not loosen our grip
pulling our parents' cultures across continents
we are reminded that we were never divided

Standing here
names and nationalities
in one hand
snapshots and stories
in the other
eyes reflecting dreams

mouths filled with hope
we gently swallow all that we are[4]

Race and School: Elementary, Middle, and High School Experiences

Until 9th grade I was sent to private Christian schools where every teacher I had was White. Because I had light skin, a European-sounding last name, and a stepdad who was White, I easily passed. I knew that my dad was Turkish but had no concept of what that meant beyond a few cultural festivals and receiving gifts or letters in need of translation from family members. I don't recall thinking much about my racial identity until middle school. However, I never felt that I fit in at school and never identified as White.

From 6th through 8th grades I found myself on the receiving end of bullying and exclusion. I was perplexed, as I was kind to all of my peers, but soon learned where it stemmed from. I still recall one of the White male students thinking it was funny to call me a n***** lover when he found out I was communicating with and interested in dating a Black peer. As I became more aware of the contradictions between the Christian doctrine preached at school and the prejudice and discrimination these same people exhibited, I began to distance myself from my classmates. Although I didn't have the language then, I now realize that the isolation and exclusion I experienced was connected to the privileging of Whiteness in these spaces. It was this preference for Whiteness that I was actually moving away from. Although I may have been able to pass as "White" to peers, my participation in interracial friendships and romantic partnerships, my darker "ethnic" features—which I was informed were unattractive in comparison to blonde classmates—and consumption of nonwhite culture (music, TV shows, films, attire, etc.) marked me as other. This would not be the last time that I felt I did not belong.

After begging my parents to let me go to public school, I was allowed to attend my local high school. I quickly connected with a small group of friends who mainly identified as Black, Mexican, and Biracial. However, I was still at an overwhelmingly White suburban school where most of my teachers were White and the curriculum was centered on European history and White perspectives. My junior and senior years I participated in my district's early college program. All was well until my White high school counselor claimed that my African American history college credits could not fulfill the high school's American history requirement. After some back and forth with my professor the course was finally accepted. Sadly, soon afterward I encountered more questioning by a White teacher regarding the acceptability of my schoolwork in relation to the high school curriculum requirements.

For my senior capstone project, I performed spoken word poetry about social issues with one of my college friends. The poems in our set referenced and critically analyzed the prison industrial complex, slavery, and racism. Although many of the grading rubrics were positive, perhaps White teachers eager to demonstrate their acceptance and colorblindness, I did receive one that left me confused. On the paper it simply said, "Appropriate?" After racking my brain for why anyone would think our performance was inappropriate, I concluded their comment likely stemmed from seeing a tall Black man with a dark complexion raising his fist, condemning racism and genocide, yelling "Fuck Hitler" in "their" White suburban school. After racking my brain for why anyone would think our performance was inappropriate, I concluded their comment likely stemmed from seeing a tall Black man with dark skin raising his fist yelling "Fuck Hitler." I became irritated and upset that they seemed to be more concerned with invoking linguistic respectability politics around cursing than denouncing xenophobia and genocide.

My voice is . . .
remnants of cultures that clash and
those that have embraced me
when my own . . . couldn't[5]

Experiences in Higher Education

My community college was a shifting point for my identity and a space where I expanded my friend group. It was the first time that I met professors and staff who identified as African American, Native American, and

Latin@. I began hearing different stories and perspectives that were counternarratives to everything I'd been taught. Two of my most influential mentors and professors were my education professor, a Black woman, and an
African American history professor, a Black man. Things started off a bit
rocky with my African American history professor. He was determined to
help me "find myself." Although well intentioned, his taking me around
campus and leaving me with Turkish people to help me "get in touch" with
my identity simply created uncomfortable short-lived conversations. His
insistence that I should have a desire to be part of Islam (as he was) became
a point of tension between us, as his jokes sometimes came across as pressure. However, he has been instrumental in my success by encouraging my
inquisitiveness, mentoring me as a future educator, and pushing me to learn
about and acknowledge all of my racial, ethnic, and cultural identities. It's
been 16 years, and we are still in contact and now laugh at the awkward
memories. He also introduced me to what ended up being my second home:
the Multicultural Center.

The Multicultural Center was extremely important to my friends and
me. It was somewhere to eat, sleep, laugh, share information, and hold student organization meetings. I met my friend Amnah there, whose mom is
White and whose dad is Middle Eastern (from Dubai). She had also been
raised in America with her mom, stepdad, and sibling. Although her stepdad
is White and Mexican, he and her sibling (her stepdad and mother's biological child) are perceived as White and generally see themselves as such. We
quickly connected with our similar backgrounds of being the only mixed
Middle Eastern members in the nuclear families we were raised by. There was
an international Middle Eastern and North African (MENA) student population, but the one thing that united many of them were their ties to Islam.
Being raised as Christians in America, neither Amnah nor I felt we truly
fit in with the Muslim Student Union. For identity-based organizations we
had two other groups to choose from—the Black Student Union (BSU) and
the Latino Student Organization (LSO). With both of us having numerous
friends in the BSU we decided to ask if we could join and were welcomed.
At the time I had no way of knowing how another group's acceptance would
lead me on a path to creating and providing services for multiracial people.
Being part of the BSU that had my African American studies professor as its
faculty adviser was how I ended up on a trip to the East Coast visiting my
future alma mater, Hampton University.

I've repeatedly been asked why I went to Hampton University, a historically Black university, as someone who is not Black and is from the West
Coast. Some of my peers thought I was on a military scholarship. Others
theorized that I was one of the "foreign" girls on a tennis team scholarship. It

quickly became apparent that, unlike the West Coast, in the Hampton Roads region of Virginia (for the most part) you were White, Black, or occasionally "foreign." On rare occasions people questioned if I was Puerto Rican, part African American, or made sense of my being there by remarking that HBCUs had also been spaces for recent immigrants. What seemed to stump them was when I told them that I was not on a scholarship and simply chose to attend a college that I liked based on the curriculum, class size, touring the campus, the professors, East Coast location, and cost of tuition in comparison to my local college options. It was confusing to the people—who saw me as White—to understand why I would not want to continue my education at a PWI. I still vividly remember the day my senior seminar professor at Hampton started off our first class by telling everyone not to be uncomfortable by the White student in the classroom. That obviously "she" wouldn't be there if "she" felt uncomfortable and to not let "her" presence change the discourse they'd otherwise have. I slowly raised my hand and asked the rhetorical question, "Are you talking about me?" She seemed surprised and replied that she was. I informed her that I was mixed, to which she responded the idea of mixed blood had racist roots and demanded if I wasn't White then what was I?

While waiting to speak with her after class, from the hallway I heard her saying in an upset tone to my friend that she didn't know what I was, but I sure looked White and she knew what I thought about her as a Black woman being my professor. Fighting back tears of frustration—of being viewed as the same as those who had also caused me pain—I walked into the room and respectfully told her that the only thing I had thought about her was that she was my professor and that I was there to learn from her. I further elaborated that I was not on a scholarship; I was taking out loans to attend school and was a first-generation college student. She replied that she usually wasn't wrong about people, but maybe in this case she was.

For the rest of the semester she treated both my friend and me as her "class favorites," but I was never sure if our interactions had changed the way she felt about me. Looking back, I can now understand how my presence made her feel uncomfortable in a place she did not expect to feel discomfort. Teaching at an HBCU was a place she could generally expect not to encounter those she'd had many negative and racist experiences with. It was a place where she didn't have to convince students of her legitimacy as a Black woman with a PhD. In some ways, my seeking out acceptance and majority POC spaces intruded on these same things for others. I learned from her personal stories that what my professor and I both had in common was being taught in educational spaces where our cultures and identities were not reflected.

This has been a constant theme for me—not finding spaces where all of my identity is accepted, represented, or invited. It is imperative that people of color and more specifically Multiracial people see ourselves in curricula, in our educators, and in extracurricular spaces and activities. The immense excitement and relief I felt going to my second student of color conference to find MAVIN, an organization and magazine created for people who identify as bi/multiracial, and hosting a session cannot fully be put into words. I was also elated the first time I saw the MENA category listed separately from White at the inaugural Critical Mixed Race Studies (CMRS) Conference. For once, I was not being asked to deny or subsume my identity under White.

Creating and Holding Space for Multiraciality in Academia

I've spent much of my career dedicated to creating spaces for mixed and underrepresented communities. I've served two terms as the community liaison on the Executive Committee for the Critical Mixed Race Studies Association (CMRSA), planning and implementing conferences and organizing arts and community programming. Previously, I was the coordinator for Multiracial and Native American/Indigenous student involvement at the University of Maryland (UMD). I was excited to be the first full-time coordinator with a role specifically identified for supporting Multiracial students. I still have not seen a similar position at another institution. While I was at UMD I worked with students, faculty, and staff to include Multiracial and Native American/Indigenous communities in the University Student Leadership Awards by creating the Mildred & Richard Loving and Sarah Winnemucca Awards. Until then both communities had been left out for more than 30 years. We also started annual Loving Day educational events designed by our student interns, expanded our student internship program so our Multiracial and Native American/Indigenous interns no longer had to share one position, implemented an annual Mixed Monologues spoken word program, and built up our Multiracial Heritage Month programming with the Multiracial Biracial Student Association (MBSA). I also created and taught a Multiracial leadership course. During my last year—coming full circle for me—we hosted the annual CMRS Conference on our campus. Although it was hard to leave a role so specifically carved out to serve my own community, now as a sociology professor I'm able to educate hundreds of students every year on the experiences, history, and representation of interracial families and multiracial people in the United States. It's not always about creating new courses but rather including the voices, experiences, and perspectives of excluded populations into the standard curriculum.

To find healing
we must do the work of remembering . . .
they [our ancestors] prayed our assimilation
would protect us,
but never become us.
That we'd never deny
where we came from
no matter how easy it might become . . .
no matter how light some of us might become.[6]

Navigating Imposter Syndrome

Another theme that has been connected to my journey has been imposter syndrome. Like many people of color, women, and first-generation college students, I've doubted my accomplishments and feared that I would be exposed as not belonging in the spaces I've earned the same credentials as others to occupy. These feelings, although sometimes unprovoked, have not always been without warrant. During my graduate school application process, I was perplexed upon receiving a conditional acceptance to a sociology program. I went to one of my Hampton professors and asked him why I would be accepted on probation when I had great writing samples, outstanding grades, and glowing recommendations. He, a White man, told me matter-of-factly that I was a community college and HBCU graduate and although I excelled in these spaces the graduate school saw them as inferior academic institutions and wasn't convinced I could succeed at their "prestigious" PWI. I did not accept their "offer." That moment stuck with me—that receiving an education in spaces where you do not feel minoritized also comes at a cost. Even now there are times where I catch myself getting ready to turn down offers to write book chapters, speak at conferences, or apply for positions because I've allowed an inkling of doubt to creep back in about my worthiness. In these moments I reacquaint my current self with my younger fearless self who moved freely, tenaciously going after things no matter how unattainable they seemed.

An imposter syndrome of sorts has also always been present in sharing my racial identity. I've felt the need to accent the "nonwhite" aspects of my identity to signal to others that I am (or am not) part of their group or community. In academic spaces this has been done through my participation on various committees focused on race and ethnicity, the topics in my writing and conference presentations, saying it outright, and through my attire. Some have asked why I don't just pass. I've been told if I didn't change my name or tell anyone about my background I could simply say I was White.

To do that I would have to deny aspects of who I am and I refuse to exist as anything less than wholly, authentically, and unapologetically.

I recently did the one thing that terrified me. I presented on being a mixed Middle Eastern American woman with a colleague at the National Conference on Race and Ethnicity in American Higher Education (NCORE). For years I'd been encouraged to "tell my story." I was scared that no one would be interested in *that* story or they'd show up only to tell me my story didn't matter and that I could and should pass and once again I'd have my identity determined for me and brushed off. What actually happened was that over 40 people came and shared their own experiences of alienation. People were/are seeking a MENA community so much so that we created a social media group and recently had another session accepted for the same conference. Had I gone along with what seemed like the easy route of passing, I would have allowed structures that privilege whiteness, prejudice, and stereotypes to go unchallenged.

> So when some ask why I don't simply pass
> why I'd reclaim a name that outs my heritage
> in a post 9/11 America
> why I fight to be categorically disaggregated from White
> why I would not simply count myself lucky
> and take full advantage of this mixed light skin
> and the ability to blend in
> why I would willingly tell
> what others desperately hide
> I respond
> Because . . . I am tired *of the forgetting.*

Notes

1. Copyright © 2015, Naliyah Kaya, *Fringers*. Reproduced with permission.
2. Term usage varies throughout chapter based on personal identification and the original context being referenced.
3. Copyright © 2019, Naliyah Kaya, *Takeouts & Tire Shops*. Reproduced with permission.
4. Copyright © 2019, Naliyah Kaya, *Second Generation*. Reproduced with permission.
5. Copyright © 2019, Naliyah Kaya, *Invoking Remembrance*. Reproduced with permission.
6. Copyright © 2019, Naliyah Kaya, *Invoking Remembrance*. Reproduced with permission.

References

Kaya, N. (2015, November 18). Part I: Reclaiming my name. *Mixed Root Stories.* https://mixedrootsstories.com/fringers/

Kaya, N. (2019). *Invoking Remembrance.* https://mixedandmena.home.blog/invoking-remembrance-poem/

Tehranian, J. (2009). *Whitewashed: America's invisible Middle Eastern minority.* New York University Press.

REFLECTIONS OF A CREOLE, INDIGENOUS, AFRO-LATIN SCHOLAR

From Community to the Classroom

Andrew Jolivétte

I was born and raised in San Francisco, California; my mother was African American, Native American (with some European ancestry) and my father was Louisiana Creole—mostly European, with French, Spanish, Italian, and Irish ancestry, but also with Opelousa and Atakapa-Ishak Indigenous as well as West African ancestry. A visual of my family is shown in Figure 10.1. Growing up, my identification changed from Black/American Indian to Louisiana Creole when I reached about 22 years of age. I think graduate school had a lot to do with coming to terms with my racial and ethnic identity over time. Being in academia has often meant "fitting everywhere" and "fitting nowhere" because some colleagues and students see me as fitting across a range of monoracial categories, including African American, Native American, Latinx, and Queer/Two-Spirit.

My research, teaching, and community work have been driven by my experiences as a multiracial person. Whether I was taking on questions of theory, politics, public health, or research methodologies, I have always inserted a multiracial analysis because it has been so lacking in most academic disciplines and also because so many students ask for work that cuts across identities. I have often over my 20-year career been asked to speak at events, conferences, rallies, and so on across the United States, Canada, Australia, and the Netherlands precisely because of my multiracial background; I don't think I would change anything about the experiences and challenges I have faced in academia or community settings. It has made me a better scholar-activist.

Figure 10.1. Contributor with his parents, Kenneth and Annetta Jolivétte.

Note. ©Andrew Jolivétte (2020). Used with permission.

Early Encounters With Race, Colorism, and Multiraciality

"I don't want those nig*** sitting next to my grandchildren" (HLJ, circa 1973). These were the words my paternal grandfather spoke to my grandmother about my older half-siblings (who are African American from their father's side and Native African American from our mother's side) sitting next to my first cousins who have a Puerto Rican father and a French Creole mother (my aunt and godmother, my father's eldest sister). This incident occurred at my grandparent's home before I was born. I can remember my father who strongly identifies as Black despite being the most "white appearing" of his siblings (he was born with blond hair, hazel eyes, and white skin) sharing this story with me at a very young age. He was called to my grandparent's home. When he arrived he ripped the phone off the wall and told my grandfather, grandmother, and his siblings that they were all "nig***" and to get over it."

Some 15 years earlier before moving from rural southwest Louisiana and the heartland of the Creole community in Opelousas my grandparents sat my dad and his four siblings down and informed them that the family would be moving to San Francisco, California. In preparing them for the move they had the children watch the 1959 film *Imitation of Life* starring Lana Turner and Juanita Moore (Hunter & Sirk, 1959). The story follows the life of a white single mother (portrayed by Turner) who is an aspiring Broadway and major film actress and her relationship with a Black housekeeper named Annie Johnson (portrayed by Moore), who is widowed with a white-presenting daughter. Annie's daughter refuses to identify as Black and clashes with her mother throughout the film and eventually leaves home and changes her name to become a performance showgirl who never reconciles with her mother until she has already died and is on her funeral procession march.

The goal of showing my father, uncle, and aunts this film was to engrain in them the "dangers" of identifying as Black when they could "pass" for white. My grandfather told them, "We are moving. We are French Canadians if anyone asks. If you want to go for something else that's up to you, but we are *just* white now." These early family stories set the stage for my identity development in many ways. There was a certain erasure in these comments that speaks to not only anti-Blackness and nihilism but also an erasure of my family's Native ancestry. And on my mother's side there was ample pride in our Native heritage but there was also an underlying anti-Blackness as well.

My mother use to tell us, "My mama is an Indian and my daddy is a Negro. . . . He's an African." Her mother's beauty seemed to always be tied to her skin color (which was light brown) and her long straight black hair (which reached to her tailbone). In contrast my maternal grandfather (who was actually about the same color or lighter than my grandmother) was celebrated for his economic success. His racialization seemed to be based on his economic status while my college-educated grandmother who was a homemaker was notable for her looks. Together these experiences and stories set the stage for me to question my racial and ethnic background but to also wonder how my own appearance set me apart from my family. Although technically I wasn't a first-generation student of color, I felt like one both because neither of my parents completed a college degree but also because it was assumed by most institutions that I was a first-generation student. I also had a different experience from all of my other siblings. My oldest siblings were all darker than me; from my father were two white-appearing older siblings who had white and white/Mexican mothers. And my two younger brothers who share the same biological parents as me are much lighter than me and often present as biracial (Black and white). My experience as a brown-skinned male with straighter hair and what others called "white" or European racial features seemed to make me stand out as more "racially ambiguous" to outsiders. I was often asked, I would say at a rate of 3 to 1, what my ethnicity was in comparison to my siblings, some of whom were assumed Black, while others were assumed white, and the youngest biracial. I, however, was often asked if I was Ethiopian, Arab, Egyptian, Mexican, Puerto Rican, Cuban, Indian/

South-Asian. I think I have heard it all to the point that people haven't believed me when I tell them that I'm not "x" to the point that they say, "Well, someone down the line must be from India . . . or Ethiopia" (the two most common things I'm asked).

The early experiences set the stage for decades of wrestling with everything from colorism to self-esteem to educational performance. I can still remember when my light ("yellow") skin turned to a very dark brown by the time I was 9 or 10 and my maternal aunt whom I hadn't seen in a number of years stated, "Wow, you got so Black!" I was stunned to say the least because I took that to mean something was now "wrong" with me. In the years that followed I would wonder often how my physical appearance has both helped and hindered my growth and experiences with others, whether as a professor, a student, an intimate partner, or an activist in multiple communities.

Elementary and High School Ethnic Dissonance and Disassociation

My elementary and high school years included many examples of external pressures to identify with certain groups that caused some dissonance and group disassociation. When I was in the first grade at my Catholic elementary school I can recall a friend's mother asking me if my father was Hispanic or Native American. I said, "I don't know. . . . I think so." I was also assumed to be biracial mixed with Black and white by elementary school teachers. I can recall in the 6th grade when talking about Puerto Rico and colonialism and mulatto identity how the teacher (a nun and member of the Daughter of Charities Order) said, "And we have two of them in our class," but I was left wondering why she was including me, because I wasn't sure if this was how I should be identified at that time. I knew I was mixed, but I didn't think of myself as biracial as much as I thought of Creoles and myself then as multiracial. The questions about my ethnic background growing up led me to eventually wonder how any one person could possibly contain so many identities without one becoming more prominent over the others. I didn't really believe it possible to be both Black and white, to be Native and European, let alone all of these things. College changed that.

Introducing Mixed Race Studies: From Undergraduate to Graduate Studies

In 1993 after I graduated from a predominantly white Catholic high school I passed over several "better schools"—the University of California (UC),

Santa Barbara, Louisiana State University (LSU), DePaul—to attend a historically Black college (HBCU), Lincoln University in Oxford, Pennsylvania. There was a big part of me that wanted to go to a UC school like some of my peers and another part of me that got excited about attending LSU, because it would mean living in Louisiana and learning more about the Creole experience. I chose to look at American Indian tribal colleges and HBCUs to get a stronger connection to either my tribal/Indigenous identity or my Black identity. Most tribal colleges offer 2-year programs, so I opted for Lincoln. It was a culture shock to say the least. What was interesting was living in the dorms (all male) where I met individuals from across the African diaspora. It was really powerful to meet Dominicans, Puerto Ricans, West and East Africans, Jamaicans, and others who looked like me. I wasn't this anomaly. I think this because the experience of many members of the African diaspora are experiences filled with miscegenation, cultural blending, and colonial violence against Black bodies. However, as people of African descent in the Americas, we have also had many relationships based on love and free choice, especially in relationships with Indigenous Peoples in North, Central, and South America, as well as in the Caribbean.

Despite being elected freshman class president, I disliked Lincoln's remote location and its dilapidated buildings. I wouldn't change the fact that I attended, but for an HBCU, I was frustrated that 50% of my professors were white. I was also concerned that this didn't seem like the journey I should take, so after a semester I transferred to the City College of San Francisco and then even though I swore I'd never attend another Catholic school I chose to finish my undergraduate studies at the University of San Francisco (USF), a private Jesuit College. I chose USF because of the small class size and because I knew I could get my classes and graduate in a timely fashion. It was at USF that I took my very first mixed race studies course in 1996, with Rebecca (Becky) Chiyoko King-O'Riain (People of Mixed Descent). I learned so much from her and finally felt a connection to both my Black and Native sides in an intellectual way. I wrote my final paper on Black-Indian and white-Indian colorism. It was a launching pad of sorts into both my graduate studies at San Francisco State University where I continued on the same topic and at UC Santa Cruz where I wrote my dissertation in 2003, titled *Creole Diaspora: (Re) Articulating the Social, Legal, Economic, and Regional Construction of American Indian Identity* (Jolivétte, 2003). There was a growing field, but it had only been about 10 years since Maria P. P. Root's (1992) *Racially Mixed People in America* had been published, and I was trying to write outside of the racial formation framework that seemed to leave out the salience of culture. In what would later become my first single authored manuscript, *Louisiana Creoles: Cultural Recovery and Mixed-Race Native American Identity* (Jolivétte, 2006),

I argued that incorporating a cultural formation analysis into racial formation would help to take into account the variations in identity experienced by not only those who identify as multiracial but also many monoracially identified peoples as well. It had become obvious especially in a place like the Bay Area that mixed race studies were a growing area of scholarly inquiry, and this became the context for my first academic appointment.

This Bridge Called My Multiracial, Queer Back: First Academic Appointment

San Francisco State has a dynamic and important history around the world. The significance of the university stems in large part from the student strikes led by the Black Student Union (BSU) and Third World Liberation Front (TWLF), along with many other students, in 1968 which subsequently led to the founding of the first College of Ethnic Studies in the United States (and in the world; there is a new College at California State University, Los Angeles, which is just starting at the time of this writing in September 2019). In 2003 I was the dean of middle school students and multicultural programs at Presidio Hill School in San Francisco and had just graduated from my doctoral program in sociology in March of that year. A position on campus at San Francisco State in mixed race studies opened up, and I was encouraged to apply, particularly because they wanted someone to work with graduate students because they had received and admitted so many new students interested in mixed race studies. I also had been teaching an American Indian studies graduate seminar for the college for about 3 years at that point. I was hired, and it became immediately apparent that I was there in some ways to be some kind of bridge between Black students and Native students and perhaps more importantly between Black faculty and other units. I was told on more than one occasion by students that faculty in different departments remarked "there's a Black man teaching in Native studies" or that there were others who thought I was going to be some kind of unicorn who would teach across Native, Black, and Latinx studies. I was expected to create new courses, and I produced many.

In my first year I created the following new classes: Mixed Race Studies, Black Indians in the Americas (cross-listed with Black studies, American Indian studies, and La Raza studies), Coloring Queer, The Urban Indian Experience, People of Color and AIDS (redeveloped), and Comparative Race and Ethnicity (cross-listed between sociology and race and resistance studies). Later I would redevelop our American Indian education course and create another new course, Native Sexualities and Queer Discourse.

I never truly felt accepted by everyone in the college as fully Native or fully Black, yet I was often asked to fill voids or needs in both communities when others would not. As someone with darker skin and clearly of African descent, I found it ironic that I was often not considered Black enough, yet I was one of maybe three faculty in the entire college who attended a historically Black college or one of half a dozen who lived in or grew up in a Black neighborhood. I was told once by a staff person that one colleague in my department said, "I looked more Black than my other Black Indian colleague." I'm like, "Why, because he has a ponytail . . . ?" Then I laughed. The fact that folks needed to even comment on these things or that I felt the pressure to create a course on Black Indians when we have no equivalent course on "White Indians" has always been ironic to me. It speaks to the privileging of white over Black and to anti-Black racism in Indian country. A colleague in La Raza Studies (now Latina/Latino Studies) also made an accusation that our department was full of a bunch of white and Black people (in other words no one was a "real Indian") during a discussion about expanding our curriculum. This accusation along with the fact that our department was often the last to come into consideration for new hires or equal time base allocations for staff and department chairs are all examples of anti-Indianness in the college as well. This was not just within our own college; it was also across the university. As someone who identifies as both Black and Native and also with my Latinx roots as a Louisiana Creole, I have felt the weight of being pulled in many directions and then questioned for decisions I've made. I will say the academic and professional choices I've made were always about serving the best interests of the students, my colleagues, the College of Ethnic Studies, and San Francisco State.

Anti-Blackness and Anti-Indianness by Any Other Name Is Still Academic Settler Violence

Ethnic studies as a field celebrated half a century of existence in 2019, and I hope that many of us are also continuing to define the field from our own community-driven histories, knowledge systems, and cultural protocols. Many books have been written about the university as a site of empire and colonialism. Scholars have remarked that American studies would mean the end of ethnic studies or that the institutionalization of the field would lead to its demise as relevant to those who fought to create it. Just this year my colleague Wei Ming Dariotis, a national leader in the field of critically mixed race studies, along with Nicole Leopardo, an adjunct professor, worked to create and implement minor in critical mixed race studies at San Francisco State, the first in the nation. Although I title this section with the words *Anti-Blackness* and *Anti-Indianness*, my career is also a testimony on the ways that anti–mixed race/heritage also exists in academia. Sadly, as someone who has also spent nearly 2 decades doing community work and diversity training work, it has been among other academics both white and of color where I have heard some of the most anti-Black, anti-Indian, and anti-Mixed comments.

The attempt by the administration at San Francisco State to rescind two tenure-track faculty positions in Africana Studies, the declining rates of African American and Native American student enrollments, the reduced administrative and institutional support for the Native American Graves and Repatriation Program, and the lack of new faculty hires in Native studies are all examples of racism and settler violence at work. When a university won't even acknowledge the land that it sits on, this is settler violence. When tribal leaders are only invited to campus to give "ceremonial" and obligatory welcoming prayers and then ignored, this is settler violence at work. One day a fellow faculty member who is African American (and who has told me and a colleague that she is also Choctaw but identifies as monoracial) walked over to my office door and pointed to a printed copy of the cover of my book, *Obama and the Biracial Factor: The Battle for a New American Majority* (Jolivétte, 2012) and said, "Why does he have to be biracial? Why can't he just be Black?" I said, "Because he is both." This comment is deeply ironic considering the faculty member is married to a Japanese American and has multiracial children.

I've also heard some cis-hetero-Black male faculty members and some cis-hetero-Latinx female faculty state that "we are admitting too many queer women into the graduate program" or on other occasions that we have to admit more Black students regardless of qualifications because the numbers are so low. Yet these same faculty members won't work with these students once they are admitted. As a mixed race, queer man of color in academia, I feel erased, and ironically this sometimes happens in the most hurtful ways in places where one might least expect it. I remember applying for a job at a university in Texas where I was a finalist. I won't go into too much detail to protect the confidentiality of the process and the institution, but the department that was focusing on these very issues ended up hiring a white male candidate who, although very qualified in several ways, was underqualified for this particular senior position. This has happened elsewhere when white-passing Native people receive offers for positions, because their whiteness doesn't necessarily erase their Nativeness in quite the same ways as my Blackness.

Beyond physical appearance, the type of scholarship one produces means so very much in the academy even though no one really reads all those peer-reviewed journal articles other than other academics. That's fine. I just wonder if the purpose of fields like critical mixed race studies and critical or relational ethnic studies should be more or at least as concerned with how our research and teaching speaks to the communities who made our careers possible.

From Community to Academia: Merging Research, the Classroom, and Activism

As a multiracial Creole, Indigenous, Afro-Latin academic my life and career have been filled with a variety of experiences, challenges, and plenty of joy as well. I strive to incorporate my community work with my research and teaching. To be completely honest I don't understand how any person of color or any Indigenous person can separate or divorce academic work in ethnic studies or related fields from community organizing work. We have a responsibility to be in dialogue with living and breathing communities and not just with the past or literary sources. We must make sure that our research and teaching methods are reflective of the communities we come from and not just from the settler societies that can shape our career trajectories. As a critical mixed race studies scholar most of my writing and community work revolves around multiraciality and the complexities of these types of identities. I have served as the board president of iPride for Multiracial Families for many years, and in that work we developed a summer program for mixed heritage youth called FUSION; it was a popular program. But as is often the case, activists and organizers are involved in so many projects that the stretch is often too great to maintain new programs. Although iPride and FUSION are no longer around, I continue to work with organizations like Speak Out and the American Indian Community Center and Black Community Collective to examine how mixed heritage experiences matter and contribute to our understanding of contemporary society and changing ethnic demographics. This also helps me to decide what is most relevant for course material in my classes. In my 20-year career I have come to see even more changes in student demographics that reflect a multiracial society. This does not mean that racism will disappear. In fact the demographic changes in this country suggest that we should continue to link the multiple identities and realities of college students, community organizers, and academics in ways that are transformative. As one of three of the first inaugural keynote speakers for the Critical Mixed Race Studies Conference in 2010, I argued that to be a critical field of research inquiry we must focus on the real-life everyday social problems facing mixed race people, including health, prison, and educational disparities.

Lessons and Messages to the Next Seven Generations

What can I say to the future generations of scholars who will come after me? Long after I am gone—I wish you love . . . I wish you joy. It is my wish that you will not have to feel like your back is a bridge between communities . . . at least not in a way that is not of your own choosing. I hope that you will be able to center without hesitation the knowledge systems of your peoples without facing questions about the legitimacy of your intellectual traditions. But please hear me now. Be your own best self-advocate. Learn the system. Publish and publish and publish. You can write for your own people and your own audience. Be proactive, not reactive. Be confident and be humble. Recognize your full humanity, and know that every single one of your identities and experiences matters and that they are indeed a gift from the creator. Everything you write and create is a gift. Don't let anyone rattle you. Life is short, so fucckk it anyway. You are responsible for the world you leave behind in small and big ways . . . just know the difference. You are a legacy. Your work is meant to be ceremony. . . . When you work with this purpose, your path will always be full.

References

Hunter, R. (Producer), & Sirk, D. (Director). (1959). *The imitation of life* [Motion picture]. United States: Universal Pictures.

Jolivétte, A. J. (2003). *Creole diaspora: (Re)articulating the social, legal, economic, and regional construction of American Indian identity* [Unpublished dissertation] University of California, Santa Cruz.

Jolivétte, A. (2006). *Louisiana Creoles: Cultural recovery and mixed-race Native American identity.* Lexington Books.

Jolivétte, A. (2012). *Obama and the biracial factor: The battle for a new American majority.* Policy Press.

Root, M. P. P. (1992). *Racially mixed people in America.* SAGE.

PART THREE

STRATEGIES AND TOOLS FOR ENHANCING MULTIRACIAL INCLUSION

CONTEXTUALIZING MULTIRACIALITY IN CAMPUS CLIMATE

Key Considerations for Transformative Diversity, Equity, and Inclusion

Chelsea Guillermo-Wann and Marc P. Johnston-Guerrero

S trategies to measure and improve campus climate have been central features of institutional transformation efforts to create diverse and inclusive colleges and universities. In particular, campus racial climate, or "the overall racial environment of the university that could potentially foster outstanding academic outcomes and graduation rates for all students but too often contributes to poor academic performance and high dropout rates for students of color" (Yosso et al., 2009, p. 664), continues to be an important area of focus for inquiry and practice. Even as colleges and universities move forward in creating more inclusive campus environments through improvement to campus racial climates (Hurtado, Alvarez et al., 2012; Hurtado, Milem et al., 1998, 1999; Milem et al., 2005), competing interests challenge such efforts. These include situating excellence in tension with equal access, free speech as a challenge to civility, autonomy against normative language, stability in resistance to change, and self-interest over the public good (Chang, 2000). Another interest that has been framed as potentially competing with or distracting from earlier racial equity work is multiraciality. Although more fluid, intersectional, and situational representations of race, class, gender, and sexuality have been emerging, recognition and use of these representations have not been without controversy or pushback (Thornton, 2009). Practical tools and resources for leaders and practitioners in the field that take multiraciality into consideration are needed, especially because the campus climate impacts students' sense of belonging, validation, and equity across student outcomes (Hurtado et al., 2012).

In this chapter, we present a revised and updated iteration of our original model, the *integrative model of multiraciality* (IMM), which incorporated multiraciality into campus climate (Guillermo-Wann & Johnston, 2012). Our new model, *contextualizing multiraciality in campus climate* (CMCC), offers further information and guidance to campus leaders, faculty, staff, and students in their efforts to better support organizational change related to campus climate for diversity that both aligns with antiracist diversity, equity, and inclusion (DEI) efforts and is inclusive of multiraciality. First, we discuss the rationale for explicit inclusion of multiraciality in campus climate. Next, we present the new model. Then we offer key considerations when applying the model by job type. Finally, we close with how the model can support broader campus DEI efforts.

Why Multiraciality?

As earlier chapters in this volume highlight, much of what we know about multiracial populations in higher education focuses on racial identity development and multiracial students' experiences. Although this literature is helpful and relevant, it tends not to consider the role of racism or specifically focus on campus climate. Our earlier review of an emerging body of mixed race research (Guillermo-Wann & Johnston, 2012) identified issues that could be used to inform a tool for assessing and improving campus climate for multiracial students, such as feelings of belonging and acceptance, high levels of prejudice, low levels of institutional support, and negative experiences related to being multiracial. These issues appeared across all five dimensions of campus climate identified by Milem et al. (2005), which are (a) the historical legacy of inclusion/exclusion, (b) the composition of different groups on campus, (c) the organizational structures and policies, (d) the psychological/perceptual aspects, and (e) the behavioral or interactional aspects of the campus environment. We also highlighted how people who identify multiracially could experience racism targeting various groups of color (and for some individuals, white privilege as well), illustrating interpersonal, institutional, and societal levels of racial power, privilege, and oppression (Guillermo-Wann, 2012).

In addition, scholars assert that higher education research tends to be atheoretical regarding race and resistant to naming racism, despite the increasing use of critical race theory (Cabrera, 2018; Harper, 2012). Research that does consider race has focused primarily on monoracially constructed groups (Johnston-Guerrero, 2017) and tends not to address how multiracial students are accounted for in the sample of a study (Harper, 2016), which are arguably manifestations of monoracism (discussed in the next section). We foreground the importance of strong theoretical grounding in racial formation (Omi & Winant, 1994), especially when considering multiraciality within campus climate, and also as context for student development. By explicitly using racial theory, educators may more effectively expose and address the roots of inequitable opportunities and outcomes across diverse groups in educational settings, including multiracial students.

Contextualizing Multiraciality in Campus Climate

In the first version of our model, we used the term *integrative* because the IMM integrated both racism and monoracism as well as insights from the literature on multiracial identity and campus climate. In the years since we debuted the IMM at the 2012 Critical Mixed Race Studies Conference, we have found some educators were able to utilize the model, but other people thought we took on too much in one model and that it was difficult to actually utilize it in research or practice. In this chapter, we build on the original work to create the CMCC model. In this section, we identify and explain the model's core components, their relationship to each other, and how the model applies to campus climate efforts (see Figure 11.1). We also discuss how the CMCC better accounts for the potential asymmetries in multiracial experiences (Johnston-Guerrero et al., 2020) by explicitly acknowledging that aspects of the model work differently based on one's racial identity (informed by ancestry, phenotype, and cultural knowledge) and ecological context (Renn, 2004).

The Rings: Linking Racial Formation and Racism With Local Contexts and Campus Climate

Colleges and universities do not exist in a vacuum—they influence and are influenced by broader societal contexts, as acknowledged in campus climate frameworks (Hurtado, Alvarez et al., 2012; Hurtado, Milem et al., 1998, 1999; Milem et al., 2005) and multiracial identity development models, particularly Renn's (2004) adaptation of Bronfenbrenner's ecological systems theory. In the outermost ring, we connect the more distal conditions of the social, economic, political, and cultural forces of racial formation (Omi & Winant, 1994, 2014) with those named by prominent higher education

Figure 11.1. CMCC model.

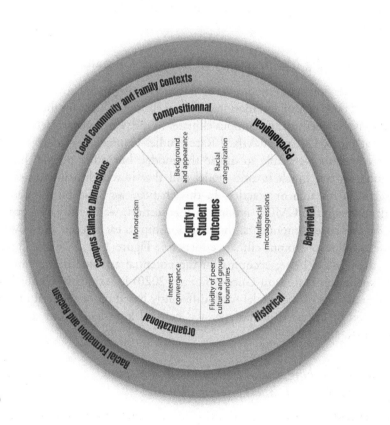

scholars such as historical trends; national, state, and local policy (Hurtado et al., 1998, 1999; Milem et al., 2005); and cultural expectations (Renn, 2004). Examples of these forces as they pertain to multiracial people in the United States include the federal legalization of all interracial marriages in 1967, the 2000 U.S. Census allowing for multiple race identification, assumptions that multiracial people were evidence of a "postracial" era during the Obama presidency, and shifting interpretations of the legacy of how so-called rules of hypodescent (e.g., the "one drop rule") work differently for different groups. These forces and cultural expectations influence perceptions of multiracial people, as well as social and identity options for them, in college contexts.

These forces also inform conceptualizations of race (and racism), where different ideas of what race means can vary from person to person. To help anchor such conversations and the CMCC, we provide guidance on the use of several terms. We understand *race* to be defined as "a power construct of collected or merged difference that lives socially" (Kendi, 2019, p. 35). This orientation differs slightly from the less explicit notion that race is socially constructed (Omi & Winant, 1994, 2014), meaning that "*race is a concept which signifies and symbolizes social conflicts and interests by referring to different types of human bodies*. . . . Race is a matter of both social structure and cultural representation" (Omi & Winant, 1994, pp. 55–56, emphasis in original). Kendi (2019) amplifies that race is a power construct moreso than a social construct. *Racial formation* is the "process by which racial categories are created, inhabited, transformed, and destroyed . . . [and is] tied to the evolution of hegemony, the way in which society is organized and ruled" (Omi & Winant, 1994, pp. 55–56), which is based in self-interest of groups with dominant power (Kendi, 2019). Related to the ensuing *racialization* process, wherein meanings are attached to a group (Omi & Winant, 1994), is *implicit bias* where those meanings become tacitly but completely embedded in the subconscious psyche after extensive exposure to broader cultural stereotypes (Banaji & Greenwald, 2016). From these perspectives, race is fluid and changing across time and place through culture and political struggle; it is not an essence, nor is it static. Rather, racial formation theory upholds antiessentialism in conceptualizing race—a key foundation for the CMCC. We therefore utilize the term *racial group(s)* instead of *race(s)* to avoid reifying the concept of race as distinct biological categories.

Falsely discrete racial categories have consistently been created and maintained throughout U.S. history through racial formation, obscuring centuries of racial intermixing. We therefore use *monoracial* as referencing, pertaining to, or ascribing to only one group racialized as a (mono)racial group in the United States (e.g., Asian American, Black/African American, Latinx, Native

American, white). Monoracial categories may or may not accurately reflect an individual's or group's ancestry or racial identity but mirror the dominant way race is currently conceptualized and operationalized in most higher education research (Johnston-Guerrero, 2017). Similarly, we use *multiracial* as referencing, pertaining to, or ascribing to the combination of two or more monoracially constructed groups (Morning, 2003). Accordingly, who or what is considered multiracial depends on what groups are considered "races" in a particular time (Daniel, 2001), keeping in mind that how people and groups are "raced" has real consequences for lived experience (Smedley & Smedley, 2005). We acknowledge here the unique and liminal positioning of Indigenous peoples as having political/tribal identities as well as being racialized (Brayboy, 2005), adding additional complexity to who is considered multiracial.

Building upon these concepts through the lens of racial formation theory, we understand *racism* to be a system of power that produces and maintains racial hegemony, including the notion of "pure races," through policies and ideas which normalize inequitable outcomes across racial groups (Kendi, 2019; Omi & Winant, 1994, 2014).[1] Racism can manifest in systemic, interpersonal, and subtle or explicit ways (see also Blum, 1999). It can target various groups, including racialized groups like Muslims (Modood, 2005) and immigrants (e.g., racist nativism; see Pérez Huber, 2010). Therefore, we acknowledge the existence of multiple racisms, which intersect with additional social positions such as class, gender, sexual orientation, and so on (Crenshaw, 1989; Garner, 2010). Explicitly acknowledging the formation of race and racism within broader societal contexts of the campus climate is a critical component of the CMCC.

The second ring represents the influence of local community contexts (Hurtado et al., 2012) and family contexts and history (Johnston-Guerrero & Pecero, 2016; Renn, 2004) on campus climate. The local ethnic communities, language(s) spoken, intergroup relations, and acceptance of multiracial people as in-group members vary by geographic region and history, as do their relations with the higher education institutions in their respective locales.

The third ring signifies the institutional campus climate for diversity, which includes historical, compositional, organizational, psychological, and behavioral dimensions (Milem et al., 2005) that account for both individual-level and institutional-level aspects of an organization (Hurtado et al., 2012). An example of an institution's *historical legacy of inclusion and exclusion* would matter in regard to how multiracial people were classified for purposes of admissions historically and how multiraciality is currently viewed, especially in the area of financial aid in relation to economic class and prior educational opportunity and consideration for diversity-related scholarships or support services. *Compositional diversity* is quite literally the numbers and percentages of demographic groups on campus, including students, staff, and faculty, and whether/how multiracial people are classified and accounted for when describing the diversity of the campus (Ford et al., 2019). The *organizational dimension* includes policies and resource allocation, as well as curriculum, an example of which would be the extent to which policies and curricular offerings reinforce monoracial norms. Finally, the *psychological and behavioral dimensions* embody individuals' values and attitudes and interpersonal and intergroup interactions, respectively. These individual-level dimensions are very intertwined; an illustration would be how members of monoracial groups categorize multiracial people potentially as in-group or out-group members (Pauker & Ambady, 2009) and the resulting implications on interactions between people who identify monoracially and multiracially.

These three rings represent ongoing racial formation dynamics between an institution's external contexts and its internal climate for diversity. These dynamics reproduce, mitigate, and challenge racial formation processes, as well as the resulting racialization of groups and systems of privilege and oppression. Racial formation takes shape both within and outside of college campuses, and these locations of racial formation recursively inform and influence one another. Structural or institutional racism (and monoracism) operates within the historical, compositional, and organizational dimensions of campus climate (i.e., institution level), and interpersonal racism is more evident in the psychological and behavioral dimensions (i.e., interpersonal level), although they are not mutually exclusive (Hurtado, Alvarez et al., 2012; Hurtado, Milem et al., 1998, 1999; Milem et al., 2005). For example, if multiracial people are not considered members of monoracial groups for purposes of affirmative action and financial aid at the institutional level, they may feel marginalized at the interpersonal level. Or, if curricular offerings largely reinforce monoracial norms and thus render multiraciality invisible at the institution level, not seeing oneself reflected in the curriculum may impact multiracial students' sense of validation and belonging, perceptions of campus climate, and racial identity development at the interpersonal level. As such, the racial dynamics represented by these outer rings collectively serve as context for the pie pieces that comprise the inner core of the model.

Pieces of a Pie: (Multi)Racialization and Identity Development Processes With Campus Climate as Context

Each slice of the pie in the core of the model represents interrelated factors to consider when planning or implementing efforts to improve the campus climate for diversity more broadly, and then specifically for multiracial students. We draw in part from Renn's (2004) ecological model for multiracial identity, which specifies proximal processes that influence student development, such as friendship groups and peer culture, classroom dynamics, curricular and cocurricular opportunities, and so on. We suggest that in these processes, educators and students can create more inclusive spaces that then collectively support transforming the campus racial climate. We also reason that the racial climate in each of those spaces and processes impacts a host of outcomes for multiracial students, similar to the campus climate research on monoracial student groups (Hurtado et al., 2012). Finally, we assert that the more proximal spaces and processes, and their respective racial dynamics, are both influenced by and are a part of ongoing racial formation and racism.

Monoracism

Whether people from nonwhite racial groups or communities can enact racism is hotly contested—this is the question of power (see chapter 4; Kendi, 2019). Racism that targets multiraciality is called *monoracism* (Hamako, 2014; Johnston & Nadal, 2010; see also chapter 4). Monoracism works to maintain the invisibility of monoracial norms and monoracial privilege, because the privileges accompanying people who fit monoracial constructions of race often go unnoticed or unchallenged. Each additional piece of the pie demonstrates different ways that monoracism and monoracial norms can manifest through the campus climate and influence student development and outcomes.

Background and Appearance

Individual-level characteristics, particularly one's physical appearance, cultural knowledge, socioeconomic status, and racial ancestry, are important factors influencing multiracial identity (Khanna, 2010; Renn, 2004, 2008; Wijeyesinghe, 2001) and are most clearly illustrative of a campus's compositional diversity. Individual-level characteristics likely influence multiracial students' perceptions and experiences of the climate for diversity. They are important factors in identity salience and development, include family and precollege socialization (Johnston-Guerrero & Pecero, 2016; Wijeyesinghe, 2001), and likely play out asymmetrically for students of different multiracial backgrounds (Harris, 2016; Johnston-Guerrero et al., 2020). These individual-level characteristics may be thought of in part as precollege characteristics, although they may also change through a student's time in college as racial identity develops (Harper, 2016). For example, a student's racial ancestry may be Native American and Latinx; if her physical appearance is racially ambiguous but she has deep cultural knowledge of both heritage groups and shares a socioeconomic status with most Native American and Latinx students at her college, she might identify with and be categorized as Native American and/or Latinx, as mixed, or her identity and categorization may shift depending on context or over time. However, if she physically appears Native American and has deep cultural knowledge of her native tribe but not her Latinx ethnic group, she might identify monoracially as Native American and be categorized as such. That said, if there are few students of color on campus, and most are Latinx, she may identify as Latinx and potentially be considered an in-group member even without deep cultural knowledge. Physical appearance, cultural knowledge, socioeconomic status, and racial ancestry may be important characteristics influencing how individuals and institutions racially categorize students and ascribe racial identities.

Racial Categorization

The classification and identity ascription of multiracial persons into racial categories may result in multiple different and sometimes contradictory categorizations. Racial classification may also depend on the extent to which there is a critical mass of multiracial students willing to organize around multiraciality, which may influence identity options in college (Renn, 2004). Racial categorization, and students' response to it, can be understood as an interaction between compositional diversity and the psychological and behavioral dimensions, including identity salience and the relative hegemony of monoracial constructions of race. Moreover, the implicit nature of cognitive frames, or categorical processing that we use to assess new experiences, may play a crucial role in how multiracial individuals may be perceived racially from one person to the next, resulting in shifting identity ascriptions and resulting racializations, based on the perceiver (Pauker & Ambady, 2009). Racial classification and identity ascription may be informed in part by cognitive flexibility, depth of intercultural competence, as well as the fluidity of peer culture and group boundaries (Gaither, 2015).

Multiracial Microaggressions

Racial classification can lead to multiracial microaggressions, which are tangible manifestations of monoracism that target students based on their mixed race status (Johnston-Guerrero & Renn, 2016). The concept of congruity is key here (Renn, 2004), as shifting racial identity ascriptions may be experienced as multiracial microaggressions or affirmations, depending in part on one's own cognitive frames and knowledge of systems of oppression (Johnston-Guerrero et al., 2020). For example, if a multiracial Asian Latinx student is perceived only as Asian but identifies as Asian, Latinx, and "mixed," the invisibility of their Latinx and mixed identities could be experienced as an invalidating multiracial microaggression. In contrast, if the same student was recognized as a multiracial Asian Latinx (congruent with their identity) and perceived to be an in-group member of either or both monoracial groups, this could result in affirmation. However, if monoracial stereotypes were attached to being Asian or Latinx, this student would also experience monoracial microaggressions in the same interaction, in which anti-Asian racism and anti-Latinx racism would manifest in addition to monoracism. Given the possibility of multiple different classifications, some multiracial students may experience a combination of multiracial microaggressions, monoracial microaggressions, *and/or* white privilege (e.g., Guillermo-Wann, 2012; Harris, 2017; Nadal et al., 2011).

Such multiplicity in experience exposes how monoracism and other forms of racism can intersect within the campus racial climate. Experiences will also differ based on additional social identities (e.g., gender), demonstrating further intersectionality (Crenshaw, 1989) and antiessentialism within multiraciality, in that multiracial people cannot be considered a single group that shares exactly the same experiences. Multiracial microaggressions have been shown to take place across multiple dimensions of the climate (Guillermo-Wann, 2012) and likely influence identity development in addition to identity salience and perceptions of campus climate (Hurtado et al., 2015).

Fluidity of Peer Culture and Group Boundaries
Fluidity of peer culture is another important factor influencing multiracial identity for college students, particularly regarding "peer-supported ability" of students to move between various social identity groups on campus (Renn, 2008, p. 19). This fluidity interacts across multiple dimensions of campus climate. In terms of psychological and behavioral dimensions, fluidity of peer culture is a combination of racial attitudes/perceptions (e.g., criteria for legitimate racial in-group status) and interactions across race (Hurtado et al., 1998, 1999). Compositional diversity of the climate may also influence the fluidity of peer culture depending on the representation of monoracially and multiracially constructed groups on campus. How one self-identifies in different contexts often depends on whom they are constructing their identity against (Wimmer, 2008), and the prevalence of monoracial norms in each context must also be considered.

Interest Convergence
Interest convergence is another key concept that offers insights into why different racial classifications may occur in varied contexts and over time. Originating from critical race theory (Bell, 1980; Delgado & Stefancic, 2001), interest convergence posits that because multiple forms of racism provide material benefits to white elites and psychological benefit to the white working class, white Americans will rarely be motivated to eradicate racism as a system of privilege and oppression. However, they may support specific

changes within the system when it serves their interests. We use interest convergence in the CMCC as a potential driving force that attaches dominant group intentions to subordinate group initiatives to produce outcomes favorable to the dominant group (Bell, 1980). For instance, the movement to allow individuals to "mark one or more" racial categories, and especially the early push to have a "multiracial box" in data collection processes, may be viewed as an example of interest convergence. That is, even if unintentional, the interests of multiracial individuals desiring more accurate identification options likely converged with monoracial white individuals (especially parents) wanting to allow multiracial people (especially their offspring) to be able to identify as something other than a person of color (particularly other than Black) (Spencer, 2010). In such ways, interest convergence with regard to multiraciality works to maintain the hierarchy of monoracially constructed whites in a more powerful social status (possibly through the creation of a middle-status multiracial group) (see Bonilla-Silva, 2010) in addition to colorism (see Kendi, 2019).

Equity in Student Outcomes
Students' perceptions of the campus climate for diversity influence numerous educational outcomes (Hurtado et al., 2012), making equity in outcomes across all demographic groups a strong driver for improving campus climate. Importantly, higher education outcomes, especially racial identity and racial consciousness as manifested by multiracial students (Malaney Brown, 2020), continually inform racial formation processes within larger society. When we start to see equity in outcomes across student groups, it may be a signal that the transformation of educational practice might be challenging the racial, cultural, and linguistic hegemony that has so plagued our nation from its beginning.

The CMCC maintains equity in student outcomes as its anchor to ensure that efforts to improve campus climate for multiraciality build and maintain strong alliances with monoracially identifying groups in the broader pursuit of DEI. These alliances will guard against previous perceptions of multiracial advocacy as being divisive, undermining, or threatening to monoracial student groups of color in particular (discussed earlier). In this sense, the CMCC acknowledges that higher education institutions, students, and the processes we engage in impact society in various ways, and places student equity and trajectories at the center.

The next section begins to apply theory to practice by offering prompts that support the use of the CMCC in campus DEI efforts that may ease the burden of toxic, racist, and monoracist environments by creating more validating and inclusive campuses. From the college president to the student affairs practitioner, student leader, professor, and beyond, each individual can make a difference every day. Whether through interactions between colleagues, staff, and students on an interpersonal level or revisions to policies and programs that teams design and implement at the institutional level, each person and role plays a part in the creation of an inclusive campus climate, subsequent racial formation, and evolution of power dynamics and culture.

Key Considerations by Job Type

This section is aimed at helping educators use positions of influence to continue to improve conditions for learning by providing key considerations for multiraciality in the form of questions, organized by three broad job types. Although certainly not exhaustive, this list of questions is designed to get individuals thinking, ideally with others in high-functioning teams (see Lencioni, 2002), about how to reexamine antiracist DEI efforts with a lens that challenges monoracial norms and includes multiraciality.

Institutional Leaders—Visioning, Planning, and Strategizing

- In what ways do the following guiding statements, documents, and entities at your institution embody a value of DEI? Is the institution's conceptualization of this value explicitly inclusive of multiraciality? What interests do various stakeholders have, and where might they converge? Where might opportunities lay to leverage interests to move DEI efforts from a multiracial standpoint forward?
  - Mission, vision, values
  - Strategic plan and other planning documents
  - Resource allocation (budget, staffing, organizational structure)
  - Policy and procedures
  - Governing board, executive leadership, middle management, staff and faculty composition and intercultural competence
- Describe the local community context of the institution, including the composition and dynamics among racial groups and potential influence on historical inclusion/exclusion and identity options. How fluid are group boundaries and cultural lines? What do leaders perceive as it relates to conflict, fear, or apathy, particularly as it relates to multiracial people or those who do not fit normative monoracial groups?
- Describe the racial composition and intergroup relations of the institution. How is the institution similar to and/or different from the

surrounding local community, particularly in relation to multiraciality? How might they influence one another? What does leadership need to be aware of in leading the institution within the local context? To what extent are the change management theories leaders use responsive to the community?

- What needs do members of monoracial and multiracial groups perceive they have? What voices are missing? What can leaders leverage to identify needs, coconstruct a vision, and plan for improvements? How can root causes of racism and monoracism be addressed through alignment with campus strategic planning processes?

- What is challenging about the CMCC model presented, both personally and professionally? Who might be trustworthy thought partners in processing these challenges and will maintain confidentiality and also support personal and professional growth?

- How do leaders' social identities inform how they lead in this context? How is each leader positioned to help implement the CMCC, based on their actual position in the organization? Based on their positionality in relation to their more and less privileged identities, including their relationship to multiraciality? How might leaders leverage privilege where they have it?

- What are three examples of institutional systems that may be reinforcing monoracial norms? What would multiracially identifying students say about these systems? (Are there ways to identify such a population, and are relationships between executive leaders and students such that executives could solicit constructive feedback?)

- To what extent are curriculum, instruction, assessment, research opportunities, and cocurricular activities structured to reinforce white privilege and monoracial privilege? To what extent are they inclusive and affirming of multiraciality and make monoracism visible?

- To what extent does leadership regularly review disaggregated data inclusive of multiraciality that provide feedback on the campus climate for diversity? How are those data embedded into institutional planning cycles? To what extent do the data contain information about various components of the CMCC?

Faculty and Staff—Working Directly With Students

- Who can faculty and staff work with to identify student needs and design potential solutions as they relate broadly to DEI and, more specifically, to multiraciality? What forms of support do faculty and staff need to engage in this work?

- List three examples of programs or practices that endorse discrete monoracial categories, maintain rigid group boundaries, or promote following of strict rules of hypodescent (e.g., the "one drop rule") in terms of racial identity and group membership. What opportunities might there be to make these programs or practices more inclusive of multiraciality?
- List three examples of existing efforts to improve campus climate for diversity. To what extent do they consider multiraciality? To what extent do they use intersectional perspectives? What opportunities might there be to make them more inclusive of multiraciality and intersectionality?
- What aspects of the CMCC model are faculty and staff interested in learning more about? How might that help teams of faculty and staff become more effective in campus DEI efforts?
- How are multiracial students classified regarding access to racial and ethnic organizations and breakout groups where race and racism are discussed? What interests might be at play in how multiracial students are classified or ascribed racial identities? To what extent do practices for engaging around race, ethnicity, and culture vary between courses and activities that already include diverse perspectives and those that do not yet incorporate diverse perspectives? What dimensions of the campus climate are at play?
- To what extent are curriculum, instruction, assessment, research opportunities, and cocurricular activities structured to reinforce white privilege, monoracial privilege, racism and monoracism? To what extent are they inclusive and affirming of multiraciality?
- To what extent is multiraciality accepted among different groups on campus? How do students experience multiraciality in relation to intersecting identities such as gender, sexual orientation, and economic status? How do you know? What evidence do you have (or not have and need)?
- How can faculty and staff ensure that student needs identified through these questions receive attention and support from campus leadership as well as students? How can root causes of racism and monoracism be addressed through alignment with campus strategic plans?

Institutional Researchers and Program Evaluators—Quantitative Data and Student Voice

- How are racial classifications decided? How is racial group and racial identity information gathered? To what extent might that policy and/ or practice contribute to how the fluidity of group boundaries may be perceived based on racial categorization in data use and storage? What flexibility exists in data collection, storage, and reporting?

- What interests might be converging that may directly and indirectly influence the ways in which individual-level characteristics are interpreted for racial categorizations? What may be the intended and unintended consequences of resulting racial classifications, particularly in the form of multiracial microaggressions? What may be some consequences of the converging interests at the institutional level?

- Does the institution promote the classification of racially mixed students as "multiracial" (e.g., through providing both a "multiracial" option and the ability to "mark one or more" on institutional racial demographic questions)? Why or why not?

- Are institutional researchers able to identify students, staff, and faculty who mark more than one racial category from demographic data? To what extent are data disaggregated or analyzed in flexible ways? How might racial categorization into or out of a monoracial group matter differently for different monoracial groups (i.e., racial asymmetries)?

- Describe qualitative data collection and analysis in relation to racial classification and campus climate for diversity. What opportunities might emerge to create flexible and inclusive practices? To what extent are student voices centered in qualitative information gathering and reporting?

- How often does the institution survey students, staff, and faculty to allow them to update their racial demographic information? How might institutions need to capture changes in multiracial identities as students develop over their time in college?

Moving Forward: Using the CMCC for Transformative DEI Efforts

The CMCC centers equity in student outcomes as the underlying reason institutions of higher education must engage in organizational transformation to improve the campus climate for diversity. It identifies key factors to consider in order to reduce toxic racial environments, particularly for multiracial students who may have been invisible due to the prevalence of monoracial norms, even in DEI-related efforts that bring a critical lens to the work. It informs the questions offered in this chapter that aid educators in applying theory to policy and practice in order to inform actual change efforts within colleges and universities. Ultimately the CMCC is both a framework and a tool that has various implications for organizational transformation around DEI.

First and foremost, the CMCC anchors campus climate for diversity and multiraciality in a broader societal context of racial formation and racialization processes (i.e., the "rings"), framing race as a social construction. This contextualization is crucial because doing so identifies multiple forms of racism as the root cause for toxic campus climates and inequitable student outcomes across racial groups. It asserts that multiraciality should be clearly established as an ally within larger efforts to dismantle all forms and systems of oppression. The CMCC also validates asymmetrical lived experiences of a campus climate among multiracially identifying groups and individuals due to the great heterogeneity among multiracial people. It charges educators with addressing institutional and interpersonal racism as a primary underlying cause for toxic racial environments and inequitable outcomes across these diverse groups and individuals.

Second, the inner core of the CMCC (i.e., the "pie pieces") names and makes visible specific phenomena that can inform how a campus approaches improving the climate for diversity. Specifically, the CMCC employs racial formation theory to clarify concepts of race, racism, and monoracism to ensure educators have a shared foundation on which to build inclusive campus climates for diversity. It highlights the importance of individuals' background and appearance in racial categorization and the fluidity of peer culture and group boundaries, which are key factors that can generate multiracial microaggressions across all dimensions of the campus climate. For example, the CMCC continues to encourage educators to consider multiple race data use and categorization in flexible ways as an aspect of the organizational dimension of campus climate, recognizing that mixed race individuals' racial identities may not align with federal and higher education racial reporting policies and practices. This categorization also needs to be considered in how students are identified for, or provided access to, information about racially conscious outreach and support programs (Johnston-Guerrero & Renn, 2016; Literte, 2010). The CMCC also highlights interest convergence as a key factor to consider in terms of interpersonal interactions as well as strategy at the institutional level for developing effective change efforts. Using the CMCC to focus on particular aspects of campus climate while also keeping in mind the larger systems at play will be helpful in organizational efforts to create diverse and inclusive campus climates for diversity.

These are some of the ways the CMCC can be used to further support higher education institutions in considering multiraciality in existing or future efforts to develop more diverse and inclusive campuses. We envision the CMCC being used in a collaborative, strategic manner to engage a broad base of key stakeholders, especially students, in planning, communicating, and implementing improvements to the campus climate for diversity. Although there may certainly be some "quick wins" easily identified and acted upon immediately with relative ease, it is crucial that those be balanced with intentional mid- and long-range planning processes at departmental and institutional levels. Depending on each campus's racial climate, how teams approach improving the campus climate may differ. Ideally, antiracist DEI efforts would become embedded into campuswide plans and actions as a lens through which all educational work is conducted, but we also recognize that some institutions may be in a place where racial climate efforts need to be developed rapidly under acute and toxic circumstances. Regardless of the approach, strong team-oriented leadership at multiple levels of an institution will facilitate deeper and more lasting organizational transformation, as systems for recursive feedback and communication will be critical for successfully implementing the CMCC. Our aspiration in considering multiraciality in campus climate is that the increasing efficacy of higher education institutions across the country will collectively contribute to the creation of a more just, equitable, and inclusive society.

Note

1. For an earlier theoretical discussion of racism in relation to the proposed model, see Guillermo-Wann and Johnston (2012).

References

Banaji, M. R., & Greenwald, A. G. (2016). *Blindspot: Hidden biases of good people.* Bantam.

Bell, D. (1980). *Brown v. Board of Education* and the interest convergence dilemma. *Harvard Law Review, 93,* 518–533. https://eric.ed.gov/?id=EJ219589

Blum, L. (1999). What is "racism" in antiracist education? *Teachers College Record, 100*(4), 860–880. https://www.tcrecord.org/Content.asp?ContentId=10345

Bonilla-Silva, E. (2010). *Racism without racists: Color-blind racism and racial inequality in contemporary America* (3rd ed.). Rowman & Littlefield.

Brayboy, B. M. J. (2005). Toward a tribal critical race theory in education. *The Urban Review, 37*(5), 425–446. https://doi.org/10.1007/s11256-005-0018-y

Cabrera, N. L. (2018). Where is the racial theory in critical race theory?: A constructive criticism of the Crits. *The Review of Higher Education, 42*(1), 209–233. https://doi.org/10.1353/rhe.2018.0038

Chang, M. J. (2000). Improving campus racial dynamics: A balancing act among competing interests. *The Review of Higher Education, 23*(2), 153–175. https://doi.org/10.1353/rhe.2000.0003

Crenshaw, K. (1989). Demarginalizing the intersection of race and sex: A Black feminist critique of antidiscrimination doctrine, feminist theory and antiracist politics. *University of Chicago Legal Forum, 1989*(1), 139–167. http://chicagoun bound.uchicago.edu/uclf/vol1989/iss1/8

Daniel, G. R. (2001). *More than Black: Multiracial identity and the new racial order.* Temple University Press.

Delgado, R., & Stefancic, J. (2001). *Critical race theory: An introduction.* NYU Press.

Ford, K. S., Patterson, A. N., & Johnston-Guerrero, M. P. (2019). Monoracial normativity in university websites: Systematic erasure and selective reclassification of multiracial students. *Journal of Diversity in Higher Education.* Advance online publication. https://doi.org/10.1037/dhe0000154

Gaither, S. E. (2015). "Mixed" results: Multiracial research and identity explorations. *Current Directions in Psychological Science, 24*(2), 114–119. https://doi .org/10.1177/0963721414558115

Garner, S. (2010). *Racisms: An introduction.* SAGE. http://dx.doi.org/10.4135/9781 446279106

Guillermo-Wann, C. (2012). *(Mixed) race matters: Racial theory, classification, and campus climate* [Doctoral dissertation, University of California, Los Angeles]. UCLA Electronic Theses and Dissertations. https://escholarship.org/uc/item/5jn7f86z

Guillermo-Wann, C., & Johnston, M. P. (2012, November). *Rethinking research on multiracial college students: Toward an integrative model of multiraciality for campus climate.* Paper presented at the Critical Mixed Race Studies Conference, Chicago, IL, United States. https://eric.ed.gov/?id=ED538027

Hamako, E. (2014). *Improving anti-racist education for Multiracial students* [Doctoral dissertation, University of Massachusetts, Amherst]. ScholarWorks. https:// scholarworks.umass.edu/dissertations_2/90

Harper, C. E. (2016). Pre-college and college predictors of longitudinal changes in multiracial college students' self-reported race. *Race Ethnicity and Education, 19*(5), 927–949. https://doi.org/10.1080/13613324.2014.911161

Harper, S. R. (2012). Race without racism: How higher education researchers minimize racist institutional norms. *The Review of Higher Education, 36*(1), 9–29. https://doi.org/10.1353/rhe.2012.0047

Harris, J. C. (2016). Toward a critical multiracial theory in education. *International Journal of Qualitative Studies in Education, 29*(6), 795–813. https://doi.org/10 .1080/09518398.2016.1162870

Harris, J. C. (2017). Multiracial college students' experiences with multiracial microaggressions. *Race Ethnicity and Education, 20*(4), 429–445. https://doi.org/10 .1080/13613324.2016.1248836

Hurtado, S., Alvarez, C. L., Guillermo-Wann, C., Cuellar, M., & Arellano, L. (2012). A model for diverse learning environments: The scholarship on creating and assessing conditions for student success. In J. C. Smart & M. B. Paulsen (Eds.), *Higher education: Handbook of theory and research* (Vol. 27, pp. 41–122). Springer. https://doi.org/10.1007/978-94-007-2950-6_2

Hurtado, S., Milem, J. F., Clayton-Pedersen, A. R., & Allen, W. R. (1998). Enhancing campus climates for racial/ethnic diversity: Educational policy and practice.

The Review of Higher Education, 21(3), 279–302. https://doi.org/10.1353/rhe.1998.0003

Hurtado, S., Milem, J. F., Clayton-Pedersen, A. R., & Allen, W. R. (1999). Enacting diverse learning environments: Improving the climate for racial/ethnic diversity in higher education. *ASHE-ERIC Higher Education Report, 26*(8). https://eric.ed.gov/?id=ED430514

Hurtado, S., Ruiz Alvarado, A., & Guillermo-Wann, C. (2015). Thinking about race: The salience of racial identity at two- and four-year colleges and the climate for diversity. *The Journal of Higher Education, 86*(1), 127–155. https://doi.org/10.1080/00221546.2015.11777359

Johnston, M. P., & Nadal, K. L. (2010). Multiracial microaggressions: Exposing monoracism in everyday life and clinical practice. In D. W. Sue (Ed.), *Microaggressions and marginality: Manifestation, dynamics and impact* (pp. 123–144). Wiley.

Johnston-Guerrero, M. P. (2017). The (mis)uses of race in research on college students: A systematic review. *JCSCORE, 3*(1), 6–41. https://doi.org/10.15763/issn.2642-2387.2017.3.1.5-41

Johnston-Guerrero, M. P., & Pecero, V. (2016). Exploring race, culture, and family in the identities of mixed heritage students. *Journal of Student Affairs Research and Practice, 53*(3), 281–293. https://doi.org/10.1080/19496591.2016.1165109

Johnston-Guerrero, M. P., & Renn, K. A. (2016). Multiracial Americans in college. In K. O. Korgen (Ed.), *Race policy and multiracial Americans* (pp. 139–154). Policy Press. https://doi.org/10.1332/policypress/9781447316459.003.0009

Johnston-Guerrero, M. P., Tran, V. T., & Combs, L. (2020). Multiracial identities and monoracism: Examining the influence of oppression. *Journal of College Student Development, 61*(1), 18–33. https://doi.org/10.1353/csd.2020.0001

Kendi, I. X. (2019). *How to be an antiracist.* One World, Penguin Random House.

Khanna, N. (2010). "If you're half black, you're just black": Reflected appraisals and the persistence of the one-drop rule. *Sociological Quarterly, 51*(1), 96–121. https://doi.org/10.1111/j.1533-8525.2009.01162.x

Lencioni, P. (2002). *The five dysfunctions of a team: A leadership fable.* Jossey-Bass.

Literte, P. E. (2010). Revising race: How biracial students are changing and challenging student services. *Journal of College Student Development, 51*(2), 115–134. https://doi.org/10.1353/csd.0.0122

Malaney Brown, V. (2020). *Exploring multiracial consciousness: Voices of multiracial students at a predominantly white institution* [Doctoral dissertation, University of Massachusetts, Amherst]. ScholarWorks. https://scholarworks.umass.edu/dissertations_2/1852

Milem, J. F., Chang, M. J., & antonio, a. j. (2005). *Making diversity work on campus: A research-based perspective.* Association of American Colleges & Universities. https://www.aacu.org/sites/default/files/files/mei/MakingDiversityWork.pdf

Modood, T. (2005). Remaking multiculturalism after 7/7. *Open Democracy, 29*(7), 1–7. https://www.opendemocracy.net/en/multiculturalism_2879jsp/

Morning, A. (2003). New faces, old faces: Counting the multiracial population past and present. In L. I. Winters & H. L. Debose (Eds.), *New faces in a changing America: Multiracial identity in the 21st century* (pp. 41–67). SAGE.

Nadal, K. L., Wong, Y., Griffin, K., Sriken, J., Vargas, V., Wideman, M., & Kola-wole, A. (2011). Microaggressions and the multiracial experience. *International Journal of Humanities and Social Sciences, 1*(7), 36–44. http://www.ijhssnet.com/journals/Vol._1_No._7_[Special_Issue_June_2011]/6.pdf

Omi, M., & Winant, H. (1994). *Racial formation in the United States: From the 1960s to the 1990s* (2nd ed.). Routledge.

Omi, M., & Winant, H. (2014). *Racial formation in the United States* (3rd ed.). Routledge.

Pauker, K., & Ambady, N. (2009). Multiracial faces: How categorization affects memory at the boundaries of race. *Journal of Social Issues, 65*(1), 69–86. https://doi.org /10.1111/j.1540-4560.2008.01588.x

Pérez Huber, L. (2010). Using Latina/o critical race theory (LatCrit) and racist nativism to explore intersectionality in the educational experiences of undocumented Chicana college students. *Educational Foundations, 24*, 77–96. https://eric.ed.gov/?id=EJ885982

Renn, K. A. (2004). *Mixed race students in college: The ecology of race, identity, and community on campus.* SUNY Press.

Renn, K. A. (2008). *Research on biracial and multiracial identity development: Overview and synthesis* (New Directions for Student Services, no. 123, pp. 13–21). Jossey-Bass. https://doi.org/10.1002/ss.282

Smedley, A., & Smedley, B. D. (2005). Race as biology is fiction, racism as a social problem is real: Anthropological and historical perspectives on the social construction of race. *American Psychologist, 60*(1), 16–26. https://doi.org/10.1037/0003-066X.60.1.16

Spencer, R. (2010). *Reproducing race: The paradox of generation mix.* Lynne Rienner.

Thornton, M. C. (2009). Policing the borderlands: White- and Black-American newspaper perceptions of multiracial heritage and the idea of race, 1996–2006. *Journal of Social Issues, 65*(1), 105–127. https://doi.org/10.1111/j.1540-4560.2008.01590.x

Wijeyesinghe, C. L. (2001). Racial identity in multiracial people: An alternative paradigm. In C. L. Wijeyesinghe & B. W. Jackson III (Eds.), *New perspectives on racial identity development: A theoretical and practical anthology* (pp. 129–152). NYU Press.

Wimmer, A. (2008). The making and unmaking of ethnic boundaries: A multilevel process theory. *American Journal of Sociology, 113*(4), 970–1022. https://doi.org/10.1086/522803

Yosso, T., Smith, W., Ceja, M., & Solórzano, D. (2009). Critical race theory, racial microaggressions, and campus racial climate for Latina/o undergraduates. *Harvard Educational Review, 79*(4), 659–691. https://doi.org/10.17763/haer.79.4.m6867014157m707l

12

BUILDING MULTIRACIAL AIKIDO

A Student Social Justice Retreat

Charlene C. Martinez and Stephanie N. Shippen

This chapter tells the story of the planning and practice of Multiracial Aikido, a weekend experiential learning retreat created for students at Oregon State University (OSU). The OSU campus is situated within the occupied territories and ancestral homelands of the Ampinefu or Marys River Band of the Kalapuya peoples, a location more commonly known as Corvallis, a small college town an hour and a half south of Portland, Oregon. In sharing the purpose, outcomes, and process of the retreat we hope to offer a model for how people and groups can create spaces to discuss the complexity of identity from multiracial perspectives. To our knowledge it is the only retreat of its kind that supports unpacking the complex interactions between multiracial identity and processes of racialization through an aikido framework, as further discussed in the following paragraphs.

Throughout the chapter we lend insights gained from several years of experience iterating the Multiracial Aikido retreat and community building efforts. We provide examples of a few activities that align with the purpose and outcomes of the retreat. Finally, we recount our approach by mapping relevant principles from adrienne maree brown's (2017) book *Emergent Strategy: Shaping Change, Changing Worlds*, in hopes of inspiring others to adopt similar methods centering adaptation, attention to relationships, and embodiment exercises.

From 2016 to 2020, we held five annual Multiracial Aikido retreats, trained 37 staff facilitators and mentors (undergraduate and graduate students), and provided opportunities for nearly 80 undergraduate and graduate students to participate in this unique experience. As documenters of

161

the development of the Multiracial Aikido retreat, we acknowledge that we were not the first people to begin talking about multiraciality in our region. Nor were we the only people involved in the creation of the retreat. It is important to note that Multiracial Aikido is made possible by handfuls of people before us doing the work of bridge building for multiracial students at OSU. However, we do see ourselves as having been critical in connecting the dots and organizing this project to come to fruition. The creation of the activities and organizing for mixed heritage communities in this region is what contributor Martinez calls a "heart hustle," or work that is fueled by the intersection of love and purpose toward social justice. Over time, shared dedication to this love and purpose helped the retreat grow through the hard work and energy of staff volunteers, along with the support of critical leaders who have come to understand the importance of our work on behalf of multiracial students. We also wish to honor the participants of Multiracial Aikido, past, present, and future, as they continue to be contributors to the evolving nature of the curriculum.

Before moving on, we offer a note on our use of terminology and language. Throughout this chapter we use a few terms interchangeably. We know that identification markers are highly subjective, problematic, and political, yet are meaningful and loaded with implications on the individual and structural levels. We initially used the term *multiracial* in the title of the retreat because it seemed to resonate with the way students of multiple races/ethnicities identified themselves. As with all terms, there is not one word that encapsulates all of the populations we serve. Students who are transracial adoptees did not quite see themselves in the name of the retreat, nor did some of those who identify as biracial or multiethnic. We use the terms *multiracial, mixed heritage*, and *mixed race* interchangeably to talk about those people who identify with more than one race or ethnicity.

Multiracial Aikido Background and History

Multiracial Aikido is modeled after the Racial Aikido retreat curriculum developed at the University of Vermont (UVM) in 2006. The UVM founders of Racial Aikido built the curriculum around the aikido martial art principles to equip students of color with tools to navigate microaggressions and learn how to shift internal energies in order to survive and thrive at their predominantly white institution (S. Kwist, personal communication, November 18, 2016). After learning about the retreat, OSU colleagues brought Racial Aikido to OSU in 2009 and have grown the program since that time. OSU's Racial Aikido maintains a reputation on campus as being a healing and transformative space for students and staff of color. A year later, in 2010 the Examining White Identity in a Multicultural World retreat was launched as an immersive learning experience to help students locate, identify, and disrupt white supremacy, culture, and privilege. These two social justice retreats, which preceded Multiracial Aikido, were constructed as learning community spaces grounded in antiracist curriculum, yet were created within monoracial frames. Shortly after Multiracial Aikido was formed came a fourth retreat, International Student Social Justice, focused on the particular needs of international students and global paradigms and experiences. Together the four retreats fall under the Social Justice Retreats Collaborative within the Division of Student Affairs at OSU.

Multiracial Aikido follows the framework of Racial Aikido, shifting the purpose slightly to create an immersive opportunity for mixed heritage identity exploration through the naming of participants' social locations and experiences and deepening self-awareness of their emotions surrounding their lived experiences as mixed people. The need for this retreat emerged out of a campus drop-in support group and multiple oral history projects in which mixed heritage students communicated their desire to do deeper learning around their experiences.

Borrowing Racial Aikido's core tenets, the Multiracial Aikido retreat follows the curricular flow of four areas: Respect, Recognize, Respond, and Replenish. The first section of the retreat, *Respect*, focuses on creating a retreat atmosphere based on respect for self and others. This includes identifying hopes and fears for the weekend, committing to group agreements, and clarifying expectations for the retreat. We introduce mindfulness practice during Respect and continue to infuse activities that encourage presence throughout the retreat. The next section, *Recognize*, explores multiracial identity concepts and dives into the contextual factors such as power, privilege, and systems of oppression that influence one's lived experience. During Recognize, we consider the impact of living in a racialized society and how each person experiences the world differently based on their multiple intersecting identities. In the third section, *Respond*, we explore basic concepts of aikido to help participants find ways to respond to harmful racialized experiences. We highlight somatic practices that help protect, deflect, counter, and heal from racism. The final section, *Replenish*, gives participants a chance to let go of hurtful experiences, build self-care practices, and have fun together.

Initially, the activities were borrowed and adapted from other practitioners, and some were generated and inspired by multiracial identity theories and research. The process has been largely experimental and has taken handfuls of facilitators to create what is currently offered today. The first team of facilitators designed the curriculum based on their understanding of

Racial Aikido. Malinda Shell and Kim McAloney were staff members who had experiences at OSU as undergraduate and graduate students. Jon Stoll was new to the campus and had a personal investment to connect with multiracial communities. All three individuals were trained as Racial Aikido facilitators at OSU. Because they had experienced Racial Aikido as multiracial individuals, they could offer firsthand ideas to contribute to the emerging Multiracial Aikido curriculum. They also had feedback from mixed heritage students who had attended Racial Aikido and were left with more questions and a desire to explore their multiracial identities. Concurrently, Shippen and Martinez began offering a weekly support group on campus for students identifying as multiethnic, multiracial, biracial, two or more races, or transracial adoptee students. During the sessions, group members expressed the need and desire for more connection, knowledge, and support. Together we (McAloney, Shell, Stoll, Martinez, and Shippen) worked to adapt the original Racial Aikido curriculum to fit the unique needs of multiracial students. Merging the Racial Aikido curriculum with the support group spirit led to the creation of the first Multiracial Aikido retreat.

Retreat Purpose and Outcomes

Although the overarching purpose and outcomes of the retreat offer a compass for our approach, the facilitation team is accustomed to tailoring the activities to the needs of each cohort. The questions from the "interest form" students fill out are intended for the participant to engage in self-reflection on their experiences as well as serve as an indicator of what to expect if selected to participate in the retreat. The purpose of the 2-and-a-half day immersive learning opportunity is to offer participants a supportive environment for students, facilitators, and mentors to lean into

- the connectedness in mixedness,
- unpacking identity, and
- all of the complexities.

By the end of the retreat, we would like participants to explore their cultural and racial identities through storytelling, become aware of systems of oppression, gain listening and empathy skills, and build a community of peers. We utilize the framework of aikido to help us achieve our purpose and outcomes.

Why Aikido?

Everyone has a spirit that can be refined, a body that can be trained in some manner, a suitable path to follow. You are here for no other purpose than to realize your inner divinity and manifest your inner enlightenment. Foster peace in your own life and then apply the Art [of Peace] to all that you encounter. (M. Ueshiba, as quoted in Dietrich & Wagner, 2015, p. 12)

The practice of aikido starts with the individual becoming aware of where one is in relation to themselves and others. This involves cultivating embodied awareness along with an amicable relationship with change and conflict and using our ability to innovate toward healing (Moon, 1997). Aikido practices require personal effort in order to achieve inner peace and effect positive change. The founder of aikido, Morihei Ueshiba, suggested that we must practice a deeper engagement with ourselves as a key component to healing ourselves and the world and that only when we know ourselves can we effectively enter combat or engage with others' energies. We must have awareness in the present moment to be able to recognize our own energy, feelings, and emotions, and where they come from. According to Moon (1997), having an amicable relationship with change means that we work with what is happening around us rather than fighting against this energy.

The spirit of aikido implores us to slow down the agenda and create a safer, braver environment for people to share their stories. As brown (2017) in *Emergent Strategy* stated, it is imperative that people "value the process as much as, if not more than, you value the outcomes" (p. 230). Wagner (2015) added that nonviolent communication requires compassion and bravery beginning with the self and expressed in community with others. Additionally, Haroun (2015) shared that

as we have become honest and sincere like a mirror, we develop wisdom and foster friendship with others. Such honesty is linked with purity and is fostered through *aikido* and *misogi* [the art of purifying our bodies]. It furthermore requires courage because it is not easy to open ourselves to others. Yet, it is crucial in order to communicate non-violently with each other. Through being aware of our presence in the here and now, having empathy and compassion, and being honest, sincere and brave, the energy of most inter-personal conflicts can be transformed from a destructive to a constructive one. (p. 110)

We use this aikido framework as a philosophy and a tool. We tell participants that the aikido principles can help them navigate challenging situations that come their way. For many participants in Multiracial Aikido this is the first time they have been able to tell their stories of being racialized. The

Multiracial Aikido curriculum prioritizes assisting students to connect with themselves by practicing exercises that ground them in the present moment. This helps them to gain access to their thoughts, feelings, and experiences related to being multiracial. We help them make meaning of their experiences within their respective communities by paying attention to how their bodies hold experiences, memories, and feelings. We encourage them to work with what is there for them without needing to change it or fight against it. And we encourage them to engage in reflective practices that activate a healing mindset.

These aikido principles work well to effectively shape our design of Multiracial Aikido. They provide a guide that helps us create an intentional space where students can process the complexities of their identities. We hear from students that they value opportunities to be with others who can connect with the complexity of mixed heritage identities, especially as students in a predominantly white institution. Our belief is that a pivot point for students is when they feel validated and affirmed for "being enough," which helps them tap into their power and facilitates the process of healing.

These aikido skills can be useful when exploring our identities and navigating difficult situations. When we are present and aware, we can work with whatever is challenging us and use our energy to respond and create the outcome that works best for us. Sadly, these skills are often not prioritized or nurtured in higher education. Yet developing them helps us connect with ourselves, decreases our sense of isolation, and protects us from the impact of harmful experiences.

Multiracial Aikido Curriculum: Selected Activities

In this section we highlight storytelling, embodiment exercises, and multiracial knowledge building as distinct curricular components that have helped us to create an environment for meaningful engagement at Multiracial Aikido. We also offer a few activities from the curriculum. Doing the important groundwork of evaluating the environment by finding out the needs and consciousness of individuals and committing to relationship building with people interested in elevating the conversation around multiraciality should precede the implementation of activities. Once the groundwork is established, one can better meet the needs of communities, especially understanding the unique and often dissimilar dynamics of mixed heritage individuals and communities in your environment.

Our retreat always begins with introductions and intention setting. Ample time is spent establishing guidelines for safer, braver spaces (Roper, 2019), inviting participants to articulate and cocreate the kind of environment needed for them to engage authentically. We draw upon brown's (2017) group agreements from her "toolkit for emergent strategy facilitation" (p. 140) to begin the conversation on how to be in community with each other in the retreat space. We also emphasize that participants can opt out of any activity and encourage them to take care of themselves (and that facilitators will check in with them as needed). By the time we begin our first small group activity, story circles, students have already shared some of their hopes and intentions, as well as expressed their needs for full engagement.

Story Circles as a Vehicle for Storytelling

Story circles originated through community organizing and popular education (Slowiak, 2017). We use the story circles protocol, adapted from the U.S. Department of Arts and Culture (2015), Slowiak (2017), and Martinez (2019), to build rapport and trust among participants during the first night. This activity is particularly powerful for creating an intentional space where each participant can bring their voices and experiences into the group by sharing personal stories related to their racial and ethnic identities (Hill, 2017).

Story circles begin when everyone is asked to "locate" a single moment or string of moments and then, in small groups, process their specific lived experiences as multiracial, multiethnic, mixed heritage, or transracial adoptee people. Facilitators begin by sharing their stories, to set the tone and provide a model. In doing so, they change the dynamic of staff serving as facilitators, as they must demonstrate and embrace their vulnerability from the start. For many of the students, this experience is the first time they have shared their respective stories among other mixed heritage individuals, or anyone at all. As one Multiracial Aikido student reflected, this moment of sharing submerged or painful experiences with others can be a powerful moment, with each story actually encouraging and prevalidating the next. One participant noted, in an evaluation of the program:

> Story circles require that each voice is treated with dignity and respect. The affirmation of each voice, each story, leads participants to a place of vulnerability that allows for the deep sharing of ourselves. Because the story circle is an established safe space, I could re-experience traumatizing episodes in my life that have to do with my mixed identity. I learned more about myself and how deeply I was impacted by the "othering" that folks have done to me. (Graduate student, Multiracial Aikido participant)

Past participants report the experience of telling stories in this format allows for genuine empathy building. Participants find that listening to someone else's story requires a deepening of their attention to see and hear another person. The energy in the group's space takes on the shape of the stories that are shared in that group. Each story circle group becomes a unique and often treasured space, opening up possibilities for new ways of being not typically experienced while on campus. These environments create opportunities for connections to form and relationships to build among diverse mixed peoples. Participants appreciate hearing the diverse experiences and, despite being mixed with different racial and ethnic combinations, often express a comfort in connecting through feelings of not belonging or "enoughness" within one's own racial or ethnic identity groups—themes evident in the words of a participant:

> Participating in story circles and sharing my story uninterrupted by others felt incredibly validating and affirming. For many of us that exist in "mixed" bodies that are marginalized by society, it is not all that often that we are heard with full attention, even by our own families. Story circles provide an opportunity for us to listen and speak fully. (Graduate student, Multiracial Aikido participant)

The depth of sharing that happens in such a short amount of time creates a culture that encourages connection through shared vulnerability. Because each individual has a unique story, participants give voice to what is salient in their social locations for that moment. What is important to each person varies, and sometimes their stories are not related to their heritage or background. For some people, geography is important to name; for others, spirituality, the role of family, or being raised in another country are central themes. Many participants resonate with hearing about stories of others who are grappling with navigating microaggressions within their respective communities. Given that the permutations of racial and ethnic backgrounds from one individual to the next are endless, the kinds of stories that are shared are vast and eye-opening. Story circles offers a way of creating a container for this varied collection of stories to surface and be held together in a humanizing way. A retreat facilitator noted:

> Participating in these story circles highlighted for me the complexity and messiness of experiencing race as a mixed-race person. But this is good messiness, the kind that generates new meaning and perspectives on aspects of my lived experience that I had not considered until I hear someone else bring them to life.

Embodiment Exercises

We aim to facilitate growth, transformation, and healing throughout the retreat. We work to achieve this by prioritizing experiential learning and then providing space for processing. Most of the weekend's activities are designed to engage participants' senses, creating unusual or unexpected approaches and thus evoking new understanding and insight. Rather than staying solely cerebral and academic, we value the wisdom that comes from turning our attention inward and sensing from within, especially because we all already have an established and "scripted" story about ourselves. After each exercise, participants use journals to explore thoughts, feelings, and ideas, and we provide ample opportunities to share in dyads, small groups, and as a large group.

We make sure that participants know when we are going to do an embodiment exercise activity and (as indicated earlier) encourage them to make alterations based on their physiological, mental, or emotional needs. This might look like inviting them to open their eyes for a closed-eye activity or moving to a location in the room that feels better to them. Participants can always opt out of activities as well. We find that embodied approaches bring the learning from the head to the heart, and participants are able to consolidate their learning more readily. Given the frequent experience of multiracial folks experiencing invalidation even from those people closest to them, this may be the first or only time they have felt seen and heard as a multiracial person. It is important to give students time to digest the new learning that is taking place by offering a variety of formats to reflect and process, which includes journaling, pair sharing, small group/large group sharing, and using art.

Using a trauma-informed lens helps us to understand the impact of racial trauma (Bryant-Davis & Ocampo, 2006). We introduce participants to basic psychoeducation regarding how racism affects a person and how one's reactions can be stored and experienced in the body and mind. The window of tolerance (Treleaven & Britton, 2018) describes the amount of space we have for coping before becoming overwhelmed or withdrawn. We use this concept to explain how trauma narrows our window, making it harder to cope with stressors in life (Treleaven & Britton, 2018). We explore ways to identify how we are each affected by racism, bringing fuller awareness to emotions and areas needing attention. We also provide strategies that help increase our capacity to cope and heal. Although some of the facilitators are mental health professionals, we are mindful that introducing this information is not a substitute for seeking mental health services, and we discuss how participants can access services as needed.

Foundational Resources for Multiracial People

After participants begin building relationships and comfort with each other, we introduce theories and practice of multiracial or mixed heritage research. Because it is an immersive retreat setting rather than a class, we aim to make the content digestible. We are constantly working to provide necessary content without cramming an entire ethnic studies curriculum into a few hours. We want this part of the retreat to be informative, accessible, and experiential. We have found that striking the right balance can be challenging as each participant comes to the retreat with varying degrees of consciousness and knowledge around racial justice issues. Although we value the exploration of one's personal identities, we see the importance of understanding our multiracial experiences within a U.S. and global context. In order to cultivate antiracist practices, we must understand how historical, institutional, systemic, and interpersonal systems of oppression directly affect each of us, depending on our social identities.

We spend time reflecting on the *Bill of Rights for People of Mixed Heritage* (originally the *Bill of Rights for Racially Mixed People*; Root, 1996), which was created by the preeminent leader in multiracial studies, Maria P. P. Root. This document serves to empower mixed heritage people to feel they have the right to choose how they view themselves and how they navigate the world. Participants often share how reading the Bill of Rights validates their experiences and helps them feel seen.

The following activities help participants place the multiracial experience within a broader context. We show sections of Shakti Butler's (2012) powerful documentary *Cracking the Codes: The System of Racial Inequity* to encourage reflection on how these systems harm and/or benefit multiracial people. We also utilize Walidah Imarisha's (2015) scholarship on the antiblack history and policies in Oregon by showing her recorded talk "Why Aren't There More Black People in Oregon?" This video sheds light on the long-standing history of anti-Black policies in Oregon that continue to influence the experience of Black people and people of color in Oregon. After presenting this material to participants, we set aside time for journaling and group discussions. While helping students map their stories onto a broader context, we invite them to consider tangible ways that they can work toward racial justice. The *Multiracial Oath of Responsibility* (Root, 2004) is a seminal document that we share with students as a way to highlight the collective responsibility that we share as racialized beings. Shifting internal energies toward healing opens the possibility of helping participants develop a change agent mindset.

Each year that we have held the retreat, students enter with the hopes of addressing privilege in multiracial identity, especially if they have light skin or white passing privilege. This conversation is particularly germane in Corvallis, Oregon. In the winter of 2019, of the 7% (1,649) of enrolled students who identified as two or more races, 94% identified as white plus another person of color group (Martinez et al., 2019). In addition to the demographics, in Martinez and Shippen's documentation of needs throughout the years, we recognized that we needed to address the conversation of being white/and with students. We introduced the *Bill of Responsibilities for Multiracial People of Color With Light Skin and White Passing Privilege* (Ito, 2019) as a way to understand skin colorism and how we may benefit or be harmed by these types of privilege. Participants have responded with appreciation in becoming aware of and attuned to literature and models which reinforce their experience and affirm their existence.

Deepening the Conversation Through the Fishbowl Exercise and Interest-Based Spaces

Activities that allow for honest and vulnerable dialogue have the biggest impact for participants. We use both fishbowl and interest-based spaces to explore topics of salience for the group. We have used the fishbowl exercise to address important topics, such as unpacking whiteness, identifying how antiblackness is maintained and perpetuated, discussing the history and complexities of Indigeneity and multiraciality, and exploring how family dynamics plays a role in the experience of multiracial people. The stories that we as the professional staff team have heard have led us to deeper discussions around how to hold space for students when it comes to complex conversations within mixed heritage communities. This has included recognizing the need for having dialogues around centering and (de)centering whiteness, antiblackness in the Asian Pacific Islander (API) community, Indigenous identity/history, and activism in college.

Another activity that students respond enthusiastically to is participation in interest-based groups. The interest-based groups are determined by issues or themes that participants mention throughout the duration of the retreat and would like to explore further. This activity was adapted from the race immersion experience held by angel Kyodo williams (2018) in Portland, Oregon. We brought this activity to Multiracial Aikido because we were inspired by being able to deepen a conversation with an interest area of salience for the participants. For instance, interest-based small group discussions combine a primary objective of the retreat, exploration of mixed heritage identity, along with another area of inquiry that is active for the participants. As the retreat goes on, facilitators track areas of interest or common themes. We begin this activity by giving participants suggestions for what the group conversations could cover and then crowdsource other ideas in real time. Topics that have been explored include queer identity, Indigeneity, antiblackness, mental health, spirituality, advancing social justice on campus, family dynamics, interracial dating, monoracism, being of multiple people of color groups, and white passing privilege.

To end the retreat, we engage participants in an exercise to articulate emerging commitments based on their areas of growth or interest. We ask the students and facilitators to contemplate the stories they have accessed during the retreat and where they would like to continue doing social change work. Participants then share these commitments out loud and do further reflection in the journals. It is also at this time that we reiterate that this is a retreat experience and refer students to resources available to them on campus for further education, including taking a course focused on race or getting involved with a variety of related cocurricular activities.

Students return from Multiracial Aikido with positive assessments of the fishbowl, interest-based discussions, and story circles. They report that these are some of the most meaningful engagements of the entire retreat. We believe that the placement of these dialogic exercises throughout the retreat is also important. We try to move from focusing our energy and attention inward to exploring thoughts, feelings, and ideas with others. This oscillation between self-reflection and community sharing maps well with the principles of aikido and how self-understanding is necessary in deepening connection with others.

Centering Emergent Strategy Principles as Our Compass

Attending to the complexity of multiracial identity requires that we use an iterative and adaptive approach to meet the needs of students. Multiracial Aikido is iterative and adaptive at its core. Each year we work to adjust the curriculum and our facilitation approach to respond to the needs articulated by students in their "interest forms" or needs that arise in the moment during the retreat. In *Emergent Strategy: Shaping Change, Changing Worlds*, adrienne maree brown's (2017) collection of philosophies draws upon the wisdom of community organizers and cultural workers who have found ways to navigate change in service of building a better, more just world. Emergent strategy philosophies parallel our design and orientation to create a dynamic and responsive retreat. Similarly, brown (2017) urges us to deeply listen to people and be willing to navigate environments with attention to organic energy and embodiment practices, to use an openness to adaptation, and to trust in the process (and each other) to develop intentional strategies responding to what matters most.

Reflecting on brown's work led us to realize that we have employed emergent strategies from the very beginning of our work. Our intentions and practices within Multiracial Aikido align closely with brown's core principles. As developers of a new program, there were times when we questioned whether or not we were attending to the right dynamics or learning outcomes. We gained confidence in our approach and growth as leaders once we saw our process reflected back to us through the emergent strategies framework. The principles now help us make meaning of our process and confidently ground our practices as we iterate for multiracial populations. In particular, the following emergent strategies continue to provide guideposts that allow us to do the work of activating multiracial individuals toward antiracist action:

- Intentional adaptation—revisiting and resetting intentions and processes
- Critical relationships over critical mass—building depth is more productive than increasing numbers
- Somatics—integrating embodiment exercises, meditations, and activities to nourish the mind, body, and soul

Because *intentional adaptation* means responding to change while centering and caring for the needs of people, we had to tinker with the purpose and outcomes until we were satisfied with the balance of personal and political objectives. In this process we asked ourselves critical questions. Was it enough to focus on identity development? Did we have the right recipe for the insertion of curriculum that addressed systemic, historical, and institutional factors of race in the United States? Was our focus on community building accurate? Did we have the tools as facilitators to attend to the process effectively? Ultimately, the postretreat conversations with participants and facilitators deepened our program's effectiveness and served as opportunities to refine our process.

Likewise, based on the events that transpired during and after past retreats, we shifted away from our original goal of "community building." We realized that just because we were all of mixed heritage did not mean we held similar perspectives and lived experiences of race in the United States. We also needed to not presume that people needed or wanted to find community, especially with this being the first time many people connected with other multiracial/ethnic or mixed heritage individuals. Although we knew this at the onset, we had to experience the retreat in real time to be able to assess the implications of our activities and how participants experienced them. Our abilities to remain present, to evaluate, and then adapt were guided by both aikido principles as well as iterative and adaptive emergent strategies.

Relationships precede the desire to move to action, not the other way around. brown (2017) emphasized that genuine community building must "move at the speed of trust" (p. 42). Thus, any successful and collaborative project needed to "focus on critical connections more than critical mass— build the resilience by building the relationships" (brown, 2017, p. 42). Our relationship building efforts with staff (especially those who would later become facilitators and supporters of the retreat) allowed us to form a professional foundation for community building around mixed heritage issues. Capacity building included understanding the tensions and needs of staff who were ambivalent about the project of elevating multiracial under-standing and awareness. This process of understanding the landscape of our campus climate allowed us to empathize with communities of color who were doing their best to retain cultural practices in the Pacific Northwest. Sometimes leaders of these cultural/ethnic/racial communities would unknowingly dismiss mixed heritage people who were of "their own" racial identity group, as well as those of other racial groups. Although it was a slow process, deepening relationships and bringing qualitative data to influential leaders who supported community building in racialized groups ultimately cultivated reciprocal relationships and mutual understanding on common ground. What crystallized for us became the need to serve students who held multiple racial and ethnic identities in more strategic ways while utilizing aikido strategies as an everyday practice.

Each year we remark on how easy it is for the facilitation team to get along and work together in a supportive and seamless manner. This isn't to say that we haven't faced stressors as we prepare for the retreat, and even once we are there. In our prioritization of *critical relationships*, however, we have invested time and energy toward cultivating a cohesive and trusting atmosphere. We challenged ourselves to do our own work as a team and were intentional about how we showed up for each other before, during, and after the retreat. When we encountered challenges and discomfort, we moved at the speed of trust. As the core group retreat facilitators transformed individu-ally and collectively as practitioners, so did our work, the curricular efforts, and outcomes of our activities. This ended up spilling beyond our immediate work, helping to also raise the consciousness of colleagues within the division of student affairs about mixed heritage students and the importance of sup-porting them in more appropriate and effective ways.

According to emergent strategies principles, we all need to be intentional and actively find ways to sustain ourselves through the long haul of social justice organizing. This requires integrating practices which center internal healing and navigational tools for personal sustainability. Discussing *somat-ics*, brown (2017) wrote about using "spells" (p. 191) and practices to assist in transforming energy. She specifically named aikido martial arts and meditation as embodied practices designed to increase one's ability to transform negative energy and trauma. These practices offer the tools to lead fully expressed resilient lives, on purpose (brown, 2017). With Shippen's training as a psychologist, therefore, we were more intentionally able to infuse embodiment exercises with a sensitivity to trauma and resiliency.

We believe that our ability to smoothly navigate through challenges results from our commitment to each other's wholeness. In higher education, all too often we put transaction before relationship. In social justice education, however, it is imperative that we lead with joy and connection at the center. After all, if we don't enact the values of liberatory practice and don't believe a better world is possible, then why are we engaging in the work?

Concluding Thoughts

Participants in Multiracial Aikido reflect back an experience that is cathartic and empowering. The stories shared during the retreat enable participants and facilitators to have unique conversations they are not typically able to have with their family, friends, classmates, instructors, or peer groups. The effects of the retreat confirm that students leave with a stronger understanding of and connection to their racial/ethnic identities, confidence in their stories, a sense of community, and value in naming and sharing emotions. These are important outcomes that can be achieved in other spaces, with other groups.

For those readers interested in creating some kind of retreat space for multiracial students, we offer the following suggestions: Go at your own speed. If you are a practitioner curious about beginning a journey of supporting students on campus, or building a community of mixed heritage folks locally, know that the path may be ambiguous but has the potential to be life-giving and rewarding. Although we drew resources from a variety of places, we also learned we need to listen to ourselves, make adjustments based on conversation and feedback, and be open to failure. All of this has been part of the iterative process. We recognize that how we enter the space and facilitate with intention carries more weight than the activities themselves. This is why we would encourage anyone to start by identifying their inner resources and creating a network of support.

In times when we were unclear about our approach, we returned to our intentions and reflected back on two of brown's core questions for returning to purpose and process: "What do we need to be and do to bring our vision to pass? How do we bring those intentions to life throughout every change, in every aspect of our work?" (brown, 2017, p. 70). Emergent strategy taught us how to refocus a liberatory framework beginning with the transformation of the individual.

Turning to what we could control, we revisited our facilitator training meetings to do deeper work with how we would show up with students. Each facilitator training meeting became an opportunity to practice storytelling with each other and develop a community of support that did not exist outside the space. This attention to the nurturance of developing our capacity to tell our own stories of mixedness became paramount in our ability to be present with ourselves and each other. This ongoing effort contributes to healing and the replenishment of faculty and staff, teaches about the complexities and nuances of race, and helps with retention at OSU. We strongly believe that how we approach this work as a facilitation team directly affects the level of depth and transformation that can occur over a 2-and-a-half-day retreat. It's not only what we offer participants in terms of activities but also how we show up for participants and each other that makes this a memorable experience.

Thus, before diving into any intervention or idea, we suggest building a small team of staff, faculty, or student leaders who are willing to contribute their strengths and continue coming to the table, especially when conversations are difficult or tense. We realize that our successes have largely been due to a committed and caring group of student affairs professionals who devoted their time and energy to developing these efforts. We have privileged those critical relationships over any drive to produce some artificially scaled-up sense of critical mass.

It is worthwhile to find a supportive off-campus network. We sought advice and expertise from Marc P. Johnston-Guerrero and Sabrina Kwist, leaders in the field around multiraciality and curriculum building. These kinds of people can check your process and give constructive feedback rooted in perspectives outside of any specific institutional culture, which can derail new ideas more quickly than most realize. When reaching out, be open to possibilities, let go of things not serving the larger purpose, and then reengage with more stories and more ideas.

It is important to build (whether as a retreat or something else) the ability and willingness to lean into tension (brown, 2017). Although it is not always easy to tackle the more difficult topics, it is absolutely necessary if we want to build stronger bridges interpersonally and systemically. We need to remind each other that we don't have to share the same perspective in order to be in connection with others. Working in coalition always means working across groups and values. This is why we focus on turning inward and doing our own work rather than focusing on the work that others need to do for themselves. This approach should bring more people with varying perspectives into the conversation.

We always feel honored to witness the growth of students, peers, and ourselves through each retreat experience. Each year we return from Multiracial Aikido inspired by the stories, connection points, and encouragement shared by participants. This dynamic experience is made possible through each cohort's energy and contributions. To witness Multiracial Aikido participants bravely engaging in the work of personal exploration, internal healing, and community engagement gives us hope that change is not only possible but happening in real time. Reflecting on these transforming and life-affirming moments, we know that seeds of societal change are planted and growing.

Living as a multiracial person in a racialized society presents many challenges. That is why it is necessary to have tools that buffer us from the negative effects of racism and promote positive change. Aikido gives us a way to work with negative energy in an intentional and harmonious way. By creating opportunities to reflect, share, and breathe, space for healing opens up. We have more energy to engage as changemakers. We return to campus with an increased sense of connection to ourselves and others. Equipped with knowledge, awareness, and empathy, we are ready to complicate ideas about race, challenge white supremacy culture, and keep making space for multiracial experiences.

References

brown, a. m. (2017). *Emergent strategy: Shaping change, changing worlds.* AK Press.

Bryant-Davis, T., & Ocampo, C. (2006). A therapeutic approach to the treatment of racist-incident-based trauma. *Journal of Emotional Abuse, 6,* 1–22. https://doi.org/10.1300/J135v06n04_01

Butler, S. (Director/Producer). (2012). *Cracking the codes: The system of racial inequity* [Documentary]. World Trust.

Dietrich, W., & Wagner, W. (2015). Introduction. In W. Wagner (Ed.), *AiKiDô: The trinity of conflict transformation* (pp. 9–14). Springer. https://doi.org/10.1007/978-3-658-10166-4_1

Haroun, R. (2015). Philosophical and spiritual roots of aikido. In W. Wagner (Ed.), *AiKiDô: The trinity of conflict transformation* (pp. 87–113). Springer. https://doi.org/10.1007/978-3-658-10166-4_4

Hill, P. S. (2017). Let my story speak for me: Story circles as a pedagogical tool. In C. Behrman, B. Lyons, P. Hill, J. Slowiak, D. Webb, & A. S. Dreussi (Eds.), *The Akron story circle project: Rethinking race in classroom and community* (pp. 51–75). University of Akron Press.

Imarisha, W. (2015, October). *Walidah Imarisha: Fearless social commentator* [Video file]. Youtube. https://www.youtube.com/watch?v=FTZlNEZ3NEw

Ito, E. (2019, October 12). *Bill of responsibilities for Multiracial people of color with light skin and white passing privilege.* https://littlekotoscloset.wixsite.com/mysite/post/bill-of-responsibilities-for-multiracial-people-of-color-with-light-skin-white-passing-privilege

Martinez, C. C. (2019). *Story circles, changing culture, and deepening leadership* (New Directions for Student Leadership, no. 163, pp. 57–71). Wiley. https://doi.org/10.1002/yd.20347

Martinez, C., Vignos, S., & Jaramillo, J. (2019, November). *Engaging in multiraciality at Oregon State University* [Poster presentation]. NASPA Western Regional Conference, Portland, OR, United States.

Moon, R. (1997). *Life in three easy lessons: Aikido, harmony, and the business of living.* Zanshin Press.

Root, M. P. P. (1996). Bill of rights for racially mixed people. In M. P. P. Root (Ed.), *The multiracial experience: Racial borders as the new frontier* (pp. 3–14). SAGE. https://doi.org/10.4135/9781483327433.n1

Root, M. P. P. (2004). *Multiracial oath of social responsibility.* https://www.apa.org/pubs/videos/4310742-oath.pdf

Roper, L. (2019). *The power of dialogue and conversation in higher education* (New Directions for Student Leadership, no. 163, pp. 15–28). Wiley. https://doi.org/10.1002/yd.20344

Slowiak, J. (2017). Introduction. In C. Behrman, B. Lyons, P. Hill, J. Slowiak, D. Webb, & A. S. Dreussi (Eds.), *The Akron story circle project: Rethinking race in classroom and community* (pp. 1–13). University of Akron Press.

Treleaven, D. A., & Britton, W. (2018). *Trauma-sensitive mindfulness: Practices for safe and transformative healing.* W.W. Norton.

United States Department of Arts and Culture. (2015). *People's state of the union toolkit.* https://usdac.us/psotu

Wagner, W. (Ed.). (2015). *AiKiDô: The trinity of conflict transformation.* Springer. https://doi.org/10.1007/978-3-658-10166-4

williams, a. K. (2018, November 17). *Radical Dharma Circle* [Facilitation and presentation]. Portland, OR. https://angelkyodowilliams.com/event/radical-dharma-circle-portland/

13

MIXED AND MULTIRACIAL STUDENT ORGANIZATIONS ON CAMPUS

The Necessity of Weaving Together Art and Critique

Orkideh Mohajeri and Heather C. Lou

This chapter contains specific activities and critical insights for faculty, student affairs administrators, and other staff who wish to create and support organizations for mixed, multiracial,[1] and transracial adoptee students on their campuses. Such groups and organizations provide spaces for support, affinity, social identity development, and activism that aids individuals with mixed and contested racial backgrounds to make sense of their various identities as well as larger social dynamics of U.S. society, at a time and space when young adults typically experience increased independence from their families of origin; are actively engaged in psychosocial development (Patton et al., 2016); and are likely living in the most diverse, semi-closed community that they will be part of for the rest of their adult years (Renn, 2003, 2004).

Our approach is distinctive and valuable in that it weaves together art and critique as two essential ingredients in doing this work well. Art is an accessible medium, and everyone can be an artist, with or without formal training. Art empowers individuals and groups to provide abstract or realistic imagery to process their lived experiences, including experiences of racialization. Critique is not merely criticism or a negative attitude but rather entails an attempt to infuse pedagogy and praxis with an awareness of both the objective and subjective nature of oppression for the ultimate aim of liberation (see Leonardo, 2009). Thus, we assert that a critical perspective must be concomitantly kept at the forefront of this work, as disrupting normative, hegemonic ideas about belonging, inclusion/exclusion, and identity is at the core of this labor.

We insist that art and critique be combined and interwoven, and the organization of this chapter reflects this weaving. Thus, we present race ideology, powerblindness, positionality, and multiracial microaggressions as four constructs necessary for critical exploration of the colonial and racialized contexts of U.S. postsecondary education. Throughout, we employ art in a variety of forms—including doodles, sketches, narratives, poetry, humor, and performance—to engage with these constructs, to foster new insights, and to illustrate how these forms push our learning forward. These art activities and creative reflections are presented in a series of labeled figures and tables.[2] Detailed instructions for each activity can be found in the appendices at the end of this chapter. Readers are encouraged to adapt the processes and activities we offer in whatever ways seem helpful. Finally, the chapter ends by highlighting additional considerations when engaging in this work.

Getting Started as an Adviser: Context Matters

Student affairs administrators, faculty, and other staff have many reasons to support undergraduate and graduate students' cocurricular activities. Sometimes it's part of their roles, and other times, advisers personally identify with a student's racial identity development (Lou, 2011). Working closely with an organization can be rewarding as advisers observe and experience student leadership development (Malaney & Danowski, 2015; Ozaki & Johnston, 2008) and become pivotal characters in students' identity formation during their collegiate years. It is important for advisers to discern the rationale for their involvement, as power dynamics among students, staff, and faculty are ever-present in postsecondary institutional settings.

Our own experiences as advisers, staff, faculty, researchers, and, most importantly, students, at six institutions (University of Vermont, San Jose State University, Smith College, University of California–Davis, University of Minnesota–Twin Cities, and West Chester University) inform our critical praxis (Freire, 1999) and recommendations for advisers to best engage and support students at their respective institutions. It is evident that context matters greatly for each student organization, as the institutional ecosystem and larger regional dynamics impact students' experiences (Renn, 2003; Wijeyesinghe, 2012). In fact, we argue that advisers must find more "inclusive critical pedagogy that allows the increasingly diverse student populations to build, share, express, and center their narratives in educational contexts that were not made for their academic and personal success" (Lou, 2018, p. 198). To that end, we name four critical constructs and demonstrate how art can be used to unveil the workings of each of them. The examples are drawn from our own experiences and research.

Race Ideology: It's the (Mono)Racial Air We Breathe!

The first critical construct that we introduce is race as ideology.

The understanding that race is socially constructed and has no consistent biological or genetic basis is increasingly acknowledged by larger segments of broader society. At the very least, it is an established understanding in the social sciences and in U.S. postsecondary institutions. With this insight comes the opportunity to more readily acknowledge race as ideology. Leonardo (2009) argued that race ideology is integral, "embedded and unrecognized in the unconscious" (p. 28). The idea that humans can be categorized into varying racial groups is commonsensical, normative, and taken for granted. Race ideology is like air; we breathe it in from moment to moment. We interact with it unconsciously. It surrounds us and we draw on it to make sense of the world.

Not only is the concept of "race" itself made up and completely false, but as a corollary, monoracial conceptualizations and categories are also completely false. No such thing as pure races exist. Humans have been mixing across borders and boundaries, real and imagined, since before recorded history, and there are no pure monoracial groups (Johnston & Nadal, 2010). Thus, if race is hegemonic ideology, this points to the need for a critical consideration of racial identity. We assert that multiracial experiences can be locations from which the spurious nature of race is more readily acknowledged. It is important to concede that this is not always the case; mixed folks are not immune to adopting the dominant ideology about race, because they also breathe the air in which it exists. However, to the extent that multiracial student organizing is grounded in critical perspectives, possibilities for troubling race ideology emerge.

Activity 1: (Mono)Racist Ideology in Your Local Context

Understanding the impact of monoracial contexts within campus is key for advisers' efforts to support students as they continue to navigate racialized landscapes. Activity 1 (see Appendix 13A) constitutes an intervention through art and data collection that can be interwoven with race ideology. We invite advisers to engage in an illustrated journal activity to reflect on their role in observing monoraciality in their social ecological environments over a 3-day period. Questions for advisers to explore through visual journaling and data collection include the following:

- What racial demographic options are available on forms, surveys, and marketing materials at your institution?
- Are there affinity- and identity-based student organizations or staff groups? If so, how are they listed or advertised? How do these groups conceptualize racial categories?
- How do you perceive the racial composition or "diversity" of students, staff, and faculty in media (websites, advertisements, social media, etc.)?
- How does your institution (colleagues, learning outcomes/goals, values, curriculum, hiring practices, etc.) address racial equity, diversity, and inclusion? Who is at the table and who is missing when strategies are discussed and decisions are made?
- When you observe interactions among students, staff, faculty, media, and so on in meetings, hallways, classrooms, or other social spaces, what assumptions do you make about people's race? To what extent do you assume/ascribe identities or narratives?

Figure 13.1 portrays an example of a day of this visually illustrated data collection journal.

Once you complete your tracking period, plot your doodles in the social-ecological model (SEM) (Dahlberg & Krug, 2002). The SEM was created to address violence as a public health epidemic by exploring relationships among individual, interpersonal/relationship, community, and social contexts. The SEM can provide perspective on ways that behaviors and attitudes are layered and manifested in micro and macro interactions. Here, it is applied to explore the trickle down/up dynamic of race as a social construct in postsecondary settings. The data from the journaling activity in Figure 13.1 are plotted in a SEM worksheet in Figure 13.2.

Powerblindness and the Construction of Responsibility

Another challenge in working with student organizations centers around the analyses of racial realities that are powerblind.

Futuristic statements such as mixed kids/folks "are gonna save the world," "can see both sides," or "can serve as a bridge" are present in larger discourses about the future of racism in the United States (Spencer, 2011; Squires, 2007). These statements imply that multiracial folks are going to

Figure 13.1. Monoracism in your local context: Day 1: Example of illustrated journaling in response to questions.

Note. 1. College application that shows demographic questions: Check all that apply and/or fill in the blank. 2. "No" symbol with a circle and line through, with the word *none* inside. Text reads, "No student organization or staff affinity group, only monoracial services." Starred: One mixed race studies course. 3. Colored-in silhouette of Turtle Island with a star and text reading, "You are here." Around the star, there is text on the coasts that says, "Not here." Around the figure, the text states, "Very Black and white. Monoracial. Refugees. Do NOT talk about race." 4. There are figures around a table. Inside the table is a word bubble from a committee that says, "We're inclusive!!!" The figures are shaded in black and white. There is a figure that is labeled "Me. No one looks like me, people keep talking over me and interrupting whenever I speak. . . . Do I belong here?" 5. Three word bubbles. Bubble 1: In a meeting, I overhear, "I don't see color." Bubble 2: In the cafeteria, I overhear, "You're mixed? Me too!" Bubble 3: In my mind, responding to a colleague, I think, "Ugh, stop trying to guess my race. Do you do this to students?"

Figure 13.2. Completed SEM worksheet.

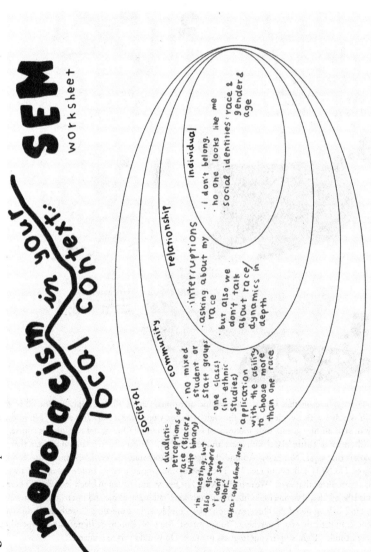

Note. Individual level: "I don't belong. No one looks like me. Social identities: race & gender & age." Relationship level: "Interruptions. Asking about my race. But also, we don't talk about race/dynamics in depth." Community level: "No mixed student or staff groups. One class! (in ethnic studies). Application with the ability to choose more than one race." Societal level: "Dualistic perceptions of race (Black & white binary). In meeting, but also elsewhere, 'I don't see color' aka: colorblind lens."

Note. Copyright © 2020, Heather C. Lou. Used with permission.

resolve all racial strife simply by their very existence. This sentiment places responsibility for healing labor on multiracial individuals, thereby absolving others of involvement. It is important to acknowledge that it is not only white monoracial people who take up this discourse of racial healing by multiracial individuals. Individuals and communities of other monoracial backgrounds, as well as mixed race individuals and communities, also take up this discourse. There's an allure to this discourse, because it conveys a rare sense of empowerment, and multiracial individuals might feel valuable and recognized—to an extent—by such statements.

Powerblindness (Castagno, 2014; Frankenberg, 1993), an offshoot of colorblindness, bars critical examination of larger, unequal, and unjust societal dynamics. It allows avoidance of the critical analysis of systematic oppression and our individual roles and responsibilities in these systems. Powerblindness produces an innocent subject position. In this case, if someone else is going to clean up racism and solve the problem, then "we" simply need to step out of the way and applaud the problem-solver's effort. Thus, "we" are positioned as innocent observers and distant supporters who evade "acknowledgement of individual complicity" (Frankenberg, 1993, p. 189) and the very difficult work of self-interrogation and owning responsibility for intentional change at systemic and individual levels.

Activity 2: Advisers Reflecting on Power
Because of the many levels of power evident in working with student organizations, it is essential that advisers reflect on, understand, and name their relationship to power and privilege. The questions in Activity 2 (Appendix 13B) will stimulate reflections around power. The construct of powerblindness is also interwoven with a reflection and poetry exercise in this activity. We challenge advisers to respond to the questions as a poetic stream of consciousness. Do not overintellectualize each response; say it plainly and however it first processes through your mind. Pay attention to which parts of your body respond to each question. Do you feel nervous and do your palms get sweaty? How would you explain your answer—not from the rational thinking part of your processing (e.g., what, why, and how), but from your emotions (feel) and your actions (do)? Lou's responses to these questions are captured in stream of consciousness in Table 13.1. Please note that once you complete your responses, they can be read aloud as a poem of positionality. In this case, Mohajeri has written a brief reflection and constructed poetry from Lou's words, which appear in the following subsection.

TABLE 13.1

Questions for Reflecting on Power

Question	Lou's Response
Why am I interested in serving as an adviser to a multiracial student organization?	i want to belong and help students belong
	provide guidance and support
What do the students need/expect from me?	space to explore identity and create affinity
	give and make space for ambiguity—to find comfort in what we don't yet know
Who is responsible for healing racism? Fostering inclusion and belonging? Witnessing multiraciality?	
What is the student organization's purpose: Belonging? Addressing mattering and marginality? Exploring identity politics? Dismantling white supremacy? Socializing? Affinity?	create community and common space to share stories ultimately to understand students' narratives as they engage on and off campus as leaders inclusion and equity are central to the institution and my role on campus (as a director) but i'm not sure how the students envision this—i need to ask more questions about their understandings and expectations of me v. adviser v. staff v. institution
How does that connect with the institutional or my own functional area's purpose?	
Who am I and where am I from?	queer, mixed, asian, white, cisgender, womxn of color, disabled, anxious, educated, middle class, jew, from the west coast/los angeles—straddling
How does this impact my own racialized experiences as I navigate postsecondary education?	between marginalization and actively marginalizing, constantly facing the ways whiteness literally lives within me, navigating guilt and empowerment simultaneously

How do my own understandings of racial identity and proximity to whiteness and white supremacy impact how I navigate my positional power (as staff, faculty, and/or adviser to a student organization)?	i am white/i can navigate this familiar structure, it is within me i am not white/i am viewed as other, on the margins i am a womxn of color/i am aggressive and a threat i am asian/i am the model minority and a nonthreat—submissive and quiet all of those things at once, butting up to what people around me expect rewarded and punished for not meeting those expectations a spy, shape shifter, crossing borders, (un)detected as one of the things not like the other
What aspects of advising a multiracial student group am I confident in? Where are my learning edges? What information and skills don't I know and how can I learn them? How do I find resources to increase my own understanding of race, racism, and intersections of identity?	i am the expert of my own experience unsettled with my owning of my whiteness still finding language around being white and not being viewed as white being asian and not being viewed as asian exploring my own biases and antiblackness striving to understand my need to be perfect—a model how do i expand my understanding of self? how do i make space for others? how do i find meaning in my journey while supporting students? read a book ask questions seek to listen and understand let the unknown settle in answers aren't in the texts remember—there are multiple truths and that is enough

Mohajeri's Reflection on Lou's Response

The questions are important to consider not only at the outset of the advising endeavor but also from time to time throughout. In my own recent advising experience, I was startled to realize that my purposes for the group were at variance with some of the more productive lines of action that students were pursuing. I spent time reflecting on my own desires and fears. Was my initial reluctance coming from the smallness of my thoughts? Was I afraid to let something organic emerge from the group, especially when my first response was to see it as a loss? Who would win and who would lose if this student initiative was supported by me in my advising role? I connect with the following phrases in Lou's reflection and have assembled them as a "found poem":

> I am aggressive and a threat.
> I am nonthreat, submissive and quiet.
> I am straddling, constantly facing
> Me v. adviser v. staff v. institution,
> Rewarded and punished shape shifter, border crosser.
>
> I need to ask more questions:
> Anti-Blackness,
> Whiteness literally lives within,
> All of those things at once.

Positionality and Counterstorytelling

Positionality is another critical construct that advisers and groups can engage with.

Positionality refers to the idea of making one's social and cultural locations explicit. It is an acknowledgment that an individual actor's biases, social advantages and disadvantages, and worldview influence what that individual perceives, understands, and concludes. Many different fields of study, from cultural anthropology (Behar, 1996, 2003) to action research (Coughlin & Brydon-Miller, 2014) to feminism (Eisenstein, as cited in Smith, 1983), law (Crenshaw, 1989, 1991), and beyond are engaged in an ongoing exploration of how our various positionalities affect what we recognize as data and as "truth."

Positionality is a necessary piece of the work of forming multiracial community on campus. Multiracial positionality is complex and can shift over time. It entails both critical self-reflection and a sharing and building of community with others, particularly through counternarrative storytelling (Solórzano & Yosso, 2002). There is a robust literature on counterstory as methodology and resistance (e.g., Yosso, 2013); however, here we use

Figure 13.3. Modified replication of Lyra's 2018 drawing of her social identities.

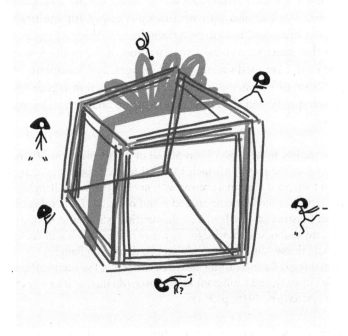

Note. An image of a box wrapped in a bow and small stick figures dancing around the box in various positions. © 2020, Heather C. Lou. Used with permission.

counterstory in a broad manner to indicate that multiracial student groups should foreground narratives and sensemaking by multiracial folks as a form of disrupting dominant, monoracial, and inaccurate understandings of race, inclusion, and belonging, among other concepts. Our examples start with Lyra's story. We use the art and narrative of Lyra, a multiracial undergraduate student who participated in a research study (Mohajeri, 2018), to guide our exploration of counterstorytelling. Lyra's positionality counterstory is captured in Figure 13.3. Then following her lead, each chapter contributor engages in parallel positionality counterstorytelling (see Figures 13.4 and 13.5). Further material that invites personal counterstorytelling is provided in Activity 3 (see Appendix 13C).

Lyra's Positionality
Lyra was one of 20 participants in a study on multiracial students at a historically white institution of higher education (Mohajeri, 2018). Lyra was a

21-year-old undergraduate student; a double major; the darkest phenotype sibling from a mixed family; an artist; and a deeply thoughtful, reflective individual. She was also part of a campus group for multiracial students. During her interview, Lyra drew a thought-provoking image in response to a prompt that solicited a visual representation of the multiple social identities that she held. Lyra used various colors, images, and metaphors and produced the depiction of her various social identities shown in Figure 13.3.

When questioned about the details of the image that she produced, Lyra explained:

> I decided to make a box. Then put all of my identities in [it], and then I also wrote the places in which I think I learned about my identities, and then I wrapped it up in a present with my favorite colors [laughs], and this is a bunch of me's dancing around it and on it. . . . I was going to imagine some bursting of [the box] . . . the dancing is a way to navigate it with, like, my embodied knowledge . . . a way to jump on it and disrupt it. . . . I could throw [the box] around, but also dress it up [laughs]. . . . It's a gift, something to be shared, and also to celebrate. . . . I've been indecisive about how I identify, and I still don't know how to do that, so it's a way to comfort that. (Mohajeri, 2018, p. 211)

Lyra's image has a generative quality. The art calls for interaction, not just observation and analysis. Some of the larger metaphors that Lyra explores can be extended beyond her own particular background and can be used as a jumping-off point for identity exploration for others. For example, Lyra used a box image and metaphor to simultaneously convey a sense of confinement and limitation, as well as a sense of gifting, celebration, and self-care. She brought a playfulness and appreciation to a topic (i.e., multiracial identity) that can often be experienced as fraught, and yet she did not deny that larger society uses social identities in power formations to constrain, label, and package. Lyra used her embodied knowledge to disrupt, play with, jump on, and move these configurations of herself. Further material that invites personal counterstorytelling is provided in Appendix 13C.

Activity 3: Positionality and Counterstorytelling
After viewing Lyra's depiction and reading her explanation, we ask ourselves the following questions: How can we follow Lyra's lead as we approach the work of helping to form student groups on campus for multiracial students? How are we read, constrained, and boxed in? Who does the "boxing?" How can we "dress up" and "throw around" these conceptualizations of difference and belonging, of identity and racial formation, of wholeness and

community? We present our own positionality drawings and counterstories in response to Lyra's prompts.

Mohajeri's Positionality

I do not identify as racially mixed, but I do identify as a person with a contested racial positioning. I am a generation 1.5 immigrant to the United States, of Iranian heritage. During my elementary and middle school years, in the Western mind, Iran and the Middle East were part of "Asia"—Western Asia, or the Near East, that is—and thus for a long time, I followed this logic of categorization and identified as "Asian." More recently, specific directions on the census and its progenies have made explicit that all people of Middle Eastern and North African descent should identify themselves as white, and thus, I have found myself, in middle age, forced to reposition myself as white.[3] This has been a disjointed transition because I am treated on a day-to-day basis as a person of color in the U.S. context, clearly positioned outside the borders of whiteness.

My children can also claim a contested racial positioning. On the one hand, they can identify as mixed because one parent is phenotypically white and the other is phenotypically "of color." On the other hand, both parents

Figure 13.4. Mohajeri's depiction of social identity.

Note. Image of a box with the word *Caution* on the outside and multicolored swirls, stars, and streaks shown emerging from the box. © 2020, Heather C. Lou. Used with permission.

currently select "white" on census forms, although one is of Anglo/European-mixed descent and the other is of Middle Eastern descent. I watch them try to make sense of U.S. racism, white supremacy, and their own racial positioning, and we learn together. This intimate grounding in racial contestation, reflected appraisals (Khanna, 2004), and contested whiteness (Mohajeri, 2018) grants me perspective on the spurious nature of racial categories and the contemporary dynamics of U.S. racial formation. In conversation with Lyra's drawing, I have produced the sketch in Figure 13.4.

I am currently engaged in a process of trying to see myself more accurately. I am trying to see past what white supremacy has trained me in. How have I spent so many years walking the planet, thinking I was marginal, foreign, incomprehensible, and in need of explanation? I was trained by white supremacy to see it so, to believe it, and to incorporate this judgment in my inner being, and I did. I obeyed the training.

Now, much later, I try to heal myself and my self-regard from what was planted and trained in me. I am tired of moving through the planet and the decades in a foggy self-regard. I pursue healing and am on the edge of being more fully alive. I am trying to break out of this ridiculous box. I am trying to step out and see the stars that come from my inner and outer being, and to celebrate each one.

Lou's Positionality

My father is Asian and my mother is white (presenting). More specifically, my father is Taishanese and my mother is an Ashkenazi Jew of Persian descent. As a racially ambiguous and multiracial womxn of color, choosing between my racial and other fluid identities has been a normed behavior—choosing to go with my father for some "ethnically" Chinese cultural events and with my mother for other events where whiteness was more palatable (shopping, going to the bank, looking at cars, student–teacher conferences, etc.). At the same time, I was told that being multiracial was to be "pretty and coveted" (Lou, 2011, p. 49), especially because I was not someone who was *just Chinese*. Model minority enough to excel academically (as expected), but also just white enough to acquiesce into ambiguous racialized spaces to be whatever the external world would want—*What are you? Filipinx? Latinx? Native? Hawaiian?* Sure, so long as this allowed me to navigate my environment with the least resistance and without having to explain my racialized experience any longer.

I internalized these beliefs of ascribing to monoraciality or assumed racial identity, thinking that my identity should be segmented and situational and that my proximity to whiteness and white supremacy was preferred. I grew up with my mother saying racial slurs about my father and grandparents—and to protect myself, I lived in layered and liminal borderlands

Figure 13.5. Lou's depiction of racialized identity.

Note. An image of half of Lou's face is superimposed on a drawing of dim sum food items and around Lou's face are the words *queer, asian, chinese, crip & disabled, anxious, sad, dragon, survivor, artist, gemini, witch, mixed, white, m.ed., mid-class, jew, west coast, persian, cisgender, educator.* © 2020, Heather C. Lou. Used with permission.

(Anzaldúa, 1987), oscillating between being invisible and hypervisible, striving to hold my identities in my hands, an offering for others to see (Figure 13.5).

The foundation of my identity is the dim sum—my "Chineseness" intermixed with a white background—the makeup of my values, culture, community, tradition. It is layered by my complex understanding of gender and sexuality, a filter of how my cisgender womxn of color and queer identities impact my relationship with my racial identities (it is important to say that I am not in relationship with my family of origin because they did not approve of my fluid sexuality and chosen partner). My own face is halved and surrounded by my identities, showing the complexity of wholeness, yet still segmented and situational. Finally, the square—my own tension between encompassing, yet suffocating, boxing in, yet pushing out. Similar to both Lyra and Mohajeri, I am making meaning of the ways that my own family, peers, and larger society ascribe identities and experiences on me based on my physical body and perceived race, yet it is more layered and liminal than what can be perceived.

Multiracial Microaggressions and Empowerment Through Pushback

Multiracial microaggressions constitute the fourth and final critical construct that we highlight in this section.

Microaggressions are everyday, commonplace slights, insults, or indignities that are leveled against various marginalized groups, either intentionally or unintentionally (Mohajeri, 2020; Sue, 2010a, 2010b). These aggressions are set apart from more egregious assaults by the implication that they operate on a lesser level, and yet the pain and trauma engendered by microaggressions are well documented (e.g., Nadal et al., 2012, 2017; Olkin et al., 2019; Sue et al., 2009; Yosso et al., 2009). Scholars have articulated taxonomies of various types of microaggressions, including racial microaggressions, gender microaggressions, disability microaggressions, and so on. Johnston and Nadal (2010) have presented a useful taxonomy of microaggressions that particularly target multiracials. As these student populations show up on campus in increasing numbers, "visible members of this group may be questionable or questioned" given the ways "their perceived external identity, or race, may be ambiguous and indecipherable to those with a monoracial lens"(Lou, 2011, p. 47). Thus, microaggressions from peers, staff, or faculty are likely not a new experience for multiracial students.

In response, multiracial student organizations can be generative spaces to practice cross-identity dialogues and utilize oppositional consciousness (Sandoval, 2000). Because the physical and emotional toll on multiracial students can be substantial, we suggest engaging in activities that allow for embodied processing and empowerment via movement and comedy, as outlined in Activity 4 (see Appendix 13D).

Activity 4: Practicing Clapbacks to Multiracial Microaggressions

The Twin Cities–based Funny Asian Womxn Kollective (FAWK) was founded in 2018 by Saymoukda Vongsay, May Lee Yang, and Naomi Ko to build community and empower Asian womxn to address internalized sexism, racism, and anti-Blackness. Part of their work is facilitating workshops on addressing microaggressions with movement and comedy. Adapted from FAWK's work around "clapping back"[4] (i.e., responding) to covert and overt oppression, participants explore microaggressions that others have enacted about their racial identity and collaborate with peers to develop creative responses. Table 13.2 demonstrates how this activity might take shape.

Some of these responses may elicit laughter, whereas others may produce silence or an audible gasp. Some of these responses can feel cathartic and

TABLE 13.2
Responding to Microaggressions

Microaggression	Clapback
"Heather Lou is such a white name and you sound so different on the phone! I wasn't expecting you to look the way you do [brown/racially ambiguous]."	"What do you mean that Heather Lou is a white name? What do people like me sound like?"
"Where are you from? No, I mean . . . where are your parents from?"	"I'm from Torrance, California. So are my parents. Where are you from?"
"Do you know kung fu [said to a person assumed to be Asian]?"	"I do know the song 'Kung Fu Fighting!'" and dances away.
"Well, I didn't think we needed a 'Mixed' option for this survey. Can't you just choose one race and stick with that?"	"I'm choosing 'Mixed' as my option. Where do I note that on this survey?"
"What part of you is _____ race?"	"My ears and my elbows are Asian. My front tooth and left eyeball is Persian Jew. Was that the answer you were looking for?"
"Mixed people are so beautiful and exotic. I want to have a partner of a different race so I can have mixed babies!"	"Beautiful and exotic like a zoo animal, right?"

comforting, and some may stimulate sadness or anger. By creating space to process, emote, practice "clapping back" at ridiculous comments, and share tools and tactics with peers, students enhance their resistance capital (Yosso, 2005). Helping students find tools that address the impact of microaggressions can empower them to engage in narrative sharing and community care in ways that retain them within the university.[5]

For student organization advisers, it may be helpful to remind students that (a) they do not always need to educate the person who microaggressed them, (b) they do not need to address every microaggression, (c) leaving the situation is okay, and (d) if microaggressions are persistent and impact their wellness or learning, other resources on campus are available for reporting these concerns. Identifying action items, sharing resources and support services, and exploring how this exercise can be used in future interactions is a powerful way to end the activity.

Further Considerations

Critical mixed race theory, according to Osei-Kofi (2012), "has the potential to fulfill the promise of education that transgresses boundaries, that inspires critical thinking, that dismantles hierarchies, [and] that moves and transforms this world" (p. 245). Student organization advisers are key in supporting multiracial and mixed students to develop not only a keen sense of multiracial consciousness but also awareness and skills to engage in radical transformation of racial politics so that white supremacy can be dismantled. In navigating advising and mentorship roles, staff and administrators working directly with students should be aware of the following considerations as they expand their practice: intersectionality, gendered concepts of labor in "womxn's work," and the danger of reinscribing other oppressions.

Intersectionality

As demonstrated throughout the activities in this chapter, an intersectional approach to social identities (Crenshaw, 1989, 1991) is key to addressing oppression when working with student organizations. Multiracial student organizations are addressing not only racism and monoracism but also other forms of oppression. A student cannot talk about their racial identity without connection to gender, sexuality, ability, class, and spirituality, among other identities. Advisers must carve out space for exploring these intersections and ultimately understand that all oppression and liberation are inherently linked. Encouraging students to explore disciplines such as postcolonial feminist and trans studies, critical whiteness studies, and critical disability studies may provide additional perspective on power, privilege, and empowerment.

"Womxn's Work"

As demonstrated in Activity 1, contexts matter. Just as racism is institutionalized, so are sexism and genderism. Across the institutions and regions in which we have gained experience, we note that it is often the queer, trans, femme, and womxn-identified undergraduate students who carry out the bulk of labor for organizing student groups, leading workshops, preparing food, sending emails, and arranging the many details of meetings and conferences. Some students with multiple marginalized and fluid sexual, gender, and racial identities may feel pressure to become "bridge builders" between communities. This emotional and psychological labor can negatively impact students. To what extent does this dynamic reflect gendered notions of womxn's caregiving work? How can we disrupt these normative conceptions of care, cleaning, and organizing labor? Are there ways in which advisers can be critical of their own assumptions and patterns around who they turn to for leadership, who they assign tasks to, who they pull into committees or task forces, and so on? As an adviser, it is important to track which students are engaging in such labor, as this can be a covert form of sexism, genderism, and internalized white supremacy. We encourage advisers to help students notice who is taking on tasks, who starts conversations, and who is expected (even unconsciously) to make their identities smaller in order to move forward the student organization's mission.

Reinscribing Other Oppressions

Each activity throughout this chapter recognizes the impact of power and privileges, as well as how powerblindness may impact the ways that student organization advisers and student leaders understand their own role within institutions. Exploring these narratives can be painful and immersive. In sharing pain, trauma, and exploring healing, how can participants avoid reinforcing other forms of oppression? Multiracial individuals and communities can still engage in sexism, homophobia, anti-Blackness, internalized white supremacy, ableism, and other forms of oppression. As members of postsecondary institutions, students, staff, and faculty become socialized to be able to recognize injustice, but not necessarily interrupt or act as active bystanders. Transparently asking critical questions; questioning your own identity, learned attitudes, and behaviors; and sharing your own growth can be simple ways to role model the value of lifelong learning.

Conclusion

This chapter has provided resources for advisers of multiracial student organizations to ground their practice by interweaving art with critical theoretical frameworks that center student racial identity development and the disruption of hegemonic notions of common sense. We presented four constructs—race as ideology, powerblindness, positionality, and multiracial microaggressions—and engaged each through various art-infused exercises. We not only interwove theory and art but also reacted to and built off of one another's work and reflections. This dynamic of engagement, reflection, composition, creation, and forging can push advisers and student organization members to discern, disrupt, and reflect more deeply, both as individuals and in community. We hope that the analysis, activities, and guidance provided herein enhance and inform your continued work on your respective campuses. As you use and modify the various activities presented in the appendices, or create new ones, please share your insights and learnings with us.

Notes

1. Throughout this chapter, we use the term *multiracial* to indicate mixed, multi-racial, and transracial folks. We capitalize the words *Black, Indigenous*, and other words meant to indicate racially minoritized populations in the U.S. context but do not capitalize *white* or *whiteness*—following the standards of Pérez Huber (2010)—as a grammatical move to decenter white dominance.
2. Each figure in this work includes an alternative text description to follow universal design imperatives that pedagogy be intentional and inclusive of people who may be visually impaired or with low vision, even in their experience of art.
3. It is important to acknowledge that Iranians have their own stories about race, including both a widespread narrative about belonging to an ancient and original Aryan whiteness and a virulent strain of anti-Blackness that runs through segments of cultural practices, literature, and art.
4. See LaBouvier (2017) for an interesting discussion on the origins of this concept.
5. Advisers can also challenge participants to organize the clapback responses into categories presented in Johnston and Nadal's (2010) taxonomy of multiracial microaggressions. Students may find this added component useful in contextualizing their experiences and providing them with theoretical frameworks with which to analyze their racialized experiences.

References

Anzaldúa, G. (1987). *Borderlands: La frontera*. Aunt Lute Books.
Behar, R. (1996). *The vulnerable observer: Anthropology that breaks your heart*. Beacon Press.
Behar, R. (2003). *Translated woman: Crossing the border with Esperanza's story* (10th university ed.). Beacon Press.
Castagno, A. E. (2014). *Educated in whiteness: Good intentions and diversity in schools*. University of Minnesota Press.
Coughlin, D., & Brydon-Miller, M. (2014). *The SAGE encyclopedia of action research*. SAGE.
Crenshaw, K. (1989). Demarginalizing the intersection of race and sex: A Black feminist critique of antidiscrimination doctrine, feminist theory, and antiracist politics. *University of Chicago Legal Forum, 1989*(1), 139–168. http://chicagounbound.uchicago.edu/uclf/vol1989/iss1/8
Crenshaw, K. (1991). Mapping the margins: Intersectionality, identity politics, and violence against women of color. *Stanford Law Review, 43*(6), 1241–1299. https://doi.org/10.2307/1229039
Dahlberg, L. L., & Krug, E. G. (2002). Violence—A global public health problem. In E. Krug, L. L. Dahlberg, J. A. Mercy, A. B. Zwi, & R. Lozano (Eds.), *World report on violence and health*. World Health Organization.

Frankenberg, R. (1993). *The social construction of whiteness: White women, race matters*. University of Minnesota Press.

Freire, P. (1999). *Pedagogy of the oppressed* (M. Bergman Ramos, Trans.). Continuum. (Original work published 1970)

Johnston, M. P., & Nadal, K. L. (2010). Multiracial microaggressions: Exposing monoracism in everyday life and clinical practice. In D. W. Sue (Ed.), *Microaggressions and marginality: Manifestation, dynamics, and impact* (pp. 123–133). Wiley.

Khanna, N. (2004). The role of reflected appraisals in racial identity: The case of multiracial Asians. *Social Psychology Quarterly, 67*(2), 115–131. https://doi .org/10.1177/019027250406700201

LaBouvier, C. (2017, May 16). The clap and the clap back: How Twitter erased Black culture from an emoji. *Vice.* https://www.vice.com/en_us/article/jpyajg/ the-clap-and-the-clap-back-how-twitter-erased-black-culture-from-an-emoji

Leonardo, Z. (2009). *Race, whiteness, and education*. Routledge.

Lou, H. C. (2011). Multiracial student acquiescence to empowerment. *The Vermont Connection, 32*(6), 46–57. https://scholarworks.uvm.edu/tvc/vol32/iss1/6

Lou, H. C. (2018). Art resists. Art heals. Art is resilience: Utilizing creativity in postsecondary education. In B. T. Kelly & C. A. Kortegast (Eds.), *Engaging images for research, pedagogy, and practice: Utilizing visual methods to understand and promote college student development* (pp. 197–212). Stylus.

Malaney, V., & Danowski, K. (2015). Mixed foundations: Supporting and empowering multiracial student organizations. *JCSCORE, 1*(2), 55–85. https://doi .org/10.15763/issn.2642-2387.2015.1.2.54-85

Mohajeri, O. (2018). *Constructions at the borders of whiteness: The discursive framing of contested white students at a predominantly white institution of higher education* [Unpublished doctoral dissertation]. University of Minnesota, Twin Cities.

Mohajeri, O. (2020). Microaggressions. In M. E. David & M. J. Amey (Eds.), *The SAGE encyclopedia of higher education* (5th ed., pp. 1042–1047). SAGE. http:// dx.doi.org/10.4135/9781529714395.n385

Nadal, K. L., Griffin, K. E., Wong, Y., Davidoff, K. C., & Davis, L. S. (2017). The injurious relationship between racial microaggressions and physical health: Implications for social work. *Journal of Ethnic & Cultural Diversity in Social Work, 26*(1–2), 6–17. https://doi.org/10.1080/15313204.2016.1263813

Nadal, K. L., Skolnik, A., & Wong, Y. (2012). Interpersonal and systemic microaggressions toward transgender people: Implications for counseling. *Journal of LGBT Issues in Counseling, 6*(1), 55–82. https://doi.org/10.1080/15538605.20 12.648583

Olkin, R., Hayward, H., Abeene, M. S., & VanHeel, G. (2019). The experiences of microaggressions against women with visible and invisible disabilities. *Journal of Social Issues, 75*(3), 757–785. https://doi.org/10.1111/josi.12342

Osei-Kofi, N. (2012). Identity, fluidity, and groupism: The construction of multiraciality in education discourse. *Review of Education, Pedagogy, and Cultural Studies, 34*(5), 245–257. https://doi.org/10.1080/10714413.2012.732782

Ozaki, C. C., & Johnston, M. (2008). *The space in between: Issues for multiracial student organizations and advising* (New Directions for Student Services, no. 123, pp. 53–61). Wiley. https://doi.org/10.1002/ss.286

Patton, L. D., Renn, K. A., Guido, F. M., & Quaye, S. J. (2016). *Student development in college: Theory, research, and practice* (3rd ed.). Jossey-Bass.

Pérez Huber, L. (2010). Using Latina/o Critical Race Theory (LatCrit) and racist nativism to explore intersectionality in the educational experiences of undocumented Chicana college students. *Educational Foundations, 24*, 77–96. https://eric.ed.gov/?id=EJ885982

Renn, K. A. (2003). Understanding the identities of mixed race college students through a developmental ecology lens. *Journal of College Student Identity Development, 44*(3), 383–403. https://doi.org/10.1353/csd.2003.0032

Renn, K. A. (2004). *Mixed race students in college: The ecology of race, identity, and community on campus.* SUNY Press.

Sandoval, C. (2000). *Methodology of the oppressed.* University of Minnesota Press.

Smith, B. (Ed.). (1983). *Home girls, a Black feminist anthology.* Kitchen Table: Women of Color Press.

Solórzano, D. G., & Yosso, T. J. (2002). Critical race methodology: Counter-storytelling as an analytical framework for education research. *Qualitative Inquiry, 8*(1), 23–44. https://doi.org/10.1177/107780040200800103

Spencer, R. (2011). *Reproducing race: The paradox of Generation Mix.* Lynne Rienner.

Squires, C. R. (2007). *Dispatches from the color line: The press and multiracial America.* SUNY Press.

Sue, D. W. (Ed.). (2010a). *Microaggressions in everyday life: Race, gender, and sexual orientation.* Wiley.

Sue, D. W. (Ed.). (2010b). *Microaggressions and marginality: Manifestation, dynamics, and impact.* Wiley.

Sue, D. W., Lin, A. I., Torino, G. C., Capodilupo, C. M., & Rivera, D. P. (2009). Racial microaggressions and difficult dialogues on race in the classroom. *Cultural Diversity and Ethnic Minority Psychology, 15*(2), 183–190. https://doi.org/10.1037/a0014191

Wijeyesinghe, C. L. (2012). The intersectional model of multiracial identity: Integrating multiracial identity theories and intersectional perspectives on social identity. In C. L. Wijeyesinghe & B. W. Jackson III (Eds.), *New perspectives on racial identity development: Integrating emerging frameworks* (2nd ed., pp. 81–107). NYU Press.

Yosso, T. J. (2005). Whose culture has capital? A critical race theory discussion of community cultural wealth. *Race Ethnicity and Education, 8*(1), 69–91. https://doi.org/10.1080/1361332052000341006

Yosso, T. J. (2013). *Critical race counterstories along the Chicana/Chicano educational pipeline.* Routledge.

Yosso, T. J., Smith, W., Ceja, M., & Solórzano, D. (2009). Critical race theory, racial microaggressions, and campus racial climate for Latina/o undergraduates. *Harvard Educational Review, 79*(4), 659–691. https://doi.org/10.17763/haer.79.4.m6867014157m707l

Monoracism in Your Local Context

Materials needed: Paper, pen, worksheets
Suggested time: 1 workweek (4–5 days)

Part 1: Illustrated Journaling

Over 3 workdays, observe your immediate surroundings—your office, meetings, interactions in hallways, social media, institutional website, marketing collateral, curriculum, and so on. Print a new copy of the worksheet on the following page (Figure 13A.1) to document what you notice in your environment. Illustrate/doodle your experiences to the following questions:

1. What racial demographic options are available on forms, surveys, and marketing materials at your respective institution?
2. Are there affinity- and identity-based student organizations or staff groups? If so, how are they listed or advertised? How do they conceptualize racial categories?
3. How do you perceive the racial composition or "diversity" of students, staff, and faculty in media (websites, advertisements, social media, etc.)?
4. How does your institution (colleagues, learning outcomes/goals, values, curriculum, hiring practices, etc.) address racial equity, diversity, and inclusion? Who is at the table and who is missing when strategies are discussed and decisions are made?
5. When you observe interactions among students, staff, faculty, media, and so on in meetings, hallways, classrooms, or other social spaces, what assumptions do you make about people's race? Are they ambiguous? Do you assume/ascribe identities or narratives?

Figure 13A.1. Monoracism in your local context.

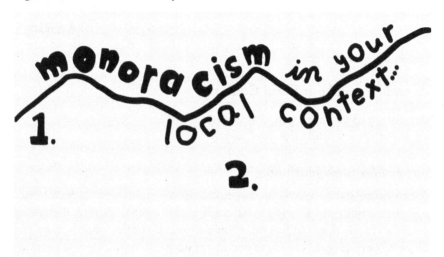

1.

2.

3.

4.

5.

Part 2: Mapping Your Observations in the Social-Ecological Model

Instructions: Once you have completed your illustrated journaling, place your observations in the social-ecological model (SEM) worksheet (Figure 13A.2), which can be reproduced as a full sheet. As you explore monoracism in your local context, notice the ways that race, (mono)racism, and intersectionality may inform the levels of your everyday ecology. How will this impact your adviser role to a mixed, multiracial, and transracial student organization?

Following are the levels of the SEM:

- Individual (attitudes, beliefs, behaviors, identities)
- Relationship (close social circle; e.g., peers/colleagues, family, mentorship, adviser, etc.)
- Community (environment/setting, e.g., department, division, institution, geographic location/neighborhood)
- Societal level (norms, group memberships, policies, etc.)

Figure 13A.2. SEM worksheet.

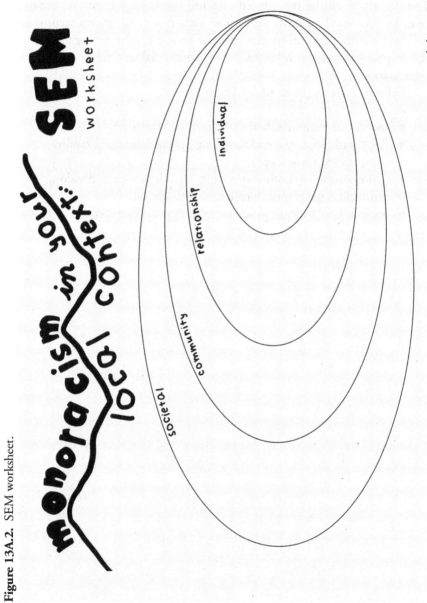

Advisers Reflecting on Power

Materials needed: Worksheet, pen/pencil, or space to process
Suggested time: 30 minutes

Instructions: Read the questions in Table 13B.1 on the following page and respond via stream of consciousness or whatever ideas come to mind. Do not focus on punctuation and grammar.

Once complete, read your response aloud to explore your positionality. Revisit this activity each time you start working with a new group of student leaders in the organization, and reflect on changes over time.

TABLE 13B.1
Reflections on Power

Question	Response
Why am I interested in serving as an adviser to a multiracial student organization? What do the students need/expect from me? Who is responsible for healing racism? Fostering inclusion and belonging? Witnessing multiraciality?	
What is the organization's purpose: • Belonging? • Addressing mattering and marginality? • Exploring identity politics? • Dismantling white supremacy? • Socializing? • Affinity? How does that connect with the institutional or my own functional area's purpose?	
Who am I and where am I from? How does this impact my own racialized experiences as I navigate postsecondary education?	
How do my own understandings of racial identity and proximity to whiteness and white supremacy impact how I navigate my positional power (as staff, faculty, and/or adviser to a student organization)?	
What aspects of advising a multiracial student group am I confident in? Where are my learning edges? What information and skills don't I know and how can I learn them? How do I find resources to increase my own understanding of race, racism, and intersections of identity?	

Positionality and Counterstorytelling

Materials needed: Paper, pencil, pens, markers for participants
Suggested time: 90–120 minutes

Instructions: Place the art items on a table for participants to access. Consider having thought-provoking questions on a dry erase board or large sticky note as directions/prompts.

(10–20 minutes) Before starting, ask students to help create community guidelines for this session. Some participants may share more vulnerable narratives, and you should explore how the group wants to hold space.

As a group, explore how participants understand the following concepts. Define the following:

- Positionality
- Identity
- Storytelling

(30–40 minutes) Using the supplies, ask students to draw a self-portrait or object that answers the following questions. If they feel stuck, feel free to share the images from chapter 13.

- Who are you? Where are you from? What are important events in your life that impact how you identify? What is your relationship to multiraciality?

(20–30 minutes) After the students complete their drawings, have them share in trios. Give each student 5 minutes to share their narratives. In their groups, they should take note of the following:

- What were themes and differences? (Words, phrases, images, etc.)
- What was difficult to share? What was easy?
- What are some takeaways from your reflections?

(30 minutes) In the large group, invite students to summarize their small group reflections. Invite the students to answer the following questions:

- What were/are pivotal experiences in your identity development that impacted your understanding of your peers' images?
- What is your relationship to multiraciality, colonization, and whiteness?
- When and how do you encounter society's injunction to heal racism? Who articulates these messages and who/where are they directed? What privileges and oppressions are at play?
- How do the dynamics of white supremacy, intersectionality, and racial formation show up in your community?
- How will you apply these learnings to your role in this student organization and beyond?

Practicing Clapbacks to Multiracial Microaggressions

Materials needed: sticky notes, markers, pens, tape
Suggested time: Up to 120 minutes

(10 minutes) Before starting, ask the students to help create community guidelines for this session. Some participants may share more vulnerable narratives—how does the group want to hold space? You may also revisit or use previous community guidelines.

(10–20 minutes) Warm up! As a group, choose some of the following exercises to start to get connected with one's body, as well as mind, emotions, and spirit.

- Moving different parts of the face and tongue (lion breath, horse breath, pushing air through lips, etc.)
- Stretching
- Making vocalizations from different parts of the body (tongue, cheeks, neck, chest, stomach) or noises (ho, hum, whee, ahh, etc.) at different volumes
- Follow the leader (where one person makes a movement and everyone mirrors/mimics)

(20 minutes) Create an agreed-upon understanding of microaggressions and monoracial microaggressions. Provide an example or two (six examples are provided in this chapter), and ask the group for two more. Invite the students to share aloud to the group or to a partner.

(15 minutes) Give each participant five to 10 sticky notes. Ask them to write a microaggression they have experienced around mixedness. This could be something someone has said to them or they have said to someone else. Once they are done, ask them to place the sticky notes on a wall. After 10 minutes, participants should view the sticky note gallery and also pick a partner. As a pair, they should pick four sticky notes and bring them back to their seats.

(20 minutes) As a facilitator, you will role model how you would like students to act out their scenes. Use one of the microaggressions provided in the chapter. Ask a participant to read the microaggression to the group. Then act out the response you have chosen.

The participants will review their sticky notes and create several "clapbacks" or responses to each. Once they have their clapbacks, they should create a brief skit of one partner sharing a microaggression and the other responding (similar to your example).

(20 minutes) Ask each group to share one to three microaggressions and their clapbacks to the group. Afterward, ask the following:

- What was that experience like for you?
- How did it feel to brainstorm clapbacks and act them out?
- How might you respond to microaggressions in the future?

(5 minutes) After each group has shared and you have debriefed the activity, we invite you to facilitate a grounding/breathing exercise to recenter people's energy and focus.

CRITICAL MIXED RACE STUDIES

Rooted in Love and Fire

Nicole Leopardo, Kira Donnell, and Wei Ming Dariotis

On May 7, 2019, the Academic Senate of San Francisco State University (SF State) approved the first degree-granting program in the field of critical mixed race studies (CMRS). The development of this historic minor in CMRS is part of a larger project of building the discipline of CMRS elucidated in "Emerging Paradigms in Critical Mixed Race Studies" (Daniel et al., 2014). In this article, the authors specified that the grassroots multiracial movement of the 1990s had "helped inform the intellectual and cultural production in the emerging field of mixed race studies" (pp. 19–20). The movement's collection of scholars, students, activists, mixed race communities, and interracial families sought to address and resist the marginalization and pathologization of their communities by interrogating monoracial norms that dominate the U.S. racial schema and prevent the full expression of mixed race identities. Activism and scholarship around the 2000 census and courses on mixed race identity being taught from the early 1990s onward contributed to the development and acceptance of CMRS as an academic discipline, blossoming in the 2010 Critical Mixed Race Studies Conference and further developing with the founding of the CMRS Association in 2015.[1] In turn, this created the environment of institutional legitimization in which a CMRS minor could exist.

Roots and Radicals

Although CMRS is framed by the intellectual and social paradigms that came out of the movement, approaches to mixedness first put forward by sociology, anthropology, English, and ethnic studies scholars provided the academic backdrop for CMRS. The curriculum, drawing from ethnic studies, humanities, critical race, sociology, and anthropology scholars, as well as mixed race activism, centers a sociocultural and legal analysis of race and racial hierarchies in various communities locally, nationally, and transnationally. In creating the CMRS minor at SF State, we aimed to offer students critical, theoretical, and methodological approaches for addressing notions of mixed race, mixed heritage, and transracial adoptee identity development and community agency in a variety of institutionalized contexts—academic and otherwise.[2]

Although some accurately argue that mixed race identity has been largely marginalized in ethnic studies spaces for a variety of reasons, the development of CMRS within the College of Ethnic Studies at SF State signifies a type of academic homecoming, as well as an observance of the original tenets of ethnic studies. Both CMRS and ethnic studies have foundations in multiracial and multicultural grassroots activism. The magnitude and function of activism differs between these academic areas: Although the 1968 SF State strike that preceded the formation of its CMRS program consisted of poor and working-class students pushing for educational equity, relevant curriculum, and more equitable access to higher education, the multiracial movement was generally made up of middle- and upper-class activists who had access to higher education because of their class status and potential proximity to whiteness. Proximity to whiteness relates to those of mixed heritage who are white passing or have features that are more Eurocentric that privilege them in certain ways. Such individuals may have white family members, especially ancestors, who may have passed on wealth, cultural knowledge, and/or a sense of privilege. Despite these privileges, mixed race activists struggled with issues of belonging and marginalization in higher education and within the U.S. racial context because of the dominance of hypodescent discourse, which emphasizes a racial binary (either/or) as opposed to a more fluid, all-encompassing (and/in addition to) racial identity.

Recognizing the relationship between these struggles, in this chapter we explore the meaning, purpose, and methodology of the process of building CMRS as an academic program at SF State, keeping in mind that the original intent of ethnic studies was to transform higher education by making it relevant and accessible, particularly to marginalized communities. Based on this history, we were guided by certain key questions as we built the CMRS minor. How does the development of academic programs in CMRS contribute to a radical transformation of higher education? What role do the concepts of solidarity and self-determination play in the institutionalization of CMRS? How do various stakeholders at SF State view the study of mixed race, mixed heritage, and transracial adoptee communities?

We begin with a brief historical context of the SF State College of Ethnic Studies. From there, we provide a detailed account of the creation of a CMRS minor in SF State's College of Ethnic Studies. In designing the minor's coursework and requirements, advocating for its place within the college, and gaining approval from the university's academic senate, we highlight the challenges of navigating institutional formalities and procedures and the importance of building solidarity throughout the process. We share our program's goals and learning outcomes and conclude by considering the lessons learned through the process of creating the minor, which we hope will help others expand CMRS as a discipline at other institutions of higher education.

Controlled Burn: From Strike to Structured Activism

In 1968, SF State College (now SF State University) was 78% white, mostly working-class students, and the faculty were even less diverse (Office of University Development, 2019). Founded as a state normal school for the education of teachers in 1899, SF State has continued to educate a majority of the teachers in the San Francisco Unified School District and significant numbers of teachers in surrounding school districts. The impact of SF State on education in the Bay Area is thus even more significant than the average 30,000 K–12 students served per year would suggest. Strikers who shut down the SF State campus from November 6, 1968, to March 21, 1969, risked (and experienced) arrest and physical violence at the hands of heavily armed police to ensure that education at SF State was "relevant" for not only the students who attended the college but also the larger Bay Area surrounding communities.

During the 1968 Third World Liberation Front strike ("the Strike") that led to the establishment of the College of Ethnic Studies, the Third World Liberation Front (TWLF) and the Black Student Union (BSU) argued for degree-granting programs as the basis for communities of color developing self-determination within the university. The SF State College of Ethnic Studies was born out of this demand for "self-determination," which ultimately meant that communities of color could have political decision-making power within academia in order to benefit their diverse communities outside the university. Strikers noted that decision-making power required equal access to public higher education, more senior faculty of color, and new curriculum centering the experiences of people of color and examining the role of race and racism in America (San Francisco State College Black Student Union, 1968).

Notwithstanding the current acceptance and indeed celebration of ethnic studies at SF State, the College of Ethnic Studies has struggled within the academy writ large against prejudice and academic elitism for the past 50 years to establish itself and the larger field of ethnic studies, as well as its subdisciplines,[3] as legitimate academic disciplines. Although SF State now espouses a mission that centers an "unwavering commitment to social justice" (San Francisco State University Academic Senate, 2015, para. 3) of which the College of Ethnic Studies is the most visible face, the college has continued to face challenges that have threatened its ability to fulfill the college's mission to liberate itself and to create conditions for the liberation of others from systemic, intersectional, and hierarchical oppressions through healing and transformative justice work (College of Ethnic Studies, n.d.; San Francisco State University Academic Senate, 2015). This struggle at the birthplace of ethnic studies is situated in the larger context of attacks against ethnic studies and related disciplines throughout the United States. These purposeful and calibrated strategies include chronic underfunding of ethnic studies programs and departments, shrinkage through faculty attrition/ administrative refusal to rehire as faculty retire, and/or the wavering support for ethnic studies graduation requirements (California State University Task Force on the Advancement of Ethnic Studies, 2016; Huben, 2018).

Strategic attacks against ethnic studies transpire even as the discipline is touted as an exemplar for student success. Recent research provides evidence that links taking ethnic studies courses with positive academic outcomes for all students and improved retention and graduation rates for students of color (California State University Task Force on the Advancement of Ethnic Studies, 2016). Within the context of these and other struggles, both fiscal and ideological, it can be challenging to create room in ethnic studies for mixed race studies, queer ethnic studies, gendered ethnic studies, and similar fields that may engage in critiques of ethnic studies and the cultural nationalism with which it is sometime invested. How, then, do we *open* ethnic studies without *destabilizing* it?

History of the CMRS Minor at SF State

In 2015, the then dean of the College of Ethnic Studies, Kenneth Monteiro, charged Wei Ming Dariotis with developing a response to an external review of the ethnic studies master's program that revealed a student desire for more structural support for an academic program in mixed race studies. At this time, college leadership, in collaboration with Dariotis, determined that rather than creating a master's program in CMRS, or a graduate-level course (although these may be developed in the future), the immediate focus would be on building an undergraduate minor in CMRS. Nicole Leopardo, a lecturer in the Department of Race and Resistance Studies at SF State, was an ethnic studies graduate student at the time of the charge from Monteiro. Leopardo (2016) completed her MA thesis *Food Rituals: An Entree Into Multiracial Family Culture*, a project grounded in CMRS intellectual paradigms, and noticed the lack of structural support for students wanting to engage in CMRS work. These observations and experiences led Leopardo to join Dariotis in designing the CMRS minor.

The creation of CMRS followed the typical model of other more recent degree-granting programs in the College of Ethnic Studies: Programs start off as minors and can be later developed into major programs. Given that SF State is a public institution with a humble budget situated in one of the most expensive cities in the world, we are faced with very limited resources (e.g., financial and available space) for new programs. Thus, we are obliged to strategically introduce smaller scale programs as a testing ground for larger academic programs. Although this approach reflects our very real budget and resource limitations, this process also ensures that academic programs in the college center student demand and interest. Quantitative data such as the number of students enrolled in a certain course or minor can dictate the expansion of programs. This process allows for ethnic studies programmatic growth and ingenuity without the risk of sinking too many resources into a larger scale program (such as a full major or master's program).

Before the proposal could be submitted, however, the college had to determine where the minor would be housed. Dariotis is a professor in the Department of Asian American Studies, in which there was strong support for the minor. Some initial discussions suggested housing the minor in Asian American Studies for this reason. The approval process within the Department of Asian American Studies would have been relatively quick and easy. However, such a structure would not have supported the deeper integration of CMRS throughout the college, which we felt was absolutely necessary both for the growth of CMRS and indeed for the development of the College of Ethnic Studies itself. So we proposed that the minor be part of the general college program instead of living in a specific department.

Thus, we began the time-consuming work of seeking approval and support for the proposed minor in each unit of the college, which consist of the four original departments—Africana (Black) Studies, American Indian Studies, Asian American Studies, and Latina/Latino (Raza) Studies—as well as Race and Resistance Studies (which became a full department in May of 2019). We created documents and presentations to communicate the need for the minor, including an extensive survey of student interest. We met with the college council (consisting of the department chairs and college leadership) and with individual departments—several more than once. No other undergraduate degree-granting program in the college has been developed through college-wide approval processes, and, indeed, this part of the project unexpectedly took more than an academic year. One of our challenges in this process was that we had to navigate between frameworks of heterogeneity and cultural nationalist paradigms that may not support multiraciality as an acceptable identity choice, let alone CMRS as a legitimate field of academic inquiry, in part due to the complex and often painful histories mixedness represents within communities of color. Locating and building solidarity while honoring the self-determination of each existing academic department and the then program (now department) of Race and Resistance Studies was key to creating a successful minor program.

The College of Ethnic Studies is built on the concept of the solidarity of the college in balance with the sovereignty of deeply heterogeneous departments. The heterogeneity of Africana Studies, Latina/Latino Studies, Asian American Studies, American Indian Studies, and Race and Resistance Studies can be seen in the names of these programs, which do not follow a standardized principle, but instead are drawn from individual disciplinary histories.[4] The various paradigms through which these departments have approached mixedness have helped to set the foundations for CMRS pedagogy, as these approaches are reflective of differential racializations faced by specific racial and ethnic groups.

For example, Africana studies, African American studies, and Black studies as disciplines primarily frame mixedness as intraracial variation among African Americans due to the history of interracial relations between African Americans, European Americans, and American Indians. Mixedness in the Africana context includes the painful history of sexual violence that Black women were subject to under slavery, as well as interracial unions between Black, European, and Indigenous peoples in the Americas. G. Reginald Daniel differentiated between African Americans who are considered "multigenerational multiracials" and "first-generation" mixed people "who have one parent that identifies as monoracially white and another that identifies as monoracially Black" (cited in Miletsky, 2012, p. 150).

Asian American studies examines the ways in which mixedness is situated within the context of violence and war after hundreds of years of European colonialism in Asia, especially in India, China, Indonesia, Southeast Asia, and the Philippines. This context has created a mixed race "buffer" class of Eurasians and Afro-Asians (Dariotis, 2013, p. 137). Williams-León and Nakashima (2001) further argued that "mixed-race Asians are vastly overrepresented among multiracial young people in the United States" (pp. 5–6).

Due to all of these factors, conversations on mixedness have been important within the context of Asian American studies, and, indeed, mixed race studies was included in Asian American studies departments and programs.[5]

The context of United States colonization and resistance has resulted in a substantial number of American Indians who are of mixed heritages. *Mixed blood* (a widely accepted, though contentious, terminology) was born of forced assimilation policies that were devised to dissolve "collectively held tribal lands into individual land allotments" (Gonzalez, 2001, p. 178). Restrictive state-sanctioned definitions of who counts as "Indian" provided the basis for land and resource allocation. In order to claim land from the U.S. government, American Indians had to be of a certain "blood" percentage. Because of this context, American Indian scholarship provides foundational scholarship on "authenticity policing" (Romo, 2017, p. 130) which is the means by which various groups that have experienced colonialism attempt to control definitions of ethnic and/or racial identity within a white-dominated racial hierarchy (Dalmage, 2000).

Chicano, "Raza," and Latina/Latino studies scholarship has included the topic of traditional *mestizaje*, a term complicated by its problematic history of privileging whiteness. Jose Vasconcelos's (1997) *La Raza Cosmica* predicted a "new race" into which current racial categories will be infused and eventually disappear, whereas Gloria Anzaldúa (1987) envisioned *mestizaje* as a cultural, racial, and linguistic "borderlands" created through histories and contemporary realities of violent colonialism. Despite concerns that multiracialism may form a slippery slope toward white supremacy, Anzaldúa's *mestizaje* does not privilege whiteness but instead critiques and disrupts internalized racism and colorism. These approaches have provided Latinx studies with a complex framework for understanding both historical mixed race identities and the contemporary population of mixed Latinxs (Hill et al., 2004).

Although these paradigms may or may not be inclusive of mixed race and transracial adoptee identities explicitly, they provide spaces in which important conversations on mixedness exist within ethnic studies. Although some ethnic studies scholarship may discuss mixed race identities, mixed heritage people and CMRS frameworks are not always centered in analysis. It is not our intention to argue that mixed people need to be centered in these disciplines. However, in order to move out of marginality within ethnic studies, people of mixed backgrounds do need academic and intellectual spaces to explore and articulate their histories, lived experiences, and identities. With the recognition that CMRS has emerged as this intellectual space, Dariotis and Leopardo sought to bring CMRS to the College of Ethnic Studies at SF State.

Defining CMRS and Developing Learning Outcomes

In order to create a new minor program, SF State requires that faculty submit a New Minor Proposal to the Office of Undergraduate Education and Academic Planning. The process is determined by SF State's Academic Senate, the policy-making body on campus. New proposals must include a list of faculty who will teach in the proposed program, a list of faculty who will serve as an advisory board, rationale for the minor program (which includes a survey of closely related curricula currently offered at SF State), a narrative explaining student demand, proposed curriculum, requirements and prerequisites, program description, and the minor's program learning outcomes (PLOs).

PLOs are programmatic goals that include the skills and larger themes that graduates of a program are expected to articulate or put into action. CMRS PLOs were informed both by the College of Ethnic Studies' PLOs and the key tenets of CMRS as a discipline. Because CMRS was to be situated as a general College of Ethnic Studies minor (and not situated under a specific department), we had to ensure that our PLO and program description language were reflective of key values and paradigms expressed by the College of Ethnic Studies, while also emphasizing the unfixed and fluid nature of racial categories.

Program Learning Outcomes

Based on these principles of interdisciplinarity, critique of structural racism and the racial hierarchy, and an emphasis on analytical skills, we (with the support from our advisory council) developed the following five learning outcomes for the program:

1. Gain an interdisciplinary understanding of the histories, cultures, and racializations of various mixed heritage communities, especially in the United States, in order to address local and global systemic injustice rooted in systems of racialization.
2. Apply critical analysis of the institutionalization of social, cultural, and political orders based on dominant conceptions of race.
3. Critique processes of racialization and social stratification based on race through an understanding of the mutability of race and the porosity of racial boundaries.
4. Apply course concepts and critical theories and methodologies to identify the structural, ideological, social, educational, scientific, and legal forces that shape the realities of mixed heritage individuals and communities and to support the self-determination of mixed heritage communities.

5. Construct evidence-based and persuasive oral and written arguments with proper citations and support from multiple forms of knowledge, including community and academic resources. Students will also develop the necessary analytical, written, and oral communication skills to prepare them to bring a racial equity lens, as well as respect for differences, to careers or graduate school.

Rationale

We were required to provide both an intellectual and a practical rationale for a minor in CMRS. Of course, challenging monoraciality and encouraging critical thinking is at the center of our intellectual focus as CMRS scholars. Additionally, we considered how we might provide a case for creating a program for a discipline that is not only more recent but also challenges deeply set assumptions about race. We had to acknowledge the idea that the increasingly astronomical financial cost and debt burden associated with a college education means that student expectations about the function of their education have shifted from "intrinsic rewards of the college experience" toward the utility or "extrinsic outcomes" of their education (Saunders, 2010, p. 43). Given the current climate of higher education, as well as shifts in the ways that students think about education, we advise that any program consider and clearly communicate the professional utility of a new academic program.

Theoretical Rationale

Through emphasizing the "mutability of race and the porosity of racial boundaries" (para. 4), CMRS courses focus on mixed race, mixed ethnicity, and transracial adoption as having profound legal, economic, social, cultural, psychological, and political impacts on all ethnic communities in the United States and transnationally (Dariotis et al. 2010). The aim of CMRS as an academic discipline is to destabilize constructions of race and racial purity that lead to models of ascribed racial status and racial and ethnic hierarchies in various communities locally, nationally, and transnationally.

Current CMRS scholarship is deeply grounded in Maria P. P. Root's (1992) essential text *Racially Mixed People in America*, which introduced the academic community to a diverse, intergenerational group of scholars in one volume challenging the U.S. racial schema and monoraciality as a norm. Root (1992) cited Paulo Freire's assertion "Marginality is not by choice, [the] marginal [person] has been expelled from and kept outside of the social system" (p. 342) in order to communicate the process of marginalization and the ways in which mixed people are pushed to occupy the liminal spaces of society in order to maintain the divisions required by the racial hierarchy. CMRS centers mixed race and transracially adopted people and, in so doing, undermines processes of marginalization and contributes to the deconstruction of the rigid racial hierarchy.

Practicality Rationale
SF State serves as a pipeline for public school teachers in San Francisco. Its School of Social Work's mission statement is "to educate diverse learners to achieve progressive development and change throughout the Bay Area and beyond" (School of Social Work, n.d, para. 1) and the university receives 600 to 700 applications for the School of Nursing's BSN program each year (Owens Viani, 2018; School of Nursing, 2014). Students working in these social services areas would benefit from a minor in CMRS as the nine-county San Francisco Bay Area overall has a relatively high mixed race population of 5.4% (as seen in the 2010 census), and even higher percentages ranging from 5% to 9.9% among Bay Area youth (Lucile Packard Foundation for Children's Health, n.d.; Metropolitan Transportation Commission & Association of Bay Area Governments, n.d.).

For those students who intend to work in the Bay Area's professional industries, CMRS holds many benefits associated with personal self-development, as well as professional knowledge that is useful in any workplace. On the individual level, research shows that identifying with all elements of one's heritage is "related to a more positive sense of identity, fewer psychological problems, and greater self-confidence" (Marsh, 2010, p. 98). CMRS offers all students opportunities to deeply connect with their multiple intersecting heritages, even if they have previously identified monoracially. For example, because CMRS is built on a critique of the racial hierarchy and of racial categories, analyzing the ethnic diversity of monoracially constructed categories (Black, Asian, white, etc.) is an important part of CMRS. Students in CMRS courses are encouraged to question what it means to belong to the categories with which they identify and to reclaim sometimes forgotten or erased legacies even within monoracially constructed identities.

A positive sense of self-identity also has vast implications for when students graduate SF State and begin their professional careers. A strong sense of identity can positively influence the ways employees deal with challenges, offer meaningful contributions, and identify opportunities for professional growth (McQuaid, 2019; Sherman et al., 2013). In addition, professionals who are able to articulate the ways in which racial hierarchy, power, and privilege shape our social world are in a unique position to contribute to important conversations on diversity, equity, and inclusion in the workplace.

Student Demand

There has long been a clearly evident and documented student demand for courses in ethnic studies that bring together multiple groups and communities. Courses on mixed race topics in the College of Ethnic Studies consistently have healthy enrollments, indicating a strong student interest in an increasingly diverse society, global economy, and transnational world. Students are increasingly looking at racial issues that connect nations, racial groups, ethnicities, and borders, as these interact with class, gender, and sexuality. In this transracial and transnational context, mixed heritage/mixed race issues, identities, and experiences are becoming increasingly relevant.

In spring 2018, the CMRS planning group surveyed 215 students and stakeholders primarily in the College of Ethnic Studies and Metro Academy.[6] The purpose of this survey was to measure student interest in a CMRS minor program. We asked if participants thought such a minor was an important educational option for SF State students, if they had ever taken a course centered on mixed race or transracial adoptee studies, and if they would declare a minor in CMRS if it were offered.

Although SF State has seen significant increases in students identifying as "two or more races,"[7] up from 5.5% in 2014 to 6.2% in 2018, this number does not capture those who might identify as multiethnic (e.g., someone who identifies as both Japanese and Hmong) nor those who are transracially adopted (San Francisco State University, 2019). This number may also not include those who make a political choice to choose one racialized category over another, when presented with limited choices. The actual number of students who are mixed race, mixed ethnicity, multigenerationally mixed heritage, and transracially adopted is probably much higher than 6.2%, if we consider mixed race to include mixed heritage/mixed race/mixed ethnicity/multigenerationally mixed or transracially adopted.

Our survey also included an open-ended qualitative portion in which respondents could add additional comments. Because there are many assumptions both about what it means to be mixed race and about who is allowed to claim mixedness, the free response portion of our survey provided space for respondents to qualify their responses. Many participants used this opportunity to share their connection to mixed race identity. Some students expressed that although they are not mixed themselves, they have mixed race or transracially adopted children or family members. Overall, students were enthusiastic about the opportunity to see curriculum that centers mixed race, mixed heritage, and transracial adoptee communities.

Other participants named that adding this minor would be yet another example of SF State's continued position as a university at the forefront of social justice education programs. Although the legacy and images of the

1968 Strike provide the context for SF State's continued commitment to social justice, new programs in Queer Ethnic Studies, critical Pacific Islands and Oceania Studies, and Race and Resistance Studies continue this legacy of cutting edge, culturally relevant education. Further, initiatives such as a faculty position in Afro-Latinidad in the Latina/Latino Studies Department and discussions about creating an Afro-Asian position in Asian American Studies demonstrate a shift in attention toward the intersections of identities that had previously been conceived of with less fluid boundaries. In this way, the spirit of CMRS fits into the context of ethnic studies at SF State despite not having been historically centered in the ethnic studies narrative.

Crafting the Minor

Merging the theoretical frameworks of antimarginality and antihierarchicalization with practice, we developed a CMRS advisory council of lecturer, junior, and senior faculty while we were in the proposal development stage of this process.[8] The task of this council was to provide necessary support and feedback through the process of building support for the minor, while also advising on the academic structure of the minor. In addition, the council was able to provide feedback on how the minor relates to the College of Ethnic Studies' other existing degree-granting programs.

In the spirit of the 1968 strikers, who claimed a place for themselves and the generations to follow in the institution through their active participation and disruption of academic hierarchy, Nicole Leopardo and Kira Donnell, both alumni of the College of Ethnic Studies' graduate programs, now continued their work and research in the college as lecturer faculty. Although lecturers are not typically empowered or expected to help create academic programs, Leopardo and Donnell actively engaged in CMRS program building. Leopardo worked closely with Dariotis in writing the proposal for the minor, learning about institutional processes along the way. The development of curriculum on transracial adoption, a foundational course for the minor, was a collaborative effort helmed by Donnell and Sophie Navarro, a graduate student in the Asian American Studies Department. With support from a student success grant from the Office of the Dean of Ethnic Studies, Donnell and Navarro organized readings, lesson plans, and student learning outcomes into a cohesive course curriculum and syllabus.

Lessons Learned

Now that we have completed the process of getting the minor through all of the layers of institutional approval, we are excited to have the opportunity to reflect back and consider the lessons we have learned. We offer the following suggestions, knowing that the situation of the SF State College of Ethnic Studies is unique. We hope that these ideas are useful to others as CMRS programs are considered and developed at other academic institutions.

Gather Support

Gaining institutional approval can be (and in this case certainly was) an exhausting process. In this case, because both Leopardo and Dariotis, the primary movers of the minor proposal, are mixed race–identified people, every point in the process opened up the possibility of rejection that we could feel in an intimate and personal way. Having each other and members of the advisory council as both personal and logistical support was critical for the ultimate success of this project. Thus, the first lesson we would like to share with others who may consider taking on such a project is to develop a strong support network. The larger extended community of CMRS scholars is an important and valuable resource; be sure to search for allies locally as well.

Gather Data

We knew that a CMRS minor was important for SF State because many students expressed that they needed a deeper understanding of mixed race and transracially adopted individuals, families, and communities. As faculty (and fellow mixed race, intersectional people) we also knew that students were experiencing the erasure of mixed race identities because of the dominance of monoracial frameworks and resulting institutional policies and practices (like data collection that only allows participants to choose one racial or ethnic category). Ask both *why* your campus needs CMRS and *how* you can best determine and support the needs of students and faculty both now and in the future. We conducted a survey. You may consider hosting a focus group or an open forum. Needs are only part of the data picture; it is also important to survey the assets of your institution. What courses, programs, resources, and/or faculty support are already in place? How can you turn the program development process into a mentoring project at your institution in order to develop identified assets?

Determine Form

Once you have analyzed the needs and assets of your particular situation, consider what form of academic program would be most appropriate given the specific demographics, structure, and assets of your institution. Institutional processes, histories, and other factors may create a pressure to determine the form of your program (as our then dean's dictum and the prevailing wisdom of various stakeholders in the college determined our program). Think about how this initial form might be tied to future development and consider how strategic partnerships may provide opportunities for programmatic development. For example, after the creation of the minor program, we partnered with the SF State development team to create a scholarship fund to support students financially and publicize the minor.

Choose a Process

Consider whether or not the easiest way is the best way. It would have been easier for the CMRS minor to be located in the Asian American Studies Department at SF State, but that would not have been best for the program. The process you choose should allow you to build alliances and community, as well as goodwill. Creating a minor program like CMRS benefits from a clear analysis of need, as well as foresight toward possible institutional, political, and individual blockages. Having a process that allows for open communication, thoughtful questioning, and collaboration will yield a successful outcome, even if it is not exactly the one that is planned at the outset. Remain open to change.

After the actual minor is created, formulate a communication plan to let people know about your new program. This plan should address multiple audiences and should be adaptable as information and audience shift. When the SF State CMRS minor passed, we created specific promotional language for various stakeholders including academic advisers, faculty, and students. The minor has also been communicated out to the larger community of CMRS scholars and activists through social media platforms and personal communications.

Be Patient

CMRS may bring up unexpected issues for individuals and programs within and outside of your institution. Be prepared to answer questions on both of those fronts. Be patient with yourself, with others, and with the process. Institutional processes are often slower than we expect. Although judicious pushing can sometimes yield positive results, it can also often backfire. Sometimes, the most important thing you can do is wait.

Be Principled

Because of our particular situation, we chose to adhere to principles of sovereignty, cooperation, antimarginality, and most importantly, antihierarchy both in how we moved through institutional processes and in how we functioned with each other and with our advisory board. Think about core principles that are valued by both you and your community. In what ways can these principles and values guide your process?

Think About Legacy and Longevity

Your thinking around program design should consider current academic and professional student needs while still considering the legacy and longevity of your CMRS program. In the context of the 50th anniversary of the founding of the College of Ethnic Studies, we were compelled to consider how CMRS might support the legacy of the college while also ensuring longevity. By questioning the boundaries that both define and sometimes limit ethnic and racial identity, CMRS initiates processes of cultural and intellectual regeneration. Establishing academic programs in CMRS opens up and makes agile ethnic studies in ways that are needed in order to push against the calcification and rigidity that institutionalization often imposes.

Room to Grow

In our increasingly multiracial America, to have a CMRS program—the first degree-granting program in CMRS in the United States—at SF State is critical. The minor's home in the College of Ethnic Studies is a reminder that CMRS is rooted in the revolutionary efforts of the strikers to advocate for self-determination and culturally relevant coursework. It is also a testament to the ways in which ethnic studies as a discipline continues to grow and transform 50 years after its founding. Keeping CMRS true to its central purpose of questioning boundaries allows ethnic studies as a whole to anticipate and prepare for transformation.

Academic programs in CMRS support the development of CMRS scholarship by providing opportunities to create more specific courses in particular areas of CMRS through which teacher-scholars can develop ideas and materials that may become scholarship. They also nurture developing student-scholars who can see that their area of intellectual inquiry is validated as a legitimate part of the academy. A generation ago, these students could read scholarship that was often created *despite*, not because of, the job descriptions or the defined areas of research of the scholars who produced them. Students then were often discouraged by the lack of institutional recognition of CMRS. The growing establishment of CMRS as a discipline creates greater security and legitimacy for present and future scholars.

As CMRS matures through the CMRS Association, the CMRS Conference, and through the establishment of CMRS academic programs, we anticipate that CMRS scholars will further develop critiques of systemic racism. CMRS as a discipline expands and questions rigid racial boundaries, including questioning who counts as "mixed" and investigating the contradictions about who belongs in each specific ethnic or racial category. CMRS also asks why these categories were created and how and why they continue to be maintained. As data collection and interpretation about mixed race populations become more nuanced and responsive to community needs and scholarly insights, we will begin to see how these intersecting identities relate to education, health, and socioeconomic outcomes. CMRS scholarship and courses will also more deeply consider cultural productions and the community's intergenerational cultural wealth.

Rooted in the radical inspiration of the Strike and fanned through the controlled burn of interracial, mixed race, and transracial adoptee community activism, CMRS is now growing rapidly in the rich soil created by these scholar and community activists. These seeds that have been released, like the SF State CMRS minor, must be nurtured with love in the recognition that they are part of a cycle that will be renewed again and again through scholarly attention and student and community activism. This chapter is a call to action: the ground is ready, so plant more CMRS seeds and help them grow!

Notes

1. Cofounded by Laura Kina, Camilla Fojas, and Wei Ming Dariotis.
2. SF State's CMRS minor consists of 18 units of undergraduate study. Mandatory courses are one introductory course (ETHS 110); three courses, no more than one from each of the Ethnic Focus sections (Asian American studies, American Indian studies, Latina/Latino studies, and Africana studies). One course is to be selected from the Comparative section. One of the applied courses (teaching, field research or internship, special study) fulfills the remaining three units needed for the minor (College of Ethnic Studies, 2019).
3. These include Africana or Black studies, Asian American studies, Chicano/Chicano or Latina/Latino or Latino studies, American Indian studies, Arab American studies, Pacific Islander American studies, and more.
4. For example, Asian American studies sought to both claim the political identity "Asian American" and distinguish itself from Asian area studies (Collier & Gonzales, 2009), whereas American Indian studies emphasizes the term *American Indian* in order to foreground colonial history rather than sanitizing it with the term *Native American* (de la Torre, 2001), which would follow a grammatical pattern more similar to Asian American studies. In recent years, the name changes from Raza studies to Latina/Latino studies (Rodriguez, 2010) and Black studies to Africana studies (Carr, 2011) were tied to specific political movements.

5. For example, a class titled The World of Amerasians by Teresa Williams-León at UCSB in 1992 (see Williams et al., 1996) and one called Asian Americans of Mixed Heritage by Malcolm Collier at SF State in 1996; UC Davis long offered a course on mixed heritage Asian Americans originally taught by Kent Ono in the late 1990s.
6. The Metro College Success Program uses targeted outreach to support first-generation, low-income, and/or historically underrepresented students in their success at SF State.
7. The CSU Chancellor's Office codes students who identify as "two or more races" as belonging to the group "Non-Underrepresented Minorities," which also includes white students and Asian/Asian American students (aggregated). The implications of this categorization of all students who identify as "two or more races"—regardless of their particular mix—as being "like white" students have yet to be fully explored but are no doubt negative.
8. The advisory council includes lecturer faculty (Jaimy Mann, Justin Woodard, Kira Donnell, Nanea Renteria, and Nicole Leopardo); Assistant Professor Maria L. Quintana; Associate Professors Andreana Clay, Dawn-Elissa Fischer, Robert Keith Collins, and Wei Ming Dariotis (now a full professor); and Professor Andrew Jolivétte (now at University of California, San Diego).

References

Anzaldúa, G. (1987). *Borderlands/La Frontera: The New Mestiza* (1st ed.). Aunt Lute Books.
California State University Task Force on the Advancement of Ethnic Studies. (2016). *Report of the California State University Task Force on the Advancement of Ethnic Studies*. California State University. https://www2.calstate.edu/impact-of-the-csu/diversity/advancement-of-ethnic-studies/Documents/ethnicstudiesreport.pdf
Carr, G. (2011). What Black Studies is not: Moving from crisis to liberation in Africana intellectual work. *Socialism and Democracy, 25*(1), 178–191. https://doi.org/10.1080/08854300.2011.569201
College of Ethnic Studies. (2019). *Critical Mixed Race Studies Minor.* https://ethnicstudies.sfsu.edu/content/critical-mixed-race-studies-minor
College of Ethnic Studies. (2020) *College of Ethnic Studies Shared Principles.* https://ethnicstudies.sfsu.edu/sites/default/files/Shared%20Principles%20Draft%20%20%282%29.pdf
Collier, M., & Gonzales, D. P. (2009). Origins: People, place, time, dreams. In J. P. Chan, M. Collier, L. Dong, D. P. Gonzales, M. K. Hom, R. Jeung, A. Tintiangco-Cubales, & W. Ueunten (Eds.), *At 40: Asian American Studies @ San Francisco State University* (pp. 7–18). Asian American Studies Department, San Francisco State University.
Dalmage, H. M. (2000). *Tripping on the color line: Black-White multiracial families in a racially divided world.* Rutgers University Press.

Daniel, G. R., Kina, L., Dariotis, W. M., & Fojas, C. (2014). Emerging paradigms in Critical Mixed Race Studies. *Journal of Critical Mixed Race Studies, 1*(1), 6–65. https://escholarship.org/uc/item/2db5652b

Dariotis, W. M. (2013). Both buffer and cosmopolitan: Eurasians, colonialism, and the new "benevolent" globalization. In L. Kina & W. M. Dariotis (Eds.), *War baby/love child: Mixed race Asian American art* (pp. 137–142). University of Washington Press.

Dariotis, W. M., Fojas, C., & Kina, L. (2010). *Welcome from the organizers.* Conference at a Glance. https://criticalmixedracestudies.files.wordpress.com/2017/01/cmrs_2010_program.pdf

de la Torre, J. (2001). From activism to academics: The evolution of American Indian Studies at San Francisco State 1968–2001. *Indigenous Nations Studies Journal, 2*(1), 11–20. https://kuscholarworks.ku.edu/bitstream/handle/1808/5763/ins.v02.n1.11-20.pdf?sequence=1&isAllowed=y

Gonzalez, A. A. (2001). Urban (trans)formations: Changes in meaning and use of American Indian identity. In K. Peters & S. Lobo (Eds.), *American Indians and the urban experience* (pp. 169–186). AltaMira Press.

Hill, L. E., Johnson, H. P., & Tafoya, S. M. (2004). California's multiracial population. *California Counts: Population Trends and Profiles, 6*(1), 20. https://www.ppic.org/content/pubs/cacounts/CC_804LHCC.pdf

Huben, A. (2018, September 14). Students and faculty protest Executive Order 1100 again. *Sundial.* https://sundial.csun.edu/121725/news/students-and-faculty-protest-executive-order-1100-again/

Leopardo, N. (2016). *Food rituals: An entrée into multiracial family culture* [Master's thesis, San Francisco State University]. San Francisco State University Digital Repository. http://sfsu-dspace.calstate.edu/bitstream/handle/10211.3/173208/AS362016ETHSTL46.pdf

Lucile Packard Foundation for Children's Health. (n.d.). *Child population, by race/ethnicity* [Database]. Kidsdata.org. https://www.kidsdata.org/topic/33/child-population-race/pie#fmt=144&loc=2,341,338&tf=108&ch=7,11,726,10,72,9,73,87&pdist=73

Marsh, M. E. (2010). "Who is really to blame?" Biracial perspectives on inequality in America. In K. O. Korgen (Ed.), *Multiracial Americans and social class: The influence of social class on racial identity* (pp. 97–112). Routledge.

McQuaid, M. (2019, February 9). Are you building a positive work identity? *Psychology Today.* https://www.psychologytoday.com/blog/functioning-flourishing/201902/are-you-building-positive-work-identity

Metropolitan Transportation Commission, & Association of Bay Area Governments. (n.d.). *San Francisco Bay Area* [Database]. Bay Area Census. http://www.bayareacensus.ca.gov/bayarea.htm

Miletsky, Z. V. (2012). Mutt like me: Barack Obama and the mixed race experience in historical perspective. In A. J. Jolivétte (Ed.), *Obama and the biracial factor: The battle for a new American majority* (pp. 141–166). Policy Press.

Office of University Development. (2019). *Juanita Tamayo Lott: A woman for all seasons*. San Francisco State University. http://develop.sfsu.edu/juanita-tamayo-lott

Owens Viani, L. (2018, February 1). SF State tackles the public school teacher shortfall. *SF State News*. https://news.sfsu.edu/news-story/sf-state-tackles-public-school-teacher-shortfall

Rodriguez, R. T. (2010). The locations of Chicano/a and Latino/a Studies. In J. C. Rowe (Ed.), *A concise companion to American studies* (pp. 190–209). Wiley-Blackwell.

Romo, R. (2017). "You're not Black or Mexican enough!": Policing racial/ethnic authenticity among Blaxicans in the United States. In J. L. Rondilla, R. P. Guevarra, & P. Spickard (Eds.), *Red and yellow, Black and brown: Decentering whiteness in mixed race studies* (pp. 127–144). Rutgers University Press.

Root, M. P. P. (Ed.). (1992). *Racially mixed people in America*. SAGE.

San Francisco State College Black Student Union. (1968). *Demands and explanations*. 1968–1969 San Francisco State College Strike Collection, Black Student Union, University Archives, J. Paul Leonard Library, San Francisco State University.

San Francisco State University. (2019). *Student data* [Database]. Office of Institutional Research. https://ir.sfsu.edu/content/students-data

San Francisco State University Academic Senate. (2015). *Revision to mission statement policy*. http://senate.sfsu.edu/policy/revision-mission-statement-policy

Saunders, D. B. (2010). Neoliberal ideology and public higher education in the United States. *Journal for Critical Education Policy Studies*, 8(1), 42–77. https://eric.ed.gov/?id=EJ896262

School of Nursing. (2014). *Fact sheet for nursing bachelor of science*. San Francisco State University. http://www.nursing.sfsu.edu/sites/default/files/BSN%20Fact%20Sheet-April2014_QR.pdf

School of Social Work, San Francisco State University. (n.d.). *School of social work*. https://socwork.sfsu.edu/content/aboutus

Sherman, D., Hartson, K., Binning, K., Purdie-Vaughns, V., Garcia, J., Taborsky-Barba, S., Tomassetti, S., Nussbaum, D., & Cohen, G. (2013). Deflecting the trajectory and changing the narrative: How self-affirmation affects academic performance and motivation under identity threat. *Journal of Personality and Social Psychology*, *104*(4), 591–618. https://doi.org/10.1037/a0031495

Vasconcelos, J. (1997). *The cosmic race/La raza cosmica*. Johns Hopkins University Press.

Williams, T. K., Nakashima, C. L., Kitahara Kich, G., & Daniel, G. R. (1996). Being different together in the university classroom: Multiracial identity as transgressive education. In M. P. P. Root (Ed.), *The multiracial experience: Racial borders as the new frontier* (pp. 359–379). SAGE. https://doi.org/10.4135/9781483327433

Williams-León, T., & Nakashima, C. L. (2001). Reconfiguring race, rearticulating ethnicity. In T. Williams-León & C. L. Nakashima (Eds.), *The sum of our parts: Mixed-heritage Asian Americans* (pp. 3–10). Temple University Press.

PART FOUR

FUTURE DIRECTIONS

15

INTERGENERATIONAL REFLECTIONS AND FUTURE DIRECTIONS

Marc P. Johnston-Guerrero, Charmaine L. Wijeyesinghe, and Lisa Combs

This closing chapter offers reflections on the theoretical material, narratives, tools, and strategies presented in the volume as well as recommendations for future work on the experiences of multiracial people in higher education. The editors, who represent different generations of scholars and writers engaging the topic of multiracial identity and experiences, are joined by an emerging scholar who provides another voice to our collective thoughts. Charmaine, who defended her dissertation in 1992, represents the experiences of those who paved the way for this emerging field of mixed race studies. Marc, who defended his dissertation in 2013, represents someone at midcareer, with a solid grounding in the scholarship and network of multiracial scholars and practitioners. And Lisa, who is just starting her PhD journey, represents the next generation of scholars, with much enthusiasm and earnestness to make their mark. Together our voices offer multigenerational viewpoints on what the chapters tell us about "future directions" for scholarship and practice. We begin the chapter with Lisa's reflection on the volume that weaves in parts of her personal narrative. Marc and Charmaine then offer their reflections, with Marc building on and adding to Lisa's thoughts and Charmaine addressing the issue of resistance. We conclude by offering a collectively built list of some of the possible future directions and important considerations for those engaging in this work moving forward.

Lisa's Narrative Reflection

Multiracial Experiences in Higher Education illuminates and complicates the ways in which multiraciality is viewed in higher education. The structure of the volume allows for a more nuanced view of what it means to be multira-cial in higher education, from different perspectives and facets of experience. I feel particularly compelled to write about how as a biracial Filipina woman, I feel seen, validated, and heard by the multiracial narratives across the higher education landscape. I *resonated* with Nick Davis when he wrote about feel-ing like he had to prove his racial identity. I felt *heard* by Victoria K. Malaney Brown when she described a fractured existence and her journey to becom-ing a scholar-practitioner. I felt *seen* when Rebecca Cepeda shared her narra-tive of not feeling racially enough or understood until her master's program. I felt *inspired* by e alexander's indigenous perspective on multiraciality. I felt *believed* when Naliyah Kaya utilized poetry to capture "existing in-between." I felt *understood* when Andrew Jolivétte used the language of "fitting nowhere" and "fitting everywhere." As an aspiring researcher, I have felt fear when talk-ing with multiracial scholars about how they have decided to move away from writing about multiraciality. I question why they have moved away. I often feel like I am telling this story so loud, yet no one hears me. However, reading these chapters motivates and challenges me as a future PhD student and scholar to think more deeply and with a more expansive lens. In this response, I will focus on four major themes that I believe call for future directions in multiracial research through the lenses of my own perspective, experiences, and narrative.

Multiracial Families and DNA Tests

One compelling point I read across the narratives and other chapters was the impact of family and DNA tests on multiracial identity. I have a vivid memory from my childhood of my parents preparing dinner for our family one summer evening. My White father was grilling steak outside, and my Filipina mother was cutting up mango slices inside as the side that would pair with our steak. I can remember it so clearly, the contrast of the charred steak and the bright yellow orange color of the mangoes. I often wonder what it could have looked like if my parents talked to me about what this meal meant and what multiracial identity was. What would my life have looked like if I had the language to describe my identity and experience back then? The lack of conversation between parents and their children was evident in one of the stories that Charmaine L. Wijeyesinghe recounts in chapter 3. I wonder about the impact of these conversations for multiracial and monoracial people alike.

Additionally, the volume often highlights the complications of DNA testing on multiraciality and perceptions of identity. Kristen A. Renn writes about these complications in chapter 2 when she discusses that DNA kits reinforce "ideas about racial biology and genetic determinism" (p. 29, this volume). I have a complicated relationship with DNA kits as I was recently connected with a family member previously unknown to me this past year because of the results. I can see how DNA tests may create empowerment or connectivity. However, I have also seen their negative impact. A colleague and friend who identifies as Afro-Latina recently received results from a DNA kit. Her results showed lower percentages in her ancestry associated with being Latina. This led to her questioning her identity as a multiracial woman. She wondered if she was Latina enough to claim an identity she has known her whole life. This phenomenon of quantifying identity is a function of White supremacy that commodifies race and equates it to a number in order to contribute to capitalism and uphold systems of oppression. These narratives and themes call for more work and research on the impact of family and DNA tests/kits on multiracial identity.

Relationship Between Monoracism, Racism, Colorism, and White Supremacy

As I sit down to write this paragraph, there is a line underneath the word *Monoracism* in the header, signaling to me as the writer that this word is not recognized by Microsoft Word. I once heard a colleague refer to this as the *squiggly line of oppression*. To me, this also illuminates the importance of teaching about and expanding upon the definition of monoracism that Jessica C. Harris, Marc P. Johnston-Guerrero, and Maxwell Pereyra convey in chapter 4. Currently, I work as a program coordinator in a multicultural affairs office where I support first-generation students and students of color. I also serve as an adviser to the Mixed Heritage Union student organization. Whenever the concept of multiraciality comes up, students' first reaction is to equate it to colorism. Colorism is a system of oppression based on skin color where folx with lighter skin tones have privilege. As a biracial woman of color, I often feel like this minimizes and erases my experience as a multiracial person because to me colorism and monoracism are two different systems of oppression that are working together to uphold White supremacy.

Harris, Johnston-Guerrero, and Pereyra assert a similar point in their chapter when they write "we see how racism and monoracism are integrally connected to rather than aligned with a false binary between monoraciality and Multiraciality" (p. 61, this volume). A limitation in chapter 4 is that the contributors did not focus on colorism and its impact and connections to multiraciality. How do we delineate colorism, racism, and monoracism as different systems of oppression without creating false binaries? How does one articulate the argument that these systems are not conflated nor are they the same or in competition with one another? Yet they cooperate with one another to reinforce White supremacy. When differentiating among these three systems, I observe an invisible competition among the three, often resembling a miniature oppression Olympics. These three systems are all symptoms of a larger system of oppression. How does one make this argument without signifying sameness in the experiencing of monoracism, colorism, and racism?

Focus on Professional Staff

I really appreciate that the volume has explicit and subtle calls to action to focus more on multiracial staff in higher education. Renn describes this in chapter 2, and Part Three of the volume explores specific and tangible tools such as story circles, student organizations, and curricular development. Renn discusses how most of the work on multiraciality centers on students and her interest in where people who were once students are now is compelling and motivating to me as a future scholar. As I mentioned earlier, I am a multiracial student affairs practitioner who works in multicultural affairs. I have experienced a lot of pushback from students of color because of my multiracial identity. Some students have voiced concerns that I am not a "real person of color," so therefore I should not be supporting students of color. My experience has been incredibly painful and invalidating. This is why I believe in the importance of sharing stories of multiracial practitioners in higher education, whether they specifically work in multicultural affairs or in other functional areas as well.

Students in the multiracial student group I advise have also experienced similar pushback. The existence of the Mixed Heritage Union is often called into question because students wonder why this group needs to exist when there are already monoracial cultural groups in place. This pushback has often left multiracial students feeling invalidated. Multiracial staff experiences impact both multiracial staff and students. This is why I also believe that sharing these stories can lead to more cocreation of strategies and tangible tools for professionals in the field. I specifically wonder what it would look like to do a study that focused on staff members utilizing the contextualizing multiraciality in campus climate model that Chelsea Guillermo-Wann and Marc P. Johnston-Guerrero write about in chapter 11.

Imaginative Thinking

Something that I truly love about this volume is that it inspires insightful thinking. The chapters provoke questions that can point to future discovery and scholarship. A point that is illuminated in the book is that multiraciality and monoracism can be utilized to tell a larger narrative about racism and White supremacy. However, the tension lies in tokenizing multiracial folx as an answer to "solving racism" or creating a "postracial" society. This complexity that Wijeyesinghe writes about in chapter 3 is fascinating to me. I often think about how a function of White supremacy reinforces the "either/or" narrative and how multiraciality is a narrative that actively works against White supremacy because multiraciality exists as a "both/and." As educators and scholars, how do we articulate that multiraciality contributes to dismantling racial constructs without putting the onus on multiracial people and without further contributing to monoracism? Another observation that I have from the text is that transracial adoptees are only mentioned a few times in the volume. This leaves me wondering, where is the place of transracial adoptees in multiracial scholarship and literature? Another thought I felt motivated by was the idea of empowerment in multiracial communities. When I was receiving my master's degree, I remember learning about Yosso's (2005) community cultural wealth model, and I felt deeply connected to the idea of navigational capital. Yosso (2005) defined *navigational capital* as "skills of maneuvering through social institutions" (p. 80). As a multiracial person, I often feel that I have access to different spaces and that I am able to navigate different spaces because of my identity which left me feeling affirmed. What would it look like to encourage multiracial folx to reflect on the ways in which they feel empowered by their multiracial identity? You may have noticed that throughout my response, I have used imaginative language such as "I wonder" or "what would it look like?" I firmly believe that this imaginative voice within me is a call to action to more expansive thinking around multiraciality. As readers, students, practitioners, and scholars, I invite you to look beyond what already exists and imagine what could be in the world of multiraciality.

Marc's Reflection

Lisa's reflection on the chapters in this volume provides a testament to the need for more voices in this area and, as she rightly points out, especially for multiracial professional staff. Given her experiences working in multicultural affairs, which she states has often been "incredibly painful and invalidating," much more research is needed to understand these dynamics playing out in a context that is intended to be a counterspace for Students of Color (Solórzano et al., 2002). Yet how much of this mission includes multiracial students (and staff)? This question has been repeatedly raised over the past 2 decades, as Renn (2000) asked: "Are services for (ostensibly) monoracial students of color equally available for multiracial students who have white heritage?" (p. 418). Across the years, investigations (e.g., Harris, 2017; Literte, 2010; Wong & Buckner, 2008) have consistently found that student services organized to support racially minoritized students are monoracially designed and that multiracial students struggle with wondering whether they can or should utilize such services. This is an ethical issue (Roper & McAloney, 2010), particularly when campuses might use multiracial students in their demographic counts of diversity (Ford et al., 2019) yet aren't matching the resources necessary to support them.

What I appreciated most from Lisa's reflection was that I could feel the emotions within her reactions. Feeling "seen," "validated," and "heard" are powerful statements that we need to pay more attention to. I for one know I am guilty of being socialized into thinking that researchers need to be objective (or as objective as possible), which we know is a symptom of a larger academic enterprise grounded in Western and colonial ideologies. Much of the past literature on multiracial people seems to be underdeveloped in terms of emotions. Part of me wonders if perhaps this underdevelopment is because of scholars not wanting their work to be conflated with stereotypes about being confused. I also remember critiques about how much of the literature in the 1990s (e.g., Root's edited volumes) was based mostly on personal narratives rather than empirical research. Perhaps we are missing opportunities to dive deeper into personal meaning and emotion by trying to be more empirical and "objective" in our scholarship.

As Lisa points out, DNA ancestry testing is an important topic brought up in several chapters but needing much more attention. I appreciated her personal story as well as the complications the testing might have for one's questioning of identity and belonging. This point rings true—that DNA test results are reinscribing quantification of our identities, which then likely reinforces questioning about whether or not we are "enough" of any identity. During my graduate studies at UCLA, I was a fellow with the Institute for Society and Genetics, which gave me opportunities to engage my bachelor's degree in human biology with my background in student affairs. It also gave me access to a growing body of research on genomics and DNA ancestry testing (e.g., Benjamin, 2015; Panofsky & Donovan, 2019), yet very few studies have actively engaged college campuses (e.g., Foeman, 2012). This area of inquiry is especially important for deconstructing misconceptions of what it means to be Native American (TallBear, 2014), as colleagues working in Native American student services have shared with me how some students try to use DNA test results to claim being Native to access resources.

Lisa accurately points out that although chapters and narratives in the volume illuminate multiple systems of oppression, including monoracism, the system of colorism is generally overlooked in the volume. This area needs much more attention to try to untangle the connections between and among racism, monoracism, and colorism. Further work may reveal just how related and interconnected these systems are, particularly in the often overlooked experiences of multiracial people from two minoritized groups, such as Blasians (Washington, 2017) and Mexipinos (Guevarra, 2012).

Reflecting on Lisa's narrative also brings me to contemplate the role and utility of the "of color" nomenclature, particularly for capturing individual versus group identity. Questions around whether multiracial people identify as People of Color or whether (monoracial) People of Color want to include multiracial people (particularly those who are also White) needs further attention. There continue to be discussions and debates about the extent to which non-Black People of Color are or should be included as People of Color (e.g., Asian Americans; see Bhangal & Poon, 2020), but I have not necessarily seen the conversation explicitly engage multiracial people. The dynamic can also be seen in the increasing usage of BIPOC (Black, Indigenous, People of Color) to center the uniqueness of the relationships between Black and Indigenous communities and whiteness (BIPOC Project, n.d.). The experiences that Lisa conveyed about her work in multicultural affairs and with the Mixed Heritage Union suggest that monoracially identifying Students of Color do not see multiracially identifying Students of Color as part of their group. There is always potential for monoracial groups to offer solidarity if doing so is not seen as taking space/resources away from the larger agenda of racial justice. Yet how do we get monoracial Communities of Color to see that dismantling monoracism is needed to dismantle racism?

As I reflected upon in my narrative from chapter 1, the relationship between (mono)racially minoritized student groups and multiracial groups seems to still be tense. Lisa's experience advising the Mixed Heritage Union and its very existence being called into question is so similar to struggles I observed in creating a new Mixed student group at MSU when I was a graduate student and staff member. How much has changed in 15 years? As Wijeyesinghe states in chapter 3: "History hasn't changed that much" (p. 38, this volume). So now, what can we learn from that history so that it doesn't keep repeating itself? My hope is that this volume, and our collective "imaginative thinking," as Lisa put it, will offer some ways to really move our field forward.

Charmaine's Reflection

This chapter and this volume include multiple generations of thinkers, and I hope readers find insights and questions to support our curiosity, our wondering, and our wandering for years to come. I value the voice and acuity of Lisa's and Marc's reflections. Like Lisa, I wonder what issues and questions are on the horizon and where the journey of investigating them will take us. Lisa and Marc have identified key areas for exploration, and additional recommendations based on our collective thoughts appear at the end of this chapter. For my concluding narrative, I chose to move in a different direction and to focus on a topic that appears in Lisa's narrative and in multiple chapters and that I believe will affect future work on Multiracial people in higher education: resistance.

Regardless of the aspects of Multiracial experiences in higher education they examine or the nature of the methods they use, scholars and practitioners will encounter some form of resistance or push back. Resistance appears in many guises, some of which were discussed in the chapters and in Lisa's narrative. It may be present when the validity of Multiracial topics is questioned or when people resist addressing monoracial norms that direct data collection or the formation of student groups. It may feed arguments that Multiracial topics reify categories and therefore centuries of oppression. Resistance is inevitable when working with and even beyond dominant representations of race, ancestry, racial groupings, and other constructs. Thus, understanding and addressing resistance will be essential componenets of strategies to advance critical knowledge and practices related to Multiracial people in higher education.

Many contributors in this volume have noted that the history of race, racial categories, and racism is complex and troubled. Systemic racism and White supremacy have created racial categories that, although representing false divisions, have been hard to dislodge from our collective narrative about race, racial identity, and racial groups. Adopting these socially constructed categories in research and work with Multiracial people in higher education highlights a challenge of using the "both/and" approach—our efforts both draw on these categories and illuminate their deceit. As we go forward, addressing how oppressive systems are served by critiques that Multiracial people reify aspects of those very same systems will be essential. It may be hard and painful work, and it requires sustained and difficult conversations and reflection. Yet our efforts may result in an analysis that, although messy and imperfect, unveils ways of discussing Multiracial lives with language and constructs independent of fixed and false categories. However, new language and concepts themselves may become sites of resistance.

As chapters in this volume have illustrated, Multiracial experiences interject complexity into analyses of identity, interactions, and systems. For example, the multiple levels and types of monoracism expand conceptualizations of the forms and effects of racism. The fluidity and liminality of identity that some Multiracial people experience and that are so eloquently reflected in the narratives in this book challenge the framing of identity as a developmental process with a preferred endpoint. Some people, including those individuals working with Multiracial topics, might find it difficult to make room for new ideas that muddy waters long thought clear based on foundational concepts (like stages of identity development). Even I struggle here—how many racisms are there now? Is "mixedness" a word? My younger colleagues gently suggest that "it's a generational thing." Even now, their wisdom and spirit make me smile. To value new and challenging ideas we have to open ourselves up to the discomfort inherent with struggling with new language, embracing new colleagues, and moving away from perspectives that may be less relevant to evolving topics and concerns.

Lisa and Marc both spoke of emotions, and I believe the history and emotion attached to certain foundational constructs leave them harder to reconsider than others. For example, about 15 years ago I was a panelist for a program on racial identity at a national conference. As I described choice of identity as an essential part of the Multiracial experience, other panelists who were authors of prominent monoracial models countered my assertion, saying, "I can't choose to be Black" and "I can't choose whether I'm Asian or not." Many Multiracial people shared with me that they've encountered similar responses to the idea of "choice." I still believe that choice is a pillar of Multiracial experience, but learning from these exchanges, I am so much more aware of the troubled histories that foster resistance to it. Choice, monoracism, and liminality can be flash points for resistance. They are also opportunities for dialogue and reflection. Within the tension that may raise, *all of us* can find ways to question, learn, and grow.

In my experience resistance, like conflict, is often seen as something to avoid or immediately challenge "head on." It's flight or fight. However, resistance is a needed force as Multiracial topics move forward and evolve. Resistance invites scholars and practitioners to revisit ideas and concepts that we've used to ground discussions of identity, experience, and systems (even as we create knowledge that contests these areas). A critical aspect of this work is an awareness of how our own social identities and locations, academic training, and personal experiences influence our beliefs and actions. Here I adapt the perspective on standpoint epistemology offered by Collins (2019) and apply it to individuals. Collins noted that "standpoint epistemology rests on claiming the integrity of theorizing from one's own experiences. This means seeing one's own knowledge as situated within social contexts." (p. 139). Numerous contributors have shared information about themselves so that readers might consider how authors' standpoints, their "distinctive angles of vision" (Collins, 2019, p. 136), have influenced the material presented in the chapters. As we go forward, scholars and practitioners might follow their example. By openly considering our standpoints we name how personal experiences based on social locations, access to knowledge, and interpretation of that knowledge inform the perspectives, methods, and beliefs we bring to research and practice. This sharing may encourage people expressing resistance to do the same. From their stories we may better understand why some people resist or even oppose Multiracial topics and find ways to respond to their concerns rather than avoid or contest them.

Finally, so much of our vision is cast toward what lies ahead. Addressing current and future resistance requires understanding the dynamics that brought us to this point. As many contributors have noted, White supremacy and racism foster competition across racial communities. There is potential for solidarity if this narrative is upended. Roots of the false messages that Multiracial people are the proverbial bridge across the racial divide or the vehicles to move America to its postracial future can be found centuries back. The same history informs the role and emboldens the use of colorism. A different history informs the hierarchy in higher education that privileges the knowledge of faculty over the wisdom offered by staff. As Lisa, Marc, I, and many contributors provide visions of the future, some of the resistance to these ideas can be understood by looking at the past.

Moving Forward

Our reflections on the collective wisdom of the volume also highlight areas that are still left underdeveloped or voices that are left out completely when considering multiracial experiences in higher education. Thus, we begin this section by offering recommendations for future directions in scholarship and practice that focus on filling the gaps within this volume. Then we discuss further considerations based on current circumstances and future trends. Finally, we offer broader suggestions and strategies for continuing to capture and support the experiences of multiracial students, staff, and faculty in higher education.

Filling the Gaps

In addition to the areas noted previously in our reflections (particularly the influence of DNA ancestry testing and colorism), we identified several gaps in topical areas and voices that provide ample opportunity for further engagement. These include the following:

- Fuller discussion of the place of transracial adoptees: As Marc Johnston-Guerrero and Charmaine L. Wijeyesinghe note in the preface, we chose not to explicitly engage transracial adoptees in this volume on multiracial experiences. There is still debate about whether transracial adoptees should be included within broader multiracial scholarship and organizing, as done by the Critical Mixed Race Studies Program described in chapter 14, or supported to create their own distinct place within higher education. More work is needed to better understand the experiences of transracial adoptees in order to avoid excluding voices but also not to solely subsume them within multiracial scholarship and practice.

- Capturing futher diversity of multiracial people: As evidenced in the narratives of this volume, being multiracial is not a monolithic experience. Further research is necessary to understand the diversity of multiracial lives based on different heritage combinations, identities, and expressions. We must also continue exploring the experiences of multiracial people who are not mixed with whiteness. Additionally, how do related factors such as immigrant and generational statuses (e.g., Waring & Purkayastha, 2017) influence multiracial people, their identities, and their experiences in higher education?

- More attention to intersectionality: As research evolves to capture distinct experiences based on social identities (e.g., how gender, sexuality, and faith influence experiences of multiracial people), we must continue to center the systems attached to these categories and their interactions with monoracism. For instance, several chapters touched on the importance of further investigating the unique experiences of multiracial Women of Color and how their intersections may or may not connect to varying levels of confidence (e.g., imposter syndrome both racially and in higher education). With this push for more intersectional research, how might work on diverse multiracial experiences (in higher education and elsewhere) contribute to intersectional theory, analysis, and practice?

- Better capturing of institutional diversity: Though the volume has tended to paint higher education in broad strokes, narratives from e alexander (chapter 8), Naliyah Kaya (chapter 9), and Andrew Jolivétte (chapter 10) highlight distinct experiences between minority-serving institutions (MSIs) and predominantly/historically White institutions. Kaya (chapter 9) and Rebecca Cepeda (chapter 7) also discuss attending and working at community colleges, respectively. How can future research and practice better uncover the nuances in the experiences of multiracial people across various institutional types?

- Centering community collaborations and virtual engagement: Though several chapters touched upon the importance of community contexts and partnerships, more attention is necessary to understand and promote working with community-based resources or building bridges between campus organizations or departments and local and even national groups. In addition, within this volume the impact of social media and virtual engagement on multiracial issues has been largely overlooked. How can technology be leveraged to connect multiracial people, and then how can the impact of these connections be researched and insights applied in various settings?
- Furthering practical and pedagogical innovations: Though chapter 4 greatly expands the understanding of monoracism, more work would further the definition and application of this concept. In addition, educating faculty, staff, and students on what monoracism is and how it manifests on campus is a crucial aspect of future work. What would it look like to include monoracism in diversity and equity curricula? Additionally, chapter 14 provides innovative approaches to curricular developments in critical mixed race studies. How can these approaches translate to other higher education and student affairs settings?

Considering Current Circumstances and Future Trends

It is important for us to acknowledge that we are writing this chapter in the midst of the COVID-19 pandemic. Forecasts about the unclear outlook ahead for higher education mean that the landscape may change drastically in the near future. Several other issues and events are also occurring while this book progresses toward publication. The insights, needs, and challenges that these forces will reveal are unknown at this time. Within this uncertainty we offer several considerations that might influence our work moving forward:

- COVID-19 pandemic: How might multiracial people (faculty, staff, students) be differentially impacted by the virus overall, and by the possible resultant changes in higher education? What began as the "great equalizer" in that the virus could infect everyone no matter one's race quickly evolved as a vehicle to broadcast the structural racism across multiple systems (workforce, health care, justice, immigration). The pandemic has had disproportionate, negative impact on Black, Latinx, and Native communities and has fueled increases in anti-Asian discrimination. As monoracially constructed advocacy groups voice their concerns and generate resources for their specific communities, there is always potential for people on the margins of those groups, who don't feel that they can access those resources, to fall through the cracks.

- Census 2020 and demographic changes: At the time of our writing, the 2020 U.S. Census collection is taking place. We anticipate that the multiracial population has changed over the past 10 years, but by how much? Whatever changes are documented in the "two or more races" population, particularly in various combinations, will likely prompt many different areas for further investigation. We should also keep in mind what these demographic changes might mean for higher education, as increases in multiracial faculty, staff, and students are anticipated. Given that most of the research focuses on multiracial students, further research is essential on multiracial staff and faculty, especially those who engage in multicultutral affairs work, and their career trajectories.

- Parenting multiracial children: If the growth of the multiracial youth propulation between 2000 and 2010 is any indicator, this demographic will likely grow again in number, and this growth will be captured in the 2020 census and subsequent counts. Thus, more attention is needed to understand faculty, staff, and students who may be parenting or raising multiracial children. Though recent work is expanding in this area (e.g., Nayani, 2020), specific attention to the role of higher education in informing parenting practices seems like an important and unique area for further study.

- Learning from and with emerging disciplines: As emerging theories and bodies of knowledge from such disciplines as critical race theory (and various offshoots), critical mixed race studies, Indigenous and decolonizing studies, and intersectionality grow, there are opportunities to explicitly engage their influence on how race, identity, and social systems are understood (e.g., Wijeyesinghe, 2012). Each discipline includes core tenets and assumptions that can both facilitate and challenge research and practice pertaining to multiracial people and their experiences. Which tenets can we draw from and which ones, which may be more difficult to enact, can we learn from moving forward?

- Evolving social and political contexts: As chapters in this book illustrate, identity, institutions, and social systems are all affected by changing dynamics, be they cultural, political, or social. National politics related to race are troublesome and troubling. How might these politics be influenced by current and future debates around nation, citizenship, and ethnicity, that frame social messages about who belongs and who does not, who is legitimate and who is not? These questions are staring us in the face during this presidential election year (especially present around Kamala Harris's racial identity) and will surely remain with us for many years. They certainly echo in the history of multiracial people across centuries.

Strategies for Doing the Work

We conclude with a few concrete suggestions related to scholarship and practice that readers may consider as they move forward with their own work. As Charmaine is fond of saying, "Take what's good and leave the rest." When engaging in future knowledge building and practice on the experiences of multiracial people in higher education and in other settings:

- Aim to understand how our work is grounded in and informed by historical contexts. Draw on historical works, where appropriate, but don't be constrained by them.
- Where needed, be clear that the goal of our work is to broaden knowledge and its application, not detract from the experiences of other racial or social groups.
- When working with newer concepts or definitions, take time and space to clearly define them, and use examples so that people with a range of learning styles and prior knowledge can grasp the intent, meaning, and significance of our work. A corollary is, when possible, to avoid "jargon" and, if newer material based on multiracial standpoints is used, ground terms and other material through explanation and examples.
- Continually consider how standpoints influence our beliefs, expectations, and responses to resistance. Engage in what Beighley et al. (2014) referred to as "thorough (sometimes painful) and constant examination" (p. 271). When others share their standpoints, encourage them to say more (rather than less) and work to truly hear and consider standpoints that may be uncomfortable or contradict our personal beliefs.
- Draw from multiple sources and voices "of expertise." As evidenced in the narratives centered in this volume, much can be learned from valuing the experiences and knowledge of staff and students, not just the empirical work from faculty. We crave more work that informs or creates visions of practice—at multiple levels and in multiple sites in higher education. And staff and students are uniquely positioned to contribute to these areas.

- Build coalitions with various groups and always adapt models to local contexts and community. The need for coalition building with (mono) racial groups and with diverse multiracial groups and communities is clear.
- Finallly, be willing to adapt Matsuda's (1996) strategy of "ask[ing] the other question" (p. 64) to unveil how our work may, even unintentionally, contribute to oppression of other racial groups—or groups based on gender, sexual orientation, gender identity, class, disability/ability, and so on. This harm can be done even as we advance what we envision as liberatory scholarship and practice.

Not all of us are able to employ these strategies, and none of us can do all of them all of the time. The responsibility for furthering research and practice and addressing resistance does not lie solely with multiracial people or their allies. We offer these recommendations with the belief and hope that they can empower us as we move forward.

Concluding Gratitude

In conclusion, we wanted to offer gratitude for the community of contributors for sharing their personal stories, keen insights, and overall time and energy. The volume as a whole, as evidenced in the work of the contributors, represents the importance of integrating theory, narrative, and practice moving forward. Although our specific identities, positions, fields, and standpoints may differ, we strengthen the presence of multiracial people in higher education through these collective contributions. Thank you to the reader, who has taken this journey with us. With much anticipation, we look forward to what the future holds for multiracial lives in higher education.

References

Beighley, C. S., Simmons, C., & West, E. (2014). Beyond identity politics: Equipping students to create systemic change. In D. Mitchell, C. Y. Simmons, & L. A. Greyerbiehl (Eds.), *Intersectionality and higher education: Theory, research, and praxis* (pp. 269–279). Peter Lang.

Benjamin, R. (2015). The emperor's new genes: Science, public policy, and the allure of objectivity. *The ANNALS of the American Academy of Political and Social Science, 661*(1), 130–142. https://doi-org.proxy.lib.ohio-state.edu/10.1177/0002716215587859

Bhangal, N., & Poon, O. (2020, January 15). Are Asian Americans White? Or People of Color? *Yes! Magazine.* https://www.yesmagazine.org/social-justice/2020/01/15/asian-americans-people-of-color/

BIPOC Project. (n.d.). *About us.* https://www.thebipocproject.org/

Collins, P. H. (2019). *Intersectionality as critical social theory.* Duke University Press.

Foeman, A. K. (2012). An intercultural project exploring the relationship among DNA ancestry profiles, family narrative, and the social construction of race. *The Journal of Negro Education, 81*(4), 307–318. https://doi.org/10.7709/jnegroeducation.81.4.0307

Ford, K. S., Patterson, A. N., & Johnston-Guerrero, M. P. (2019). Monoracial normativity in university websites: Systematic erasure and selective reclassification of multiracial students. *Journal of Diversity in Higher Education.* Advance online publication. https://doi.org/10.1037/dhe0000154

Guevarra, R. P. Jr. (2012). *Becoming Mexipino: Multiethnic identities and communities in San Diego.* Rutgers University Press.

Harris, J. C. (2017). Multiracial college students' experiences with multiracial microaggressions. *Race Ethnicity and Education, 20*(4), 429–445. https://doi.org/10.1080/13613324.2016.1248836

Literte, P. E. (2010). Revising race: How biracial students are changing and challenging student services. *Journal of College Student Development, 51*(2), 115–134. https://doi.org/10.1353/csd.0.0122

Matusda, M. J. (1996). *Where is your body?: And other essays on race, gender and the law.* Beacon Press.

Nayani, F. (2020). *Raising multiracial children: Tools for nurturing identity in a racialized world.* North Atlantic Books.

Panofsky, A., & Donovan, J. (2019). Genetic ancestry testing among white nationalists: From identity repair to citizen science. *Social Studies of Science, 49*(5), 653–681. https://doi.org/10.1177/0306312719861434

Renn, K. A. (2000). Patterns of situational identity among biracial and multiracial college students. *The Review of Higher Education, 23*(4), 399–420. https://doi.org/10.1353/rhe.2000.0019

Roper, L. D., & McAloney, K. (2010). Is the design for our cultural programs ethical? *Journal of College and Character, 11*(4), 1–3. https://doi.org/10.2202/1940-1639.1743

Solórzano, D., Allen, W. R., & Carroll, G. (2002). Keeping race in place: Racial microaggressions and campus racial climate at the University of California, Berkeley. *Chicano-Latino Law Review, 23,* 15–112. https://escholarship.org/uc/item/5b52m9r3

TallBear, K. (2014). The emergence, politics and marketplace of Native American DNA. In D. L. Kleinman & K. Moore (Eds.), *Routledge handbook of science, technology, and society* (pp. 21–37). Routledge.

Waring, C. D. L., & Purkayastha, B. (2017). "I'm a different kind of biracial": How black/white biracial Americans with immigrant parents negotiate race. *Social Identities, 23*(5), 614–630. https://doi.org/10.1080/13504630.2016.1271739

Washington, M. S. (2017). *Blasian invasion: Racial mixing in the celebrity industrial complex.* University Press of Mississippi.

Wijeyesinghe, C. L. (2012). The intersectional model of multiracial identity: Integrating multiracial identity theories and intersectional perspectives on social identity. In C. L. Wijeyesinghe & B. W. Jackson III (Eds.), *New perspectives on racial identity development* (2nd ed., pp. 81–107). NYU Press.

Wong, M. P. A., & Buckner, J. (2008). *Multiracial student services come of age: The state of multiracial student services in higher education in the United States* (New Directions for Student Services, no. 123, pp. 43–51). Wiley. https://doi.org/10.1002/ss.285

Yosso, T. J. (2005). Whose culture has capital? A critical race theory discussion of community cultural wealth. *Race Ethnicity and Education, 8*(1), 69–91. https://doi.org/10.1080/1361332052000341006

EDITORS AND CONTRIBUTORS

Editors

Marc P. Johnston-Guerrero serves as assistant chair for enrollment management in the department of educational studies at The Ohio State University. He is also an associate professor in the higher education and student affairs program and affiliated faculty with the Asian American studies program. He completed a PhD in education (with an emphasis in higher education and organizational change) from the University of California, Los Angeles (UCLA), where he did assessment work for UCLA's Office of Residential Life and served as a graduate fellow in UCLA's Institute for Society and Genetics. These experiences integrated his background in human biology (BS, Michigan State University) and student affairs administration (MA, Michigan State University). Johnston-Guerrero has worked in multicultural affairs units across several institutions, including the University of Arizona and New York University. His research interests focus on diversity and social justice issues in higher education and student affairs, with specific attention to college students making meaning of race and racism and Multiracial/mixed race issues. He serves the field of higher education through his involvement in the American College Personnel Association (ACPA) Governing Board as Member-at-Large, Faculty.

Charmaine L. Wijeyesinghe, EdD, is a consultant with over 35 years of experience lecturing and writing on social justice, racial and social identity, intersectionality, and conflict resolution. She has held several positons in student affairs, including staff associate to the vice chancellor of student affairs and assistant ombudsperson at the University of Massachusetts Amherst and dean of students at Mount Holyoke College. In addition to authoring book chapters and articles, Wijeyesinghe served as volume coeditor (with Bailey Jackson) for two editions of *New Perspectives on Racial Identity Development* (New York University Press, 2001, 2012) and volume editor for *Enacting Intersectionality in Students Affairs: New Directions for Student Services* (Jossey-Bass, 2017) and *The Complexities of Race: Identity, Power, and Justice in an Evolving America* (New York University Press, forthcoming). She served on the editorial board of the *Journal Committed to Social Change on Race and Ethnicity* and was the inaugural recipient of the NCORE Social Justice Award for Scholarship in 2017. Her doctoral research yielded one of the first models of Multiracial identity. This tool was adopted by the Anti-Defamation League (ADL) for its anti-bias curriculum.

Contributors

e alexander, MSW, is a doctoral candidate in higher education and student affairs at The Ohio State University. Their professional experience is in college administration, at both minority-serving and predominantly white institutions, and in social services. Through queer, Black existentialist, Trans-Atlantic/Indigenous, and anticolonial womxnist frameworks, alexander's scholarship interrogates western academia as a global neocolonial project and nonwestern womxn's survivance therein. It also centers embodiment in education scholarship through therapeutic, ethnocultural, geospatial, and arts-based knowledge.

Rebecca Cepeda, MEd, is a doctoral student in higher education and student affairs at The Ohio State University. She completed her BA in political science with a minor in Chicana/o studies at the University of California, Los Angeles and her MEd in educational counseling at the University of Southern California. Cepeda's research interests include understanding and validating the experiences of People of Color and community college students within higher education settings. Her experiences as a first-generation Mexipina have driven her commitments toward calling out racism and white supremacy and advocating for equitable policies and practices for minoritized populations.

Lisa Combs, MS (she/her/hers), recently transitioned from her role as program coordinator in the Student Diversity and Multicultural Affairs Office at Loyola University Chicago to become a doctoral student at The Ohio State University in the higher education and student affairs program. Her research interests include identity interconnections, multiraciality in higher education, and Filipinx identity development. She has been published in the *Journal of College Student Development* and serves as the cochair for the Multiracial Network in ACPA. She received her BA from The Ohio State University and her MS from Miami University in Oxford, Ohio.

Wei Ming Dariotis is faculty director of the Center for Equity and Excellence in Teaching and Learning, professor of Asian American studies, and affiliate faculty of the Educational Leadership Doctoral Program at San Francisco State University. With Laura Kina and Camilla Fojas, she coordinated the

Inaugural Critical Mixed Race Studies Conference (DePaul University, 2010), and cofounded the *Journal of Critical Mixed Race Studies*. She serves on the editorial board of *Asian American Literatures: Discourses and Pedagogies*. Her publications include *War Baby/Love Child: Mixed Race Asian American Art* (University of Wisconsin Press, 2013) and *Fight the Tower: Asian American Women Scholars' Resistance and Renewal in the Academy* (Rutgers University Press, 2019).

Nick Davis is a recent graduate of Northwestern University's Department of Sociology. He has presented at numerous conferences on topics ranging from student racial identity development to how racial anxieties are portrayed in sci-fi films to urban agriculture. Davis has worked as a youth empowerment consultant with the Obama Foundation, Aspen Institute, and the Academy Group, and he is a founding member of Amplify Chicago, a career pipeline organization for formerly incarcerated youth.

Kira Donnell, PhD, is a transnational, transracial Korean adoptee scholar, educator, and advocate. Her research focuses on Korean adoptees as individuals with agency and the development of an individual and collective Korean adoptee identity particularly as expressed through analysis of cultural productions. Donnell is a lecturer in the Asian American Studies Department at San Francisco State University, where she developed the university's first course on transracial adoption, which is a foundational course in the fulfillment of the College of Ethnic Studies' newly developed minor in critical mixed race studies.

Chelsea Guillermo-Wann, PhD, is an educator and leader based in California with nearly 20 years of professional experience spanning K–12, community college, and 4-year institutions. She approaches systems leadership, strategic planning, and program evaluation as a multiracial woman with Filipino, Mexican, and white American heritage. She recently coedited *Mixed Race Student Politics: A Rising "Third Wave" Movement at UCLA* (Lulu Publishing Services, 2019) and has published and presented on campus climate, multiraciality, and intergroup relations. At UCLA, she earned a PhD in higher education and organizational change and an MA in race and ethnic studies in education; her BA in Spanish is from Westmont College.

Jessica C. Harris, PhD, is an assistant professor of higher education in the Graduate School of Education and Information Studies at University of California, Los Angeles. Through her research, Harris interrogates race, racism, and its intersections in higher education. Her research is concentrated on three areas: race and campus sexual violence, multiraciality in higher education, and the (mis)use of theory in advancing racial equity in postsecondary contexts.

Andrew Jolivétte (Atakapa-Ishak/Creole of the Tsikip Clan) is professor and department chair of Ethnic Studies at the University of California, San Diego and the inaugural founding director of Native American and Indigenous Studies at UCSD. Jolivétte is the 2020–21 Scholar in Residence of the MultiRacial Network/ACPA and series editor of Black Indigenous Futures and Speculations at Routledge. He is the author or editor of nine books in print or forthcoming, including *Louisiana Creoles: Cultural Recovery and Mixed-Race Native American Identity* (Lexington Books, 2007) and *Indian Blood: HIV and Colonial Trauma in San Francisco's Two-Spirit Community* (University of Washington Press, 2016). He is a former professor and department chair of American Indian Studies at San Francisco State University and one of the first keynote speakers at the inaugural conference of the Critical Mixed Race Studies Association.

Naliyah Kaya, PhD, is an associate professor of sociology at Montgomery College in Takoma Park, Maryland. She previously served as the coordinator for multiracial and Native American/Indigenous student involvement at the University of Maryland, where she also created a Multiracial Leadership course and continues to facilitate TOTUS Spoken Word Experience. Kaya identifies as a poetic public sociologist centering her energy on the intersections of art and activism. She organizes arts programming in her role on the Critical Mixed Race Studies Association Executive Committee. Kaya is an alumna of Shoreline Community College, Hampton University, and George Mason University.

Nicole Leopardo, MA, is a scholar-activist based in San Francisco. She is a lecturer in the Race and Resistance Studies Department and cofounder of the Critical Mixed Race Studies (CMRS) minor program at San Francisco State University. Leopardo is also a senior consultant with the Oakland-based social impact consultancy The Justice Collective (TJC). She received her MA in ethnic studies from San Francisco State University with specializations in critical mixed race studies and food studies. Leopardo holds a BA from University of California, Santa Barbara, in political science and minors in Black studies and writing: business communication.

Heather C. Lou, MEd (she/her/hers), is an angry, gemini earth dragon, Multiracial, Asian, queer, cisgender, disabled, depressed, anxious, and survivor/ing womxn of color artist and educator based in Minnesota. Her art and radical scholarship include love, hope, critical mixed race studies, art as an assessment/evaluation technique, womxnism, and gender equity. Lou's art is a form of intergenerational healing, transformation, and liberation and directly challenges/dismantles white supremacy in all of its forms. In her spare time, she enjoys birdwatching, adventuring with her family, cuddling with her dogs and cat, and eating her favorite dim sum items.

Victoria K. Malaney Brown currently serves as the inaugural director of academic integrity for undergraduates at Columbia University. She earned her BA in English-Spanish with minors in dance and Latin American studies from Skidmore College. Malaney Brown received her higher education PhD from the College of Education at the University of Massachusetts Amherst. Her qualitative dissertation explored critical consciousness in the narratives of multiracial collegians at a predominantly White institution. A scholar-practitioner, Malaney Brown's research interests focus on the racialized experiences of multiracial undergraduate students in higher education, intergroup dialogue, and college student activism.

Charlene C. Martinez, MEd, is an equity consultant, educator, Multiracial, Taiwanese-Colombian American. Her professional work includes student and multicultural affairs at Oregon State University (OSU), Sacramento State, Mills College, Contra Costa College, the University of California-San Diego, and the nonprofit Rockwood Leadership Program. She is cofounder of OSU's Multiracial Aikido retreat, intended for participants to explore mixed heritage and understand their agency as emerging leaders. Martinez was awarded the 2017 Professional of the Year Award from the ACPA-Multiracial Network, for innovations in multiracial student initiatives. She is passionate about storytelling and integrative methodologies for personal and collective healing.

Orkideh Mohajeri, PhD, is an assistant professor at West Chester University. Her current research focuses on the discursive construction of race and subjectivity for various populations on college and university campuses. Mohajeri is a generation 1.5 immigrant to the United States, hailing from a long line of immigrants in the Southwest Asian/North African region. She identifies as a person of color in the U.S. context but is obligated to select "Caucasian" on forms and state technologies of categorization. She is a motherscholar to two mixed race children, who accompany her in learning and growth.

Maxwell Pereyra (he/him/his) is a PhD student in the division of higher education and organizational change at the University of California, Los Angeles (UCLA). His academic background (with training in both education and engineering) has shaped his unique, multidisciplinary perspective on higher education research. Presently, his scholarship utilizes critical theories to explore the experiences of minoritized college students, as well as sexual violence prevention and response on college campuses. As a queer, Mixed Race/Filipino scholar, he believes his work must be committed to dismantling systems of domination within postsecondary education, as well as in society at large.

Kristen A. Renn, PhD (she/her/hers), is a professor of higher, adult, and lifelong education at Michigan State University, where she also serves as associate dean of undergraduate studies for student success research. She graduated from Mount Holyoke College and received her PhD in higher education at Boston College. Prior to working at Michigan State University she was a dean in the Office of Student Life at Brown University. Renn teaches courses on college students and student development, history of higher education, and diversity and equity in postsecondary education. Her research focuses on the intersection of student success with issues of identity in higher education, including studies of mixed race identities, LGBTQ students, and leaders of identity-based student organizations. She recently completed a landmark study of women's colleges and universities worldwide.

Stephanie N. Shippen, PsyD, is a multiracial Thai American. She lives and practices as a licensed clinical psychologist in Sydney, Australia. Prior to moving, she served as the practicum coordinator at Oregon State University Counseling and Psychological Services and also worked in private practice. She uses trauma-informed practices to support clients in their healing. She is cocreator of the annual Oregon State University Multiracial Aikido social justice retreat for multiracial students. She received her BA degree from the University of California, Santa Cruz and her MS and PsyD degrees in clinical psychology at the PGSP-Stanford PsyD Consortium in Palo Alto, California.

students, multiracial, 18, 237–38.
See also specific topics
affairs, 8
experiences, 19–24
identities, 19–24, 106
organizations, 12–13, 134,
186–87
programs and services, 24–25
at SF State, 221
student success coach, 105
studies, ix, xvi, 17, 18, 19–20,
21–22. *See also* critical mixed
race studies
advances in, xvii–xviii
African American, 87
analysis of, 26–29
applications of, 29–30
Chicana/o, 101–2
conclusions of, 30–31
ethnic, 135–36, 212–16, 225,
226nn3–4
mixed race, x, 132–34
on multiracial faculty, 25–26
of multiraciality, 95
Sue, D. W., 59
supplemental information, 10
support, ix, 223
networks, 176
organizations, xiv
supremacy, white, 62, 63, 71, 112,
192, 235–36
in academia, 107
either/or narrative, 237
monoracism and disruption of,
66–68
surveys, 28, 31, 86, 221
surviving, strategies for, 14–15
S.W.A.N.A. *See* Southwest Asian/
North African
symbol, "No," 183n2
syndrome, imposter, 126–27

synthesis, 15, 47
systems, 43–44
belief, 22, 65
of domination, 65–66, 68–70
ecosystems, 46
foster care, 105
institutional, 153
of oppression, 67–68, 70–71,
238–39

Tagalog, 7, 99
talking back, through multiraciality,
114–15
Tashiro, Cathy, 27–28
technology, advances in, 28–29
tenets, Multiracial Aikido, 163
tension, 37, 62–70, 71, 176–77
tension points, monoracism, 62–70,
71
terms
defining, 145–46, 162, 198n1,
226n4
grammatical styles for, 3
tests
cultural authenticity, 120
DNA, 29, 234–35, 238
themes, guiding, 9–10
theoretical rationale, for CMRS,
219–20
theories, critical race, 142–43, 150,
196
thinking, imaginative, 236–37
Third World Liberation Front
strike, 213
thriving, strategies for, 14–15
time, weaponizing, 112
traits, phenotypical, xv
transgender, 59
transnational mixed experiences,
118–19
transracial adoptees, 243

Faculty Development books from Stylus Publishing

Advancing the Culture of Teaching on Campus
ow a Teaching Center Can Make a Difference
Edited by Constance Cook and Matthew Kaplan
Foreword by Lester P. Monts

Faculty Mentoring
*A Practical Manual for Mentors, Mentees, Administrators,
and Faculty Developers*
Susan L. Phillips and Susan T. Dennison
Foreword by Milton D. Cox

Faculty Retirement
Best Practices for Navigating the Transition
Edited by Claire Van Ummersen, Jean McLaughlin and
Lauren Duranleau
Foreword by Lotte Bailyn

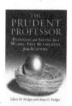

The Prudent Professor
*Planning and Saving for a Worry-Free Retirement from
Academe*
Edwin M. Bridges and Brian D. Bridges

Teaching Across Cultural Strengths
*A Guide to Balancing Integrated and Individuated Cultural
Frameworks in College Teaching*
Alicia Fedelina Chávez and Susan Diana Longerbeam
Foreword by Joseph L. White

Why Students Resist Learning
A Practical Model for Understanding and Helping Students
Edited by Anton O. Tolman and Janine Kremling
Foreword by John Tagg

Professional Development books from Stylus Publishing

Adjunct Faculty Voices
Cultivating Professional Development and Community at the Front Lines of Higher Education
Edited by Roy Fuller, Marie Kendall Brown and Kimberly Smith
Foreword by Adrianna Kezar

Authoring Your Life
Developing an INTERNAL VOICE to Navigate Life's Challenges
Marcia B. Baxter Magolda Foreword by Sharon Daloz Parks
Illustrated by Matthew Henry Hall

The Coach's Guide for Women Professors
Who Want a Successful Career and a Well-Balanced Life
Rena Seltzer
Foreword by Frances Rosenbluth

Contingent Academic Labor
Evaluating Conditions to Improve Student Outcomes
Daniel B. Davis
Foreword by Adrianna Kezar

Shaping Your Career
A Guide for Early Career Faculty
Don Haviland, Anna M. Ortiz and Laura Henriques
Foreword by Ann E. Austin

What They Didn't Teach You in Graduate School
299 Helpful Hints for Success in Your Academic Career
Paul Gray and David E. Drew
Illustrated by Matthew Henry Hall
Foreword by Laurie Richlin and Steadman Upham

Race & Diversity books from Stylus Publishing

Building on Resilience
Models and Frameworks of Black Male Success Across the P-20 Pipeline
Edited by Fred A. Bonner II
Foreword by Tim King

Diverse Millennial Students in College
Implications for Faculty and Student Affairs
Edited by Fred A. Bonner II, Aretha F. Marbley, and Mary F. Howard-Hamilton

Answering the Call
African American Women in Higher Education Leadership
Beverly L. Bower and Mimi Wolverton

The Department Chair as Transformative Diversity Leader
Building Inclusive Learning Environments in Higher Education
Edna Chun and Alvin Evans Foreword by Walter H. Gmelch

Multiculturalism on Campus
Theory, Models, and Practices for Understanding Diversity and Creating Inclusion
Edited by Michael J. Cuyjet, Chris Linder, Mary F. Howard-Hamilton, and Diane L. Cooper

Creating the Path to Success in the Classroom
Teaching to Close the Graduation Gap for Minority, First-Generation, and Academically Unprepared Students
Kathleen F. Gabriel
Foreword by Stephen Carroll

Race & Diversity books from Stylus Publishing

Advancing Black Male Student Success From Preschool Through Ph.D.
Edited by Shaun R. Harper and J. Luke Wood

Contested Issues in Troubled Times
Student Affairs Dialogues on Equity, Civility, and Safety
Edited by Peter M. Magolda, Marcia B. Baxter Magolda
and Rozana Carducci
Foreword by Lori Patton Davis

Critical Race Spatial Analysis
Mapping to Understand and Address Educational Inequity
Edited by Deb Morrison, Subini Ancy Annamma, and
Darrell D. Jackson

Closing the Opportunity Gap
*Identity-Conscious Strategies for Retention and Student
Success*
Edited by Vijay Pendakur
Foreword by Shaun R. Harper

Beyond Access
Indigenizing Programs for Native American Student Success
Edited by Stephanie J. Waterman, Shelly C. Lowe, and
Heather J. Shotton
Foreword by George S. McClellan

Critical Mentoring
A Practical Guide
Torie Weiston-Serdan
Foreword by Bernadette Sánchez

Teaching and Learning books from Stylus Publishing

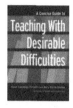

A Concise Guide to Teaching With Desirable Difficulties
Diane Cummings Persellin and Mary Blythe Daniels
Foreword by Mary-Ann Winkelmes

Hitting Pause
65 Lecture Breaks to Refresh and Reinforce Learning
Gail Taylor Rice
Foreword by Kevin Barry

Connected Teaching
Relationships, Power, and Mattering in Higher Education
Harriet L. Schwartz
Foreword by Laurent A. Daloz
Afterword by Judith V. Jordan

POGIL
An Introduction to Process Oriented Guided Inquiry Learning for Those Who Wish to Empower Learners
Edited by Shawn R. Simonson

Teaching as the Art of Staging
A Scenario-Based College Pedagogy in Action
Anthony Weston
Foreword by Peter Felten

Project-Based Learning in the First Year
Beyond All Expectations
Edited by Kristin K. Wobbe and Elisabeth A. Stoddard
Foreword by Randall Bass

Also available from Stylus

Transformative Practices for Minority Student Success

Accomplishments of Asian American and Native American Pacific Islander–Serving Institutions

Edited by Dina C. Maramba and Timothy P. Fong

Foreword by Robert T. Teranishi

"For far too long the Asian American and Pacific Islander (AAPI) student population has been left out of conversations about student success, forgotten due to the model minority myth. Maramba and Fong have brought to the surface key issues for all in higher education to discuss and learn from. The contributors they have assembled have both the scholarly background and practice-based knowledge to help the field move forward in its understanding of AAPI students and Asian American and Native American Pacific Islander–serving institutions."—*Marybeth Gasman, Judy & Howard Berkowitz Professor of Education, University of Pennsylvania*

Difficult Subjects

Insights and Strategies for Teaching About Race, Sexuality, and Gender

Edited by Badia Ahad-Legardy and OiYan A. Poon

Foreword by Lori Patton Davis

"*Difficult Subjects* could not have come at a better time. It offers keen insights and guidance without being prescriptive. It offers critical social analysis while still being pragmatic and accessible. As educators grapple with the tensions the current administration poses, this text serves as a beautiful and necessary counterbalance as we collectively try to regain our humanity."—*Nolan Cabrera, Associate Professor, Center for the Study of Higher Education, University of Arizona*

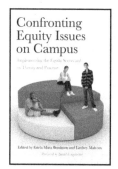

Confronting Equity Issues on Campus

Implementing the Equity Scorecard in Theory and Practice

Edited by Estela Mara Bensimon and Lindsey Malcom

Foreword by David Longanecker

"This volume examines how colleges and universities are using the Center for Urban Education's Equity Scorecard to create racial equity on campus. With in-depth examinations of the Equity Scorecard process as well as reflections from practitioner teams and researchers, the book is a testament to the role thoughtful data assessment can play in generating more racially equitable outcomes for students. The book calls educators and administrators to take personal responsibility for their roles in moving from deficit model to an equity model and provides helpful context for anyone currently using or considering the scorecard as a tool for change."—*Diversity & Democracy*

Designing Transformative Multicultural Initiatives

Theoretical Foundations, Practical Applications, and Facilitator Considerations

Edited by Sherry K. Watt

Foreword by Marybeth Gasman

"Sherry K. Watt has assembled talented 'conscious scholar practitioners' to address the growing need to design university policies, programming, and classroom pedagogies that address difference. This book addresses both the theoretical and practical aspects of multicultural teaching. As the preferred term *conscious scholar practitioners* suggests, both aspects are vital for developing multicultural policies and teaching practices.

For those scholars who want to deepen and center difference in their classroom and across their university, this book strikes me as incredibly valuable. For departments of theology and religious studies seeking to form stronger links with other departments, staff members, and administrators, this volume can provide a common vocabulary and methodology."—*Reflective Teaching (Wabash Center)*

22883 Quicksilver Drive

Sterling, VA 20166-2019   Subscribe to our e-mail alerts: www.Styluspub.com